THE GUINNESS BOOK OF SEA FISHING

Light Tackle Technique
for British Waters

One of England's most famous bass fishing locations, beneath the towering chalk cliffs of Beachy Head in Sussex. The angler, Nick Cranfield, has taken many big, hard-fighting fish here.

THE GUINNESS BOOK OF SEA FISHING

Light Tackle Technique for British Waters

Brian Harris

GUINNESS BOOKS

Editor: Beatrice Frei
Picture Editor: Alex Goldberg
Design and Layout: Alan Hamp

First published as *Saltwater Angling* 1977
Second impression 1982
This edition published 1989

Published in Great Britain by Guinness Publishing Ltd,
33 London Road, Enfield, Middlesex

Set in Meridien 10/12 by Ace Filmsetting Ltd
Printed and bound in Italy by New Interlitho SpA, Milan

'Guinness' is a registered trade mark of
Guinness Superlatives Ltd

British Library Cataloguing in Publication Data
Harris, Brian, *1937–*
    Guinness guide to sea fishing. — 2nd ed.
    1. Great Britain. Coastal waters. Sea angling.
    Manuals
    I. Title   II. Harris, Brian, *1937–*. Guinness guide to
    saltwater angling
799.1'6

ISBN 0-85112-349-X

Contents

Foreword

There is little doubt the sea angler is a hardy breed of sportsman. Throughout the year, regardless of weather conditions, he stands on desolate beaches, often at night, braving the biting wind and penetrating spray from heavy surf. Furthermore, with the quality of fishing improving considerably during autumn and winter months, a boat angler fares little better. On many occasions, often in open boats, he is tossed around from dawn to dusk, the only comfort a flask of coffee and sandwiches.

Even on more pleasant occasions I often wonder at the patience shown by the angler as he gazes intently at the rod tip, almost, it seems, willing a fish to take his bait. Little wonder, therefore, the angler is the butt of the cartoonist and considered slightly crazy by the general public.

Somewhat eccentric the sea angler may be, but the deep affection he has for his chosen sport allows him quickly to identify sound, sincere angling writing.

There are journalists, often quite professional, who seem more concerned with the flow and arrangement of words, rather than the subject itself; often they attempt to write with authority on subjects well outside their experience. Such shallow words are quickly ignored by the sensible anglers.

On the other hand there is the true angling journalist, writers such as Brian Harris who have fished all their lives with dedication, affection and concern for the sport; such enthusiasm can be instantly recognised by the accuracy and sincerity of their words.

I remember Brian in his late teens fishing my patch from the steeply shelving beaches of Dungeness through to the rocky ledges of Winchelsea. Even in those days he had this enquiring mind bordering on the nuisance. My most enduring recollection is of him walking along the beach, spade and rod in one hand, with a bucket of worms, crabs and razor fish in the other.

From the practical down-to-earth task of bait digging to the editor of a successful magazine in a few short years is no mean feat, and a sure indication of

The late Leslie Moncrieff.

the author's competence in the sea angling field. His obvious love of our sport is the reason I am happy to contribute a foreword to this excellent book, 'The Guinness Book of Sea Fishing – Light Tackle Technique for British Waters'. The author has not made the mistake of over stretching the subject matter but confines himself to discussing 24 of the most popular sporting saltwater fish in detail. The fish included are the most popular found around the British Isles. Their natural environment, methods of capture, including bait and tackle are described in depth. The amount of colour work with excellent photographs and line drawings, printed on high quality paper, are quite outstanding.

Brian Harris's approach to sea angling is very much my own, simple and direct. It is not always an easy task to explain on paper, at least in understandable terms, the important details that make the difference between the average and the outstanding angler.

This book, however, is a distillation of a practical angler's knowledge that must prove invaluable to both beginners and experienced anglers alike.

Leslie J. Moncrieff

Acknowledgements

Illustrations

Thanks are due to all who supplied photographs for this book, including Russ Symons, Bob Cox, Dave and Kay Steuart, John Darling, the late Ian Gillespie, John Cooper, Terry Hill, Keith Linsell, the late Reg Quest, the late Bill Keal and especially to Neil Nevison, whose professional skill, enthusiasm and patience are gratefully appreciated.

The author would also like to acknowledge the help and skill of many friends with whom so many happy angling hours have been spent.

Neil Nevison.

Colour illustrations supplied by:
John Cooper
Bob Cox
John Darling
Ian Gillespie
Terry Hill
Trevor Housby
Keith Linsell
Mike Millman Photo Services
Neil Nevison
Reg Quest
Kay Steuart
Russ Symons
The International Game Fish Association
Mick Toomer

Introduction
to previous editions

The rate at which mankind is consuming the world's natural resources continues to accelerate. Over-population and a widespread belief that an affluent society is the key to happiness have, together with greed and political factors, drained to an alarming level what land and sea are able to produce and provide.

Cousteau blames the trawl for most of the destruction of marine life and its environment. Add to the seabed slaughter the effects of pollution, sophisticated modern fish-location systems and equally refined fish-catching methods, and the dangerous situation may be envisaged.

Suddenly, world governments have become concerned, having ignored the warnings of their marine biologists for many years, and are imposing territorial fishery limits, though they cannot agree to a worldwide fishing policy. Some scientists believe it is already too late to save some fish species which have fallen in numbers to an extent that natural regeneration is impeded.

Against this background sportfishing is an important and growing part of saltwater angling. The sportfisher, appreciating that there are fewer fish to catch, is content to catch fewer than many other heavy-tackle anglers, but makes sure he gets maximum enjoyment from each fish. It is a natural sequence of events, therefore, for him to decide that some fish fight harder than others, some are more demanding of skill to catch than are others, and that henceforth he will choose to fish only with light and sporting tackle for the kinds of fish that fulfil his requirements.

This book aims to encourage more saltwater anglers to adopt the sportfisher's attitude since this will be both a move towards conservation and – due to the self-imposed problems that have to be overcome – it leads to lasting interest and fulfilment.

Sportfishing elevates what has for too long been regarded as a 'thick-eared branch of angling' to something of an art.

Brian Harris

Introduction to this edition

Those few paragraphs, written just over 12 years ago when I was editor of the now-defunct national monthly magazine, *Angling*, are as apposite today as they were when the first edition of this book was published.

Fish stocks, particularly those species more frequently caught from the shore, and in the shallower inshore waters, have been further depleted by commercial fishing, despite quota restrictions imposed – many of which are blatantly ignored – and, many of us believe, by the insidious pollution of the saltwater environment.

There are grounds to suspect, too, that our warming climate has had an effect on the distribution of inshore fish stocks. For example, the recent mild winters have made autumn and winter cod fishing

from some of the favoured shores, specially those in the south-east of England, almost a waste of time. Famous beaches like those of the Dungeness promontory in Kent, which used to yield a hundredweight or so of cod, many weighing in the teens of pounds, to individual anglers, in the 1988/89 winter did not reward anglers with that weight of cod from late September to early January, the former prime period.

However, out in the deep water, in that part of the English Channel between the Thames Estuary and the Isle of Wight, there were plenty of good cod caught, generally over wrecks and rocky ground. Deep water stays cool while the inshore shallows fluctuate more in line with air temperatures, of course.

At the same time, species of fish which like warmer water, tended to be around inshore far later than was previously the case. Bass, soles and conger, for example, were taken well into the winter.

Against this background, it seems strange, perhaps, that since 1977, when the first edition of this book went on sale, there have been 79 new sea-fishing boat- and shore-caught records accepted by the British Record (Rod-Caught) Fish Committee, 45 of those records taken by shore fishing.

Is there a logical explanation? I believe there is, and my opinion is that today's sea anglers are not only more record-conscious, and thus tend to make more claims for the big fish they catch, but that the improvement in their high-tech tackle, plus their higher standard in its optimum use, get them any good fish that are around.

There were no commercially produced graphite (carbon-fibre) rods for surfcasting in 1977, though rods for flyfishing had begun to appear in the tackle shops. We were then happily using hollow glass-fibre rods, and catching plenty of fish with them. But with the new graphite and graphite-glass composite casting rods now being used by an increasing number of anglers, and being used competently with better multiplier and fixed-spool reels, with spools and frames moulded from graphite composites and titanium alloys for other parts, the average range of the shore caster has greatly increased.

Long casting is not always the key to rewarding fishing, but in some areas and in some periods of the sea-angler's season, it is the only means of making good catches. Proficient use of the modern rods and reels, coupled with some important advances in terminal tackle that can reduce the drag of the baited hook or hooks in flight, have increased casting distances by many metres. The 150-metre (164-yard) cast from the beach, with a couple of short-snood hooks, is no longer the comparative rarity it was a decade ago.

Boat-fishing tackle has improved, too, though the improvements have not had the profound effect that they have had on shore fishing. There is not much more one can do than drop the tackle overboard and be able to bring to the boat any hard-fighting big fish hooked, though there is a wider use of uptide casting from boats anchored in shallow water, the technique pioneered in the Thames Estuary by John Rawle and Bob Cox and which was included in the first edition of this book. It is in the reels, of which there are now an increasing number of models incorporating sensitive lever-operated disc drag systems which yield line very smoothly to a fighting fish, that there has been the greatest progress. Boating big fish is now easier than it used to be.

Perhaps one of the biggest changes experienced by sea anglers over the past 10 years or so has been the decline in the supply of bait, notably lugworms, king ragworms, razorfish, red-nosed cockles and butterfish – the shellfish, not the little rockfish that bears the same name. For despite the decline in the available inshore fish, specially the winter species, though other species, previously fairly commonly caught from the shore – turbot, smooth-hounds, tope and lesser-spotted dogfish to name a few – are also a rarity today, the number of sea-fishing addicts has increased.

There are a number of reasons for the reduced availability of baits, including over-exploitation of the bait-beds by commercial diggers, changing patterns in the make-up of the sand-and-mud mixtures of our shores, due to shifting tidal streams, land-drainage carrying silt into the inshore waters in increasing amounts and, so far as some of the shellfish are concerned, their inability to recover from that very cold winter of 1963/64, when vast numbers perished.

Despite all the problems facing sea anglers today, the sport is flourishing. The rough-and-tumble of a winter cod beach; the roar of surf on a whitewater storm beach in summer; the promise of great things as the boat drops anchor over a wreck or reef; and the beauty of the changing patterns of sea and sky – all these things are part and parcel of why so many prefer to fish in the sea than in freshwater.

Some of the men who helped lift the sport from the thick-eared image of the 1950s and inspired its development to the present day, have passed on. Leslie Moncrieff, that doyen of beach fishermen who kindly wrote the foreword to the original edition, and with whom I shared so many happy times on beach and boat, in all seasons, here and abroad, died three years ago but left us a wealth of inventions and good tactical sense. Ian Gillespie, that impish East Anglian, inventor with Nigel Forrest of the breakaway lead, among other good ideas, whose big heart gave out when he was in his prime years, is another. Whenever I stand on a lonely shore and watch the rod tip bowing to the surf against a black velvet sky, pricked with stars, and listen to the song of the waves and the soughing of the wind in the taut line, I can still hear that voice exclaiming 'Good 'ere, ennit!'

All of us who love sea fishing know that he was right.

Brian Harris

PART ONE

Attitude and principles: tackle and baits

Previous page: Evening flood-tide, an ideal time for shore cod. Anglers wait for action – hot drinks, warm clothes and lamps at the ready.

Even youngsters can bring big fish to the boat on light gear. This 26 lb (11.7 kg) cod was beaten on 15 lb (6.8 kg) test line in a strong tidal stream by the author's son Stuart, then aged 12.

1 Sportfishing principles

Sheer size or weight in a fish is of little importance to the sportfisher in his assessment of whether it qualifies for his interest or not. For example, the fighting abilities of a 3 lb (1.3 kg) grey mullet and a 3 lb whiting, both hooked on the same tackle, are inarguably so far apart that any experienced sea angler who has taken plenty of both species will find even the suggestion of a comparison laughable. The poor old whiting is not in the same league, neither would it be were the comparison to be made between a 3 lb grey mullet and a 6 lb (2.7 kg) whiting.

When considering which fish rate the interest of sportfishermen, it is generally accepted that the round fish rather than the flat fish are more popular. This is to be expected since fish with a fusiform body shape are agile, fast swimmers while those with bodies flattened in a horizontal plane are more fitted to lying on or being partially buried in the sea-bed, the tidal flow passing over them easily.

A number of flatfish do earn the sportfishers' interest and are included in this book, while there are omissions of a number of round-bodied fish, the whiting being one, of course, which cannot be of interest. While sheer size or weight of a fish is of little importance when giving it a rating as a sporting fish, there are some species which do depend upon their size to a certain extent as to whether they are fished for. For example, a 3 lb (1.3 kg) codling (cod under about 5 lb (2.26 kg) are called codling in most parts of Britain) would not be a very interesting proposition for a sportfisher, but a cod of 10 lb (4.5 kg) or more would be, since its extra weight helps it resist the tackle.

The speed at which a fish can swim, the speed and the depth of its dives, whether it leaps from the water, or whether it can stay deep in the water and resist by dogged pulling the resistance exerted by the angler's rod and line, are all characteristics by which sporting species are judged. Aesthetic appeal enters the picture, too: whether a fish is beautiful to look at or just 'plain ugly'. Paradoxically, one or two ugly customers are included in these pages because they can swim fast and pull, or both.

A fast-taper 2–3 oz (56.5–85 g) casting bass rod bends over as Hampshire angler Jack Austin drags a nice bass through the swash at Inch Strand, County Kerry, Ireland.

Here, then, is our list of sporting saltwater fish that may be caught in their seasons round the shores of the British Isles and the Irish Republic, as well as in other parts of north-west Europe: porbeagle shark, blue shark, mako shark, thresher shark, tope, smooth-hounds (two species), conger eel, common skate, stingray, cod, pollack, coalfish, halibut, bass, thick-lipped grey mullet, thin-lipped grey mullet, ballan wrasse, black bream, red bream, mackerel, garfish, plaice and flounder.

Twenty-four species. Many saltwater anglers no doubt feel that some of these should not be listed, while others should. The blue shark, for example, is a borderline case and is included on the grounds that, though it fights less well than even the tope or

13

A good place to pull in the gaff on a cod is near the gill covers, since edible meat is not spoiled and lifting against water resistance is easy.

smooth-hound, size for size, it is prolific, grows to a good size and can be quite fun on light tackle. Haddock might have been included but the species has a very limited range and reaches no great size. Species that attain heavy weights, such as monkfish and anglerfish, both capable of being taken frequently at weights of 30–40 lb (13.6–18.1 kg) are both dour on the hook and among the ugliest fish in our seas.

To make catching the 24 selected species consistently interesting and enjoyable and, to a certain extent, difficult (in that clumsiness in tackle handling will weigh against success) it is necessary to use tackle that is light in weight and of a strength that makes fighting an average-size specimen a relatively equal contest, yet will still enable an angler to exercise skill in overcoming the occasional fish that is well above average size. Balanced tackle is the term used to describe the gear used by sportfishers in the sea. It is nothing new, yet, strangely enough, fewer than half the anglers in Britain have discovered the delights of using balanced, lightweight tackle.

There is a great deal of misunderstanding about light tackle fishing in the sea: old habits die hard and in spite of the fact, for example, that enlightened anglers have regularly been catching cod to 30 lb

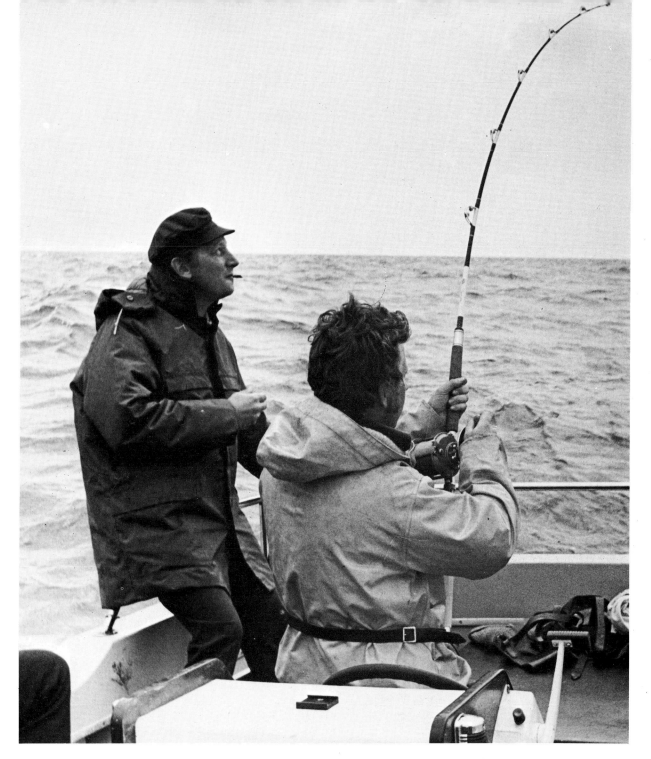

(13.6 kg) on light rods and lines of 15 lb (6.8 kg) test and conger eels of up to 80 lb (36.2 kg) on 30 lb test lines, many will not try the system. They continue to haul up their multi-hooked paternosters, each hook adorned with an almost undetectable pouting or dab, on rods and lines twice as stiff and as strong as those used by anglers catching the big cod or congers.

Some of the resistance to light tackle sportfishing in the sea has been brought about by a few light-tackle addicts taking their technique too far, such as seeking to catch cod with weights in double figures on line testing 5 lb (2.26 kg), or porbeagle sharks known to average well over 100 lb (45.3 kg) on lines of 10 lb (4.5 kg) test. The author, having been guilty a time or two of trying the latter smart trick, now

An angler playing his first shark on light tackle, in this case a 30 lb (13.6 kg) combination. This is the stern of the Q22 craft designed on the Isle of Wight and ideal for shark fishing in those waters.

believes that 25 lb (11.3 kg) test should be the minimum for tackling porbeagles that may be expected to range between weights of 80–200 lb (36–90 kg) in the hands of a skilled angler.

Using ridiculously light tackle does lead to criticism, and with justification. Quite apart from the fact that it is not clever to leave fish swimming around with hooks, leads and yards of line trailing from their mouths, there is the matter of such tackle interfering with the pleasure of fellow anglers near whom one is fishing. Nothing can be more relied upon to get tempers flaring, than an angler in a party of eight or so on a 30-foot (9.1 m) plus boat, who is using tackle much lighter than that which his fellows deem necessary to hold bottom. His gear drifts and tangles, unless he is made to fish at the extreme stern of an anchored boat, or he spends so much time playing each fish he hooks, that his companions have to spend much of their time with their tackle out of the water and out of his way; and, of course, out of the fish's way!

Thus it may be seen that light-tackle sportfishing on a boat has to be carefully planned: either one goes with a party of like-minded friends, all of whom realise that fishing time is wasted when one of the party is playing a good fish, or, if the intent is to fish really light – for example with 25 lb (11.3 kg) test line for big porbeagle sharks – then only one or two anglers may fish. That makes the cost of a day's sport very expensive indeed. In fact, such fishing really calls for a special type of boat and experienced skipper, of which more in chapter 5.

Sportfishing then, as it is described in this book is demanding of skill, a suitable mental attitude and the knowledge that it is either necessary to pick your boat fishing companions with care, or spend a lot more than most non-specialist sea anglers do on charterboat fees. Your tackle, too, will tend to cost more, though there are many items, including rods, that may be made at home and thus save a great deal of money.

It is necessary to pay a great deal of attention to the choice of tackle for sportfishing and its maintenance. The various items needed to cover the whole scene are the subject of the next chapter.

2 Tackle and accessories

To many people, sea angling conjures a mind-picture of stout rods and reels, with heavy weights and thick lines, either being lowered over the side of a boat or heaved out to sea from a beach or pier. But modern sea fishing is not like that. It has advanced from the thick-eared image of the past to become a branch of angling every bit as skilful as flyfishing or high-class coarse fishing at its top level.

Nor does sea fishing only involve fishing a baited hook, or hooks, on the seabed, held down by a lead weight. The species dealt with in this book demand many other techniques, in addition to bottom fishing, including float fishing, spinning, trolling (sometimes called trailing), drift-lining, jigging or pirking and even flyfishing. Such techniques require a diversity of tackle, not only because of the need to cover the dif-

The Atlantic strands of County Kerry can provide magnificent surf for the bass angler, and solitude in beautiful surroundings. This is Derrynane, where there is also fine rock fishing for pollack, tope, wrasse, conger eels, mackerel and garfish.

Action from a large trawler off Ireland's South-West coast as an angler bends into a fish deep down in a rocky gully between rock pinnacles.

ferent feeding habits and habitat preferences of the species, but to be able to enjoy maximum sport from fish whose weights range between a pound (450 g) or so up to over 200 lb (90.7 kg) – mackerel, garfish and black bream at the lower end of the scale to conger, sharks and halibut at the other.

Different fishing techniques are required even to tackle one species in different environments and when feeding in different ways. Take the bass, perhaps the most truly sporting of our British saltwater fish, as an example. When they are feeding in the surf of whitewater Atlantic storm beaches, such as are found in Ireland's south-west, and in the English West Country, or in the shorter surf of English Chan-

nel beaches, in the currents of estuaries or along rocky shores, a legered bait – soft or peeler crab, lugworm, ragworm, sand-eel, small dead fish or strips cut from mackerel or herring, and whole small squid or cuttlefish, or strips or heads and tentacles from those two creatures – is the usual method.

From rocky headlands, piers and from boats over offshore sandbanks, reefs and wrecks, bass will feed on small fish and sand-eels, so spinning, trolling and driftlining is the answer, even flyfishing with a long, slim fly that simulates their prey. And from similar places, specially from piers, rocky headlands with deepish water, and tide-rips, harbour walls and vantage points in estuaries, float fishing with a live sand-eel, live prawn, bunches of ragworms or small live pouting and other fish – even fish strips – is effective. The modern sea angler needs many strings to his bow.

From the foregoing, it may be seen that sea fishing

is a sport of extremes. At the delicate end of the sport is, for example, the use of a lightweight trout-spinning rod and a fixed-spool reel loaded with line of 4–6 lb (1.8–2.7 kg) test and a small lure, from the shore or a small boat, to catch mackerel, garfish, bass or small pollack and coalfish, for example. At the rugged end is the pursuit from a boat over deep water, drifting or at anchor, of sharks, common skate, conger or halibut, all of which can weigh over 100 lb (45.3 kg) and some of which can weigh more than five times that figure.

It must be admitted that, if the angler is solely fishing for the pot, thus not really interested in rod-bending and reel-screaming excitement in pitting his skill with light gear against hard-fighting fish, even big ones that would seem to be too much for the tackle to overcome, a couple of outfits, one for shore, one for boat, would just about suffice. A casting rod of about 11 ft (3.3 m), for leads weighing 4–6 oz (113.3–170 g), used with a multiplier or fixed-spool reel holding about 250 yards (228.5 m) of 15 lb (6.8 kg) line, can be used to catch fish as varied as dabs, codling and school bass weighing no more than about 4 lb (1.8 kg) up to tope, cod, conger and stingray, which can exceed 30 lb (13.6 kg) from the shore quite frequently. The tope, conger and big cod will prove quite a handful on that outfit, but the little fish may be wound in with the angler hardly knowing they are on his hook.

Similarly, on a boat, a 7 ft (2.1 m) rod equipped with a strong multiplier reel holding about 400 yards (365.7 m) of 30 lb (13.6 kg) test line will serve to catch blue and porbeagle sharks to well over 100 lb (45.3 kg), and will reel up small whiting, pollack or codling like a crane!

The sea fisherman who wishes to get the most fun from the sport, in addition to some fine fish for the table, will try to be selective in his choice of tackle, to match the weight and species of the fish he seeks, as well as the conditions in which he must fish for them.

'About 95 per cent of saltwater fishing rods are today made from glass-fibre. It is a very suitable material that has been in use for making fishing rods for the past 20 years or so and refined to a very high standard.' That sentence was written for the first edition of this book, but today it is no longer true. Carbon-fibre, and other materials since developed, including kevlar, are now the basis for most sea rods, for shore casting and boat work. Glass-fibre rods, in both solid and tubular construction, are still widely used, specially by we greybeards over the age of 50, though fewer are available today. The younger pace-setters of the modern sea fishig scene are deeply 'into'

About a mile up the estuary of the Hampshire Avon there is excellent fishing for thick-lipped grey mullet. This is best done from a dinghy. This lad has just beaten a good mullet on light float tackle.

rods made from graphite fibres in a big way, and those in which other materials, like kevlar, are incorporated in the graphite construction.

However, though graphite rod construction, which gives greater stiffness – and quicker recovery from bending – and lightness in the hand, has taken the sea fishing world by storm, increasing casting distances in tournaments to more than 250 yards (228.5 m), such refined rods can only perform to their capacity in the hands of a skilled angler. As in other fields, where a top rifle will not make a poor marksman an expert, nor a fine golf club convert a hacker into a scratch player, only competency in their use will maximise the capabilities of high-tech casting rods.

Many casters, in fact, have found graphite rods too stiff and strange in action, and to meet their requirements – as well as for technical construction reasons – there are a number of rods made with graphite lower sections with glass-fibre built in for the last three feet or so, to soften the tip action and increase the caster's 'feel' of the lead as he builds up rod compression. The use of a proportion of glass mixed with graphite also renders a casting rod – and boat rods, too – less liable to fracture, though this problem of breakage is being overcome by the use of other materials, including kevlar, to bolster the graphite.

The reduction in weight of a rod made from graphite, rather than glass, and graphite's faster recovery when the rod unleashes its compression curve, are factors more important in rods used for casting, for shore and boat-casting work, than for pure bottom fishing from a boat. Reduction in weight is less important in the short lengths in which boat rods are made than in rods of from 9 to 12 ft (2.7–3.6 m) and in rods constantly held while fishing. Graphite, then, is best used in heavy and light surfcasting rods, uptide boat rods and pier rods, and in rods meant for float fishing, spinning and flyfishing techniques.

There have also been improvements in the rings used on sea rods, with stronger, one-piece frames than the old soldered or welded hard-chromed and stainless-steel ones have. The modern rings have centres of metallic oxides, developed by the Japanese company, Fuji, which are very hard and smooth and tough as well. They last for years.

Reel seats have been developed, mainly in Japan, too. They have graphite in their construction, plus stainless steel, which makes them light, tough and corrosion resistant – an important facet of tackle to be subjected to the rigours of saltwater fishing. There are also simple hose-clip type rings made from nylon and hard plastic that permit a reel to be firmly attached anywhere along the length of a rod's handle – much better than the old hose clips and adapted clip fittings we used 10 years ago.

Since the first edition of this book was published, my opinions have changed somewhat concerning the most rugged of the outfits needed to cope with British boat fishing way offshore. I now believe that a rod-and-reel combination able to impose maximum strain on up to 50 lb (22.6 kg) test line is needed, but only to tackle comparatively few species: big common skate that can exceed 200 lb (90.7 kg), porbeagle, thresher and mako sharks that can be twice as heavy, as well as halibut, that can reach astonishing weights, certainly well above those achieved by most sharks. And though many congers over 80 lb (36.2 kg) have been boated on lines testing less than 30 lb (13.6 kg), the species grows to such a size, and inhabits such rough ground, including wrecks and reefs, that 50 lb (22.6 kg) line and a matching rod and reel combination must be included in the all-round angler's tackle collection.

To be fully equipped for sporting sea fishing, from shore and boat, I believe that 10 or 11 separate outfits are required, though at a pinch, some may be used to double for other techniques and species, even though they might not be considered ideal for the job. We all have to compromise to meet our budgets.

First, then, let us look at the rods, reels and sundry equipment needed to cover most sporting shore fishing. I reckon five rod-and-reel combinations are about right.

For winter cod fishing, and summer work for

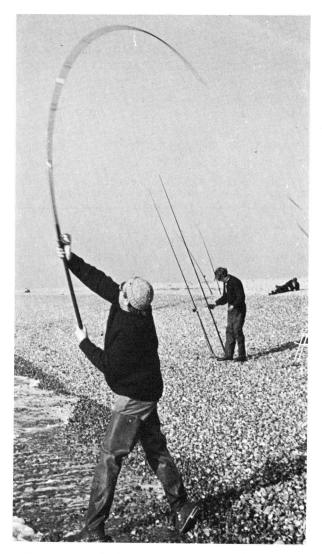

Hollow glass surfcasting rods can absorb tremendous strain without breaking. Here the author punches out light tackle on a Kentish cod beach in autumn. Note the short distance between the hands.

such heavyweights as stingray, tope, conger, common skate, among others that might happen along, a rod of 12–13 ft (3.6–3.9 m) to cast weights of 4–6 oz (113.3–170 g) up to 150 yards (137.1 m) with baited hook or hooks is about right. Such a rod will, with the right reel, cast well over that maximum distance in competent hands, putting two lugworm-baited hooks way out from steep shingle beaches, such as are found in East Anglia, Kent and East Sussex and a few places farther west, in Dorset and in Wales, to take big autumn and winter cod.

It will also put a big fillet of fish, such as mackerel, herring, or garfish, or a whole big sand-eel, small pouting, silver whiting, or a whole small squid, or strips cut from them or from cuttlefish, maybe over

100 yards (91.4 m) to catch tope, rays, common skate, conger and bass and cod, when fishing from beaches, rocky stances giving way to deep water over sand, and sand/rock mixtures.

The best reel for this rod and its relatively heavy casting weights is a smooth-running multiplier. It should have a smooth drag system, for fighting big and often fast-running fish, and a spool capacity of about 300 yards (274.3 m) of 15 lb (6.8 kg) nylon monofilament line, though for tackling big shore conger, tope and common skate, such as are within range from beaches, rocky promontories and pierheads, it may be wise to use line up to 30 lb (13.6 kg).

There is a vast difference between playing out a fast-running fish, like a tope for example, than in battling with the bulk and sluggish weight of a conger or a big ray or common skate, though even those species will sometimes make quite long runs along the bottom. Line of 15 lb (6.8 kg), used intelligently, will usually subdue a big tope, because its fast runs will eventually tire it. But the stubborn kind of resistance, specially among rocky or snaggy ground, put up by a common skate or a conger needs more muscle over a sustained period to bring to the shore.

Plenty of these big fish have been successfully tackled for many years on good quality hollow-glass rods, but modern trends involve the use of graphite or graphite/glass rods, which are far more expensive. Expect to pay well over £100 – even up to £50 more – for a quality graphite rod equipped with good rings and reel fitting, with glass rods about half that price range.

Most rods of this type are made in two sections, joined by some form of spigot joint, though many of them are constructed from about nine feet (2.7 m) of graphite, graphite composite or glass with a separate stiff-handle section made from either high-tensile aluminium tube or of the same material as the blank – graphite or glass.

The rings should be strongly made, lined with one of the modern hard centres (like aluminium oxide or titanium), and have large centres near the reel tapering down to quite small ones near the rod tip. The handle area is usually covered with some form of rubber or plastic, glued on, with either a rugged reel fitting equipped with a screw-up clasp, or special clamps with which the reel can be positioned at any chosen point along the handle's length to suit the caster.

It is possible to save quite a considerable outlay by buying the blank and the requisite rings, plastic handle covering and reel fittings and building the rod yourself. Such work is very simple, and all the rods

The multiplier is used on top of the rod. This is a Policansky Monitor Number 4 lever-drag reel firmly anchored with braces to a 30 lb (13.6 kg) class rod. The butt cap of the rod is slotted and fits into the bar on the groin protector, which prevents the rod from turning when playing a fish.

listed can be made at home. Details of how to do this follow later.

The second rod required for lighter shore fishing – casting weights of 2–3 oz (56.5–85 g) – is usually between 10½–11½ ft (3.2–3.5 m) in length. It needs to be lighter in the hand, since unlike the stiffer rod just mentioned, which is fished in a rod-rest or laid down on rocks or against pier rails, this one may need to be held for long periods. Its main quarry is the bass, arguably the most sought-after shore fish in the British Isles, though the rod will also do very well for smooth-hounds and rays, and in competent hands, will cope with tope, modest conger and other heavy fish.

The reason such a rod needs to be light, for long periods of being held while fishing in the surf, or from rocky stances, is that bass often take a baited hook very delicately, and unless one is ready, sometimes to yield line to a biting fish, at others to strike home the hook immediately, many chances will be missed.

This rod is ideally equipped with a small, salmon or pike-size multiplier, the type which holds about 200 yards (182.8 m) of 15 lb (6.8 kg) line, though most bass fishing will be done with lines of 8–12 lb (3.6–5.4 kg) test. The rod also doubles well for tackling big ballan wrasse from rocky ledges, or even heavy lure fishing for pollack and coalfish in similar situations.

The third rod I would recommend is one of between 9 and 10 ft (2.6–3 m) or a little longer, to be

Rod 1, the powerful surfcasting rod, with one of the matching reels suggested, the ABU Ambassadeur 7000. This rod casts up to 6 oz (170 g) long distances for cod, tope, conger, stingray and even common skate on occasions.

This light surf rod (rod 2 in the list) is uncluttered with 'hardware' and weighs just over 12 oz (340 g). The only luxury is a length of rubbery plastic to hold. The butt is equipped with a rubber walking stick pad. The matching reel is an Ambassadeur 6000C.

Rod 3 is a 9–10 ft (2.7–3 m) weapon of the salmon (spring) spinning or carp type. This one is excellent, though it would be better with a screw reel fitting instead of the sliding rings. The rings are, in fact, of nylon and therefore not subject to corrosion. The reel is a medium size fixed-spool type of Japanese origin.

Rod 4 with a matching ABU Cardinal 44X fixed-spool reel. The rod in this case is 7 ft (2.1 m) long and was made from a fly rod blank. It weighs 4 oz (113.3 g) and has been used by the author to catch bonefish in the Bahamas, seatrout, mackerel, pollack, black bream and mullet in Britain. Its rings have never needed replacement. They are Pezon et Michel Chromex.

A sound design of lightweight ring for surfcasting rods is this centre-supported model with a hard chromed finish that resists both line abrasion and corrosion by saltwater. It is also very strong.

Long, unjointed surfcasting rods – or jointed rods assembled – may be carried on a variety of racks that fit to roof gutters on cars.

used for float-fishing and heavy spinning from rocks, piers and cliff ledges. The quarry will be bass, ballan wrasse, pollack and coalfish, as a rule, and the rod may also be used for similar fishing from a boat. A salmon/pike spinning rod is about right, or one of the modern salmon bait-fishing rods. Lines of about 7–10 lb (3.1–4.5 kg) will be suitable in most cases and though many people will prefer to use a saltwater-proof fixed-spool reel with a 200-yard (18.2 m) capacity, my preference for the spinning technique is a small multiplier.

Bass, mackerel, garfish, smaller school bass, small pollack and coalfish – fish, in fact, running from a little over a pound (0.45 kg) up to maybe 5 lb (2.26 kg) – are best taken on a much lighter and shorter spinning rod, of the type used in freshwater fishing for trout, seatrout, perch and chub. Usually from 7–8 ft (2.1–2.4 m), very light and flexible and for use with lines of 3–6 lb (1.3–2.7 kg) test on a smaller fixed-spool reel than the one used on the previous rod, this little wand makes light spinning tremendous fun and may, of course, be used from a boat for the same species and with the same reel and lines.

The fifth rod for the shore-fisher's armoury is a

Left: A spigot joint on a hollow glass bass rod is fitted together. The gap left when assembled is to permit the joint to remain stable after the glass wears a little with years of use. The whippings are made very firmly to prevent casting and fishing stresses splitting the rod blank.

Rod 5, the freshwater Avon type, for mullet etc. It is used in the open sea, in brackish water, even in pure freshwater for thin-lipped grey mullet. The reels are a Black Cat open centrepin (on the rod), a Rapidex caged centrepin, and a Mitchell 300 fixed-spool reel.

The High Bells Life ring, best for the mullet-type rod.

freshwater Avon-type trotting rod. Most are about 11 ft (3.3 m) in length and very light and flexible, for use with lines of 3–5 lb (1.3–2.2 kg) on either the fixed-spool reel suggested for the trout-spinning rod above or, for some purists such as myself, a centre-pin reel. The main quarry is mullet, either up the tidal reaches of rivers (sometimes beyond the influence of the salt) or from rocks and piers in the sea, though it will also be great fun when float-fishing for mackerel, school bass, garfish, and even flounders in muddy estuarine creeks. Such fish, even flounders, are a revelation on such tackle.

I estimate that fewer than one per cent of British sea anglers have fished for saltwater fish with a fly rod and line, but though the opportunities for using such an outfit in our waters are few, I would not wish to be without one. A graphite reservoir trout rod for use with weight-forward and shooting-taper lines of 7–8 weight, and about 9 ft (2.7 m) in length, equipped with a graphite reel like the Leeda LC 80, carrying 50 or more yards (45.7 m) of 20 lb (9.07 kg) braided Terylene backing spliced to it, will provide tremendous fun with school bass, mackerel and garfish, and maybe the odd seatrout, when fishing fry-imitating streamer-type flies, from rocky vantage points along the shore or in estuaries, even from open beaches giving way to reasonably deep water. And from a small dinghy, either at anchor in a spot chosen to ambush the quarry, or drifting, the fly can be a great killer.

Boat fishing calls for a range of about five rods, three of which should be ordinary boat rods of about

When fishing for bass in the Atlantic surf there is nowhere to rest the rod, since one is standing in the surf most of the time. A light rod tires the angler less than a heavy one and adds to both fish-fighting enjoyment and ease of handling.

7 ft (2.1 m) in total length, and in International Game Fish Association (IGFA) line-classes 20, 30 and 50 lb (9.0, 13.6 and 22.6 kg) for use with rugged multiplier reels, ideally equipped with smooth lever-drag systems – though good star-drag reels will still do the job to a degree. The same reel, with different spools, can be made to cope with the 20 and 30 lb lines, but a larger one is needed for the 50 lb class. Each should hold an adequate quantity of line: 400 yards (365 m).

The rods, though very similar in general make-up, have different resistance to bending into about a quarter-circle, at which shape each will protect its selected test of line by absorbing shocks. With the reel drag adjusted to just yield line when the rod is in a quarter-circle, a big fish will have great difficulty in breaking the line, though the angler must be able to handle his rod and reel competently to complete the system.

Most such rods have a glass, graphite or graphite/glass tip of about 5½ ft (1.67 m) in length which is ferruled or has a special screw-locking connection into a strong butt about 18 inches (45.7 cm) long and which has at its front end the strong, locking reel seat. The ferrule on the flexible tip section fits into the front, open end of the reel seat. There is a cork or resilient foam plastic foregrip on the base of the tip, and the stiff butt is usually covered with some form of plastic, or may have a cork grip just behind the reel seat. At the extreme end of the butt piece there should be a rubber button or a slotted metal butt cap which fits into a plain cup-shaped holder strapped around the angler's waist, to provide support when fighting a fish. The better holders have a crossbar into which the slots on the rod butt-cap locate, to prevent the rod from turning under tension, due to the reel being fished on top of the rod, as multipliers are.

At the very least, these three rods should have good quality roller rings at tip and butt (Aftco, made in America, are superb), with very rugged, hard ceramic-type lined or hard-metal intermediate rings – at least six of them, to distribute the considerable bending stresses the rods must accept. Roller rings enable the angler to recover line more easily and smoothly when it is under great tension, more important at the rod's tip, where the line angles over the ring.

Personally, I favour all roller rings on such rods, which make it possible to tackle the real giants of the sea, and afford the ability to fish with wire lines

Left: This still-water trout fly rod has big hard chromed snake rings on it to facilitate line shooting when casting for distance with shooting-head lines. The reel is an Intrepid Rimfly with all the paint stripped off and the aluminium alloy polished. It is washed after use and wiped with a soft cloth soaked with WD40.

Centre: The 30 lb (13.6 kg) class boat rod and a matching reel: the rod is an American Berkley Regulation model, the reel the Policansky Monitor Number 4. The slots in the

butt cap of the rod may be clearly seen: they fit into a crossbar in the groin protector to prevent the rod from rolling when fighting fish.

Right: A lighter boat combination, the 20 lb (9.0 kg) class rod and a suitable matching reel: the ABU Ambassadeur 9000C. The rod is a Puma by Martin Ashby of Going Brothers, the specialist Southend-on-Sea tackle shop. Only butt and tip rollers are fitted, but rollers throughout are fitted on request at extra cost.

in deep water and fast tides where normal lines may demand the use of lead weights far too heavy for most to use. Wire lines can get the bait down with much less lead, but such lines need roller rings if work-hardening – and subsequent line kinking and breakage – are to be avoided.

I would rather have a glass boat rod with the cash saved on graphite used to provide roller rings throughout, than to have a modern graphite-composite blank with only a roller tip ring.

The 20 lb (9 kg) class rod is fine for bottom fishing for cod, rays, tope, smooth-hounds and inshore conger with lines from 17–20 lb (7.7–9.0 kg) test, as well as jigging or pirk fishing over wrecks or reefs for cod, pollack, coalfish and even big bass, plus trolling natural baits, like sand-eels, or artificials over similar deep-water grounds.

The 30 lb (13.6 kg) class rod will tackle similar species, both bottom fishing, fishing pirks, feather or plastic squid-type jigs, and is also good for tope in strong tidal currents or very deep water where the stronger line can be a bonus. With careful handling, a quality 30 lb class combination will also handle blue, porbeagle and thresher sharks up to 200 lb (90.7 kg) or so, and conger eels up to 80 lb (36.4 kg) have been boated on such light tackle. However, tackling such heavy conger, as well as common skate and halibut, is not as easy as tackling the free-swimming surface fish, like the sharks. You have to pull, with a certain amount of brute force, a big conger, skate or halibut up to the surface, usually in very deep water over rocky ground or a wreck, and sometimes you are hampered by strong tidal flow. Sharks will make fast runs, often in midwater to close to the surface, and this tires them, so that very much bigger running fish may be taken successfully on 20 and 30 lb class tackle rather than what should be used for halibut, common skate and big congers.

I did not include a 50 lb (22.68 kg) class rod-and-reel outfit in earlier editions because I had personally rarely found a use for one in a lifetime of sea fishing in the United Kingdom and in Caribbean and other warm-sea fishing. In fact, I have used a 50 lb outfit only for halibut fishing in the Orkney Islands, for common-skate fishing and, over deep-water wrecks known to hold huge conger, on maybe a dozen occasions.

However, with better-equipped big angling boats going many miles offshore and finding new grounds, including wrecks and reefs, the chances of finding a use for the 50 lb class outfit are now increased. For example, the record British rod-caught records for halibut, common skate, conger, and mako and porbeagle sharks are, respectively, now 234 lb

(106.1 kg), 227 lb (102.9 kg), 109 lb 6 oz (49.5 kg), 500 lb (226.8 kg) and 465 lb (210.9 kg), and there can be little doubt that bigger specimens will be encountered.

Because of the combination of sheer weight, plus the strong pulling power of these huge fish, specially in deep, fast water, a 50 lb class rod must have roller-rings throughout, and the reel, which really needs to be of the lever-drag type, with a very smooth drag at that, should be capable of holding about 400 yards (365.76 m) of 50 lb (22.68 kg) test line.

If you might one day like to enter a fish for a record under the International Game Fish Association rules, bear in mind that the line used must test no more than the class entered, and a test-sample must be included with a claim. This is why anglers fishing to IGFA classes select lines known to test a couple of pounds or so less than the class limit. Also, in all three line classes I have mentioned, the actual working tip section of the rod may be no longer than 5 ft (1.5 m) and the butt sections for the 20 and 30 lb (9 and 13.6 kg) rods be no longer than 18 inches (45.7 cm); the butt of the 50 lb rod must not exceed 27 inches (68.5 cm).

The fourth rod in the boat-fishing range is rather a specialised one. Termed an uptide rod, it is for fishing from an anchored boat in shallow water and casting the baited tackle uptide, maybe as far as 50 yards (45.72 m) from the boat. This casting achieves several advantages. It puts the bait away from the boat, which may, by its shadow cast on the seabed, or by noises made by the occupants, otherwise scare fish in such shallow and sometimes clear water. And because the wired anchor lead's front end faces the tidal flow, the force of the flow on the line pulls the anchor wires into the seabed rather than out of it, thus firmly anchoring the tackle with less lead than when fishing downtide.

There is also one more advantage, which is that, when a fish takes the bait and moves downtide with it towards the boat, it is first brought up short by the anchored lead, which, if your hook is very sharp – as it should be, of course – will begin to set the point in the fish's mouth. The usual bite signal when uptide fishing is a sudden slackening of the line, and the rod is quickly picked up, the slack line wound up as fast as possible until the weight of the fish is felt, when a good firm strike is made. Few bites are missed when fishing thus.

Uptide rods need to cast from 4–8 oz (113.3–226.7 g) and are ideally about 9–10 ft (2.7–3.0 m) in length with flexible tips, to give a good bite indication as well as keeping the lead from being yanked from its anchorage by sudden boat movements. A good surfcasting multiplier of the more rugged, larger type, loaded with line of about 15 lb (6.8 kg), is a good partner for this rod.

Cod, stingrays and bass, plus thornback rays, are the usual quarry of the uptide angler.

Finally, the very sporting little rod for fishing from a boat, usually at anchor but also on a slow drift, for black and red bream, plaice and flounder, bass, small pollack and coalfish, even smooth-hounds, is a crank-handle freshwater baitcaster of the type used by American and Canadian anglers to cast lures for large and smallmouth bass, pike, muskellunge, walleye and the like.

Such rods are usually made for use with lines vary-

The baitcaster, shown with a suitable reel: the Ambassadeur 5000C. This combination is excellent for black bream, red bream, plaice and smooth-hounds from a boat.

ing from about 5 lb (2.26 kg) test to about 15 lb (6.8 kg) test, and are in one or two pieces and between 6 and 6½ ft (1.8 and 1.98 m). I suggest one of the lighter ones, to fish lines from 5–10 lb (2.26–4.5 kg) test.

A small multiplier partners this rod – one that has a smooth drag system and which will hold about 150 yards (137.1 m) of the chosen nylon monofilament line. I have used ABU Ambassadeur 5000 and 6000 series reels for many years and cannot fault them.

The fishing may be light legering, or driftlining, or even trolling, but catching black bream and plaice on such an outfit can be quite a revelation to those who have used heavier boat tackle in the past. If you choose to acquire such a rod, of hollow-glass or graphite, it is likely to have freshwater rings and fittings on it, which may corrode when used in salt water. Wash the whole rod thoroughly in fresh, warm water after every trip to avoid the problem, though I suggest you do the same with all your tackle used in the sea. It is a chore that will keep tackle in excellent condition for a lifetime.

There is a vast range of casting and boat-fishing sea rods in Britain today, made from graphite, graphite composite of several types and glass. Besides the complete rods turned out by the major companies, including Daiwa, Shakespeare, ABU, Normark, Century Composites and Cono-flex, there are many good specialist tackle shops where sound advice on choice of a blank and components may be obtained, either for the rod to be built to your requirements or for you to do the job yourself.

Unless you have no time – and little time is needed – to build your own rods, I would always suggest you select blanks and components and build your own rods. Not only does this save about a third of the cost of a ready made or custom-built rod, but is a very enjoyable job. And learning to properly assemble tubular rods means that, when you have accidental damage to your rods, like a ring being broken or coming loose, or joints needing tight-whipping, you can do it yourself and maintain your gear in optimum condition.

Doing the work yourself, and selecting the blank, handle, reel fitting and handle covering yourself, permits you to have exactly what you want – from the thickness of the handle, the position of the reel on it, even the length and colour of the ring and joint whippings and the number and positioning of the rings.

Let's see how easy, and quick, it is to assemble one of the three IGFA boat rods from parts bought at the tackle shop. All three rods can be the same, in terms of parts needed and the way the work is done. Only the stiffness of the working tip, whose length may be

Above: Typical construction of the tip to butt junction of a well made boat rod. The Vee in the tube on the tip locates into a transverse bar inside the reel fitting, the two then being locked by the knurled collar shown up against the cork foregrip. This construction is very strong and stops the tip from turning in the butt section when using a multiplier and there is tension from a big fish.

as short as 5 ft (1.5 m) or as long as 6 ft (1.8 m), differs.

Butt and tip combinations are available from the shop, as is a specially strong screw reel fitting combined with a male ferrule which is fitted to the base of the tip section and which slides into the open end of the tubular chromed brass or stainless-steel reel fitting, the best of them having a locking nut which screws down over the assembled joint, to hold the tip and butt firmly together. The fixed clip of the reel fitting is the part into which the ferrule on the tip fits.

Butt sections may be of tubular graphite, heavy-wall glass, carbon-glass composite or high-tensile duralumin tube. Butt sections are simply there to put the reel in such a position that the winding hand is in a comfortable position when the end of the butt is rested in the groin, to give leverage when fighting a fish. Therefore, I like the overall length of the butt, including the glued-on reel seat, to be no longer than 18 inches (45.7 cm). My arms are 22 inches (55.8 cm) long from armpit to wrist and a 16-inch (40.6 cm) butt (including the reel seat in position) suits me best, placing my front hand comfortably on the front grip, glued to the butt of the working tip, when the button or slotted gimbal on the butt's extremity is in my groin (in a groin protector or belly pad).

First of all, fit the male ferrule to the tip, making sure it is a firm push-fit by testing without any glue. Clean any grease or metal turnings from the inside of the ferrule with petrol, alcohol or cellulose thinner on a cloth wrapped round a suitable length and thickness of dowel. Failure to do this (and on the inside of the reel seat tube) is likely to result in the adhesive

failing to bond properly. If the fit is not quite tight enough, find a suitable thickness of thread that, when wrapped tightly over the blank, will take up the slack. Apply a thin coat of Araldite to the area of the blank that will be inside the ferrule, and push the blank right home to the end of the ferrule, pressing the ferrule on the floor or against any other firm surface. Wipe off any extruded adhesive with a cloth.

Leave the job for about 24 hours for the adhesive to cure properly, before fitting the reel seat to your butt section.

Butt sections can be obtained in lengths of 18–24 inches (45.7–60.9 cm) and you can then, after fitting the reel seat, cut off the appropriate bit from the other end to suit you. First, test the length of the male ferrule that goes into the reel seat's open end and, with the ferrule still firmly home, slide the butt section into the other end of the real seat's tube. When the butt and male ferrule meet in the reel seat tube, mark the butt about a quarter-inch (6 mm) forward of this point. This will allow for future wear of the male ferrule and the inside of the reel seat tube, thus maintaining a tight fit for years to come, as well as leaving a gap for any extruded adhesive, which might otherwise cause a problem in assembly. Apply a thin coat of Araldite to the butt section to the mark you have made, and slide the reel seat into position. Again, leave to set for 24 hours.

Since you will be saving a lot of money by building the rod yourself, it makes sense to have the best rings you can buy, so choose a set of Aftco rollers, which come with a large double butt roller, and smaller single rollers diminishing in size towards the slim tip of the blank, with a roller tip. You will have bought the correct size tip roller to match the diameter of the blank so the roller's tube is a good fit.

But before you whip on the rings, you have to decide on what kind of forward grip you want, since you have to slide it down into position, butted up to the male-ferrule collar, from the thin end of the tip. Despite the wide choice of specially made foamed plastic and rubber grips available for sea rods today, not to mention the cycle, mower, scythe and other type grips that can be used, I still prefer the traditional handle of good, solid cork. Buy cork rings that have as few holes in their surfaces as you can find, and with bores that will fit very tightly to the blank when slid down into position. Apply Araldite to the first half-inch of blank above the male-ferrule reinforcing band, then a little to the edge of the cork facing towards the rod tip. Slide it into position firmly. Wipe off any extruded adhesive around the ferrule. Now coat the next inch of blank and slide on the next cork ring. Glue will exude between it and the one already in position, which will ensure that each cork is glued to the next as well as to the blank's surface. Push each cork very hard, with the rod's ferrule against a firm surface. You want no joins to show between the corks.

Continue sliding down corks until you have the length of handle you want. About 10 inches (25.4 cm) will do nicely. Give the last cork a really good push, then tightly apply a rough temporary lashing of string round the blank and tight up against the cork, to hold everything compressed while the Araldite cures. Leave the job to set for 24 hours.

Shaping is very easy. Use a sharp, small Surform first to work all round the uneven corks, to form a neat parallel-sided outline. The blobs of adhesive will come off as well. Work on a bench or old table, constantly turning the blank to ensure the blank is centralised in the cork. The usual handle shape for a boat rod, and the one I prefer, is a simple gently sloping one, from about an inch (2.54 cm) near the ferrule and along most of its length before sloping down to meet the bank. A metal collar, of chromed brass or stainless steel, is then slid down and glued in place on the sloping front corks, to finish the handle off neatly, and protect the front of the handle from damage.

Shaping the corks is done with sandpaper on a sanding block, turning the blank as before. To get a smooth finish, use finer grades of abrasive paper before you think you need to do so. Give the corks a filling of 'deal' coloured plastic wood, then finally smooth with fine silicon-carbide paper, used dry.

For a 5½-foot (1.67 m) working tip, you will need a roller tip ring and five or six intermediate rollers, including the double-roller butt ring. Make sure when you buy them that the tube on the tip roller is a good fit on your blank. Positioning the rollers should be carried out so that the first roller down from the tip one is no more than six inches (15.24 cm) distant and with the double-roller butt ring about 18–20 inches (45.7–50.7 cm) from the front of the reel when it is clamped on the reel seat. Position the others in diminishing distances apart from butt to tip. The idea is to distribute stress evenly over the rod when it is bent into a fighting fish and to keep line clear of the rod blank itself.

Before doing any positioning, however, grind or file down the ends of the base (foot) of each roller on the upper sides, so that a feather edge is formed sloping down to the rod surface when the ring is in place. This will avoid an unsightly bulge in the whipping and also avoids the possibility of the sharp edge wearing through the whippings at times when the rod is flexing to the fight of a fish.

Rods with fast-taper tips need more rings posi-

Top: Detail of the single roller tip ring on the Puma 20 lb (9.0 kg) class rod.

Above: Roller butt ring for a light tackle boat rod, showing the way in which the line should be passed through. The reel is on the left out of the photograph. The underwhipping can be clearly seen.

tioned quite close to each other near the tip while slower tapers can have their rings fairly evenly distributed. Most modern boat-rod blanks have a fast-taper construction, since the flexibility of the last 18 inches (45.7 cm) helps to prevent line breakage, due to sudden shocks imposed by a fish, while providing better leverage for the angler when lifting to get a fish to the surface.

Having decided on where each roller ring will go, and having marked the blank, with pencil or masking tape over the distance the base of each ring will cover, plus that essential quarter-inch (6 mm) on either side, whip the rod tightly with a reasonably strong rod-whipping thread made from nylon or Terylene (Dacron in American terminology) between the marks made. This whipping forms a firm bedding for the base of each roller-ring, so that when the bases are whipped firmly down on top of the bedding, there is less tendency for them to loosen in use, plus the fact that the blank surface itself is given protection against abrasion from the bases when the rod is fully arched. This is known as underwhipping.

When beginning the underwhipping, trap a turn of thread with a forefinger, then turn the rod while guiding the next turns of thread over the tag-end. When about half-a-dozen turns have been made, trim off the tag end and continue turning the rod away from you, laying each turn of thread under as much tension as you can exert tightly up against the previous turn. To finish off a whipping, insert a six-inch (15 cm) length of 10 lb (4.5 kg) nylon monofilament under the last 10 turns and thread the end of the thread through the looped nylon. Pull on the monofilament loop until the tag is hard up against the turns around the rod and then, with a very sharp blade, held at a right angle to the blank's surface, cut the tag as close as possible to the looped monofilament. Continue pulling on the monofilament, which drags the tag-end of the whipping

Personal comfort when the water surges waist deep on the wild Atlantic surf beaches of south-west Ireland is the key to enjoyment. Here the angler fights a bass in a gathering storm over Mount Brandon on the Dingle Peninsula.

This angler fishing a rocky cove in North Cornwall has taken the precaution of wearing non-slip footwear on his rocky stance, and also has a one-piece blaze-orange suit to protect him from the drenching waves. The suit would also permit him to be easily seen by rescuers should he slip in or be stranded by the tide.

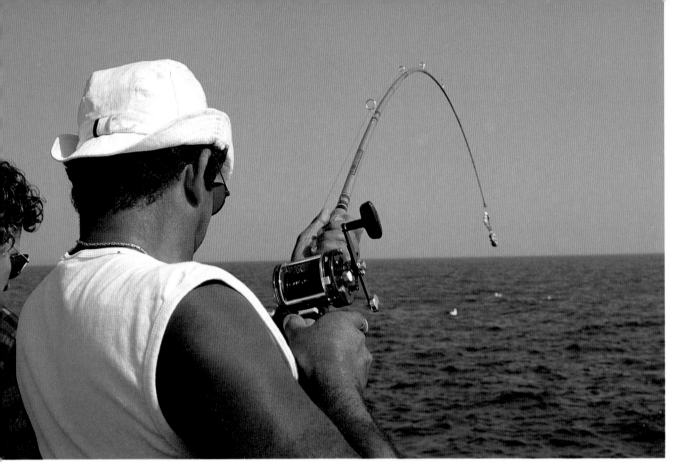

Light rods like this permit anglers to use low breaking strain lines against heavy fish. The rod takes the shocks and, aided by the reel's drag system makes life easy for the angler.

Right: Slim modern beach-casting rods can be impressively flexed by good casting technique and project bait and terminal tackle a long way out.

This fine bass has been fooled into taking this modified sand-eel as the real thing. The soft plastic artificial wriggles attractively in the water and looks like other sand-eels swimming near by.

There are about one thousand pounds worth of graphite surfcasting rods in this photograph. These are the famous Zziplex rods ready to leave the Kent factory.

Right: A good selection of lures for spinning and trolling. Top three are flexible plastic Wagtails. The same wriggling principle is used on the Red Gill plastic sand-eels down the left side of the group, which are separated from the Wagtails by a deep-diving plug coloured like a small mackerel. This is a Rapala plug from Finland, and excellent for bass and pollack. It may be fished with an uptrace lead for deep work, especially when trolling. On the right, top to bottom, are various wobbling spoons – ABU Rick, ABU Ellips, ABU Toby, ABU Koster, a British wobbler with a weedguard, three heavyweight Sild-type wobblers, and a Mepps Comet number two bar-spoon. All the lures in the right column cast very well and are suitable for bass, pollack, coalfish, mackerel and garfish, in appropriate sizes, though the Mepps is most suitable for mackerel and school-bass, and will also take seatrout – not included in this book but a very welcome bonus when encountered on light spinning gear.

Keeping the rod in a smooth curve is the mark of an experienced angler. This man has hooked a large smoothhound and is applying additional braking pressure with his thumb on the spool of his reel.

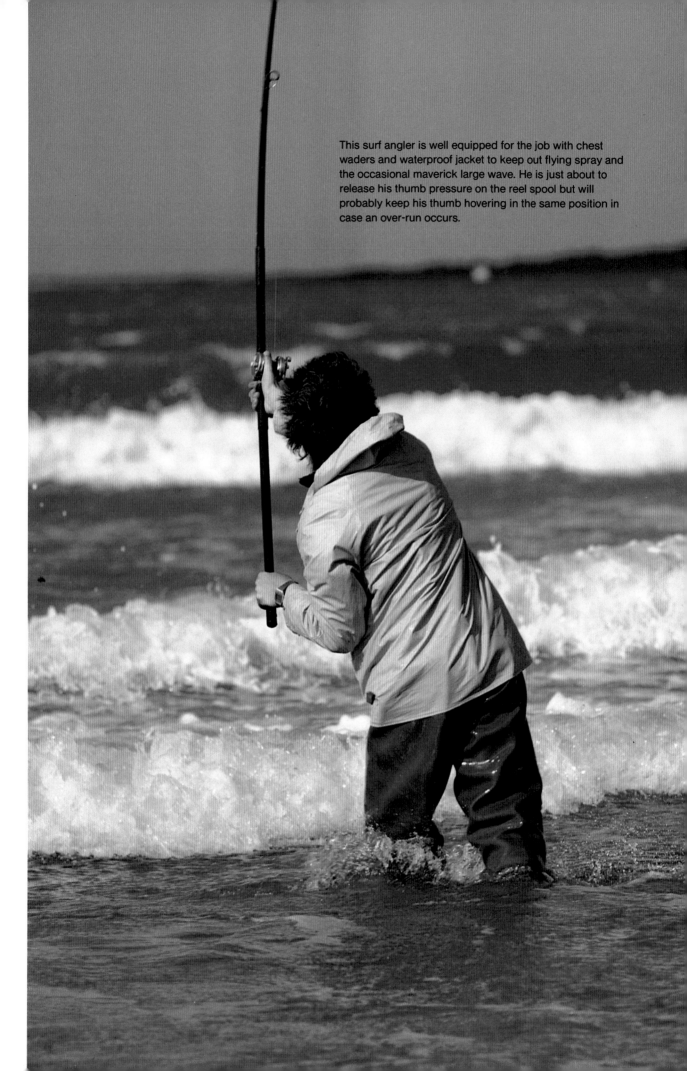

This surf angler is well equipped for the job with chest waders and waterproof jacket to keep out flying spray and the occasional maverick large wave. He is just about to release his thumb pressure on the reel spool but will probably keep his thumb hovering in the same position in case an over-run occurs.

Lugworms can be various colours but are mainly reddish pink ranging through brown to almost jet black. The red ones, especially when they are small, are known as blowers.

Below: The common shore crab, like all crabs, grows by shedding its old shell when it becomes too small and growing another. This one's old shell can be clearly seen to be smaller than the soft crab which has recently crawled out of it. In the soft stage, or just before it sheds its shell (when it is known as a peeler) the crab is a favoured bait for bass, cod, smoothhounds among other fish.

thread under the final turns of whipping, but does not, as in some methods, pull the tag-end out between the turns of whipping. By this method, there is no emergent tag-end of thread to cut off and a very smooth, secure whipping is the result. When the tag-end is pulled right through, as some people suggest, it is very difficult to trim off the tag-end close enough to avoid a bump being formed in the subsequent coats of varnish applied to the whippings.

Having whipped between the marked points

where the rings will go, give each whipping a coat of polyurethane varnish (Humbrol is good) rubbed in well with the tip of a forefinger, so that it penetrates the thread to the rod surface. Leave to dry overnight.

The roller-rings may next be whipped in position, centred in the underwhippings. Begin with the double-roller butt ring, but first fit the butt and tip together and put the reel in position on the butt. Sighting along from the reel, tape the butt roller in position, checking several times to ensure that the

1. Whipping on a ring. Begin by moistening the first three inches with saliva, which prevents the threads from slipping on the shiny blank, then lay the thread on the rod just ahead of the sloping ring leg, holding it with the forefinger.

3. Continue to turn the blank, keeping the spool of thread under considerable tension for a tight whipping. At this stage the trapped tag end may be cut off by see-sawing across it on the glass surface with a very sharp scalpel or knife.

2. Rotate the blank, holding down the end of the thread, and trap the end with the first turn of the thread round the blank. Use plenty of tension, both with the thread and with finger pressure on the tag of thread.

4. About six turns from the point at which the whipping will end, insert a loop made from a separate piece of thread.

41

5. When the remaining turns of whipping have been completed, keep all the turns firmly anchored by finger pressure and tuck the end of the thread – after cutting off from the spool – through the loop.

6. Pull on the ends of the loop, still holding all whipping turns secure, to drag the tag end under the tight turns of thread.

7. Pull the tag end firmly at a right angle and trim flush with the surface of the whipping.

rollers are in line with the middle of the reel's spool. Then, beginning on the rod blank side of the underwhipping, begin whipping towards the base of the ring (the one left without a wrapping of tape) so that turns of thread climb up the slope you have carefully ground or filed down. Proceed as for the underwhipping, but do ensure that you retain as much tension on the thread as you find possible. Many commercially built rods are whipped by women who lack the manual strength necessary to maintain sufficient tension (though they do a neat job) and such rings may turn in their whippings under great stress. The photographs of whipping on an ordinary rod ring show how the work proceeds.

Boat rods take a great deal of punishment. They are leaned against gunwales, along which they often slide when the boat pitches or rolls, and varnish can be scraped off whippings, leading to fraying and the eventual loosening of the coils of thread. So carefully coat the ring whippings with at least four coats of polyurethane varnish – small cans of Humbrol brand stocked by model-makers' shops are good – applied with a flat, soft brush. Let each coat harden for at least 24 hours.

The surface of most graphite and glass rod blanks that are sold in Britain are smoothly finished and sealed with various hard lacquers, sometimes heat-treated. They are best left as they are, only the whippings being varnished. It is unlikely you will be able to improve on the blank-maker's finish, though you may wish to apply a coat of tough lacquer if the rod's finish becomes badly scraped and chipped after several seasons of hard use. Always rub down the original finish with silicon-carbide 'wet and dry' abrasive paper, used wet, before re-finishing. The rubbing-down provides a key for the new coat of lacquer or varnish.

Just as boat rods are easily assembled at home, so are the other types of rods listed for shore fishing. The shore-casting rods simply need a set of hard-centred rings whipping on, plus either a cork or plastic or rubber handle – sleeve type or taped with the last two mentioned – and something to hold the reel on the butt in the required position.

The big surfcasting rod will need about 10 rings, plus a tubed and strut-supported tip ring. The butt ring, with an inside diameter of about an inch (2.54 cm) for multiplier reels and twice that size for fixed-spool reels, should be positioned about two feet (60.9 cm) above the reel position, for a multiplier, and about 40 inches (101.6 cm) for a fixed-spool reel. With the next ring down from the tip ring positioned about 5 inches (12.7 cm) from the tip, grade the other rings in increasing spacings. One of my hollow-glass surf rods has the following spacings (from the tip ring) and has always worked well: 5 in (12.7 cm), 6 in (15.2 cm), 7 in (17.7 cm), 8 in (20.3 cm), 9 in (22.8 cm), 10 in (25.4 cm), 11 in (27.9 cm), 12 in (30.4 cm), 14½ in (36.8 cm) and 17 in (43.1 cm). That rod is quite a fast-taper one, casting up to 5 oz (141.7 g).

Because that rod has a stiff piece of duralumin alloy joined to the butt end of the glass blank to make up into a two-piece 12½ ft (3.8 m) weapon, and because I use on it a multiplier which is equipped with a clamp which fits it firmly to the rod butt, I have no screw reel fitting on the butt. I simply joined the glass to the duralumin with a strong hardwood dowel, glued into each with Araldite, and covered the duralumin and a few inches of the glass with neoprene tape, wrapped edge-to-edge over Araldite. The reel clamps firmly on to the plastic-covered metal.

But I do not favour such a method when clamping a reel straight on to the butt of a rod which is hollow glass or hollow graphite, since there would be a likelihood of crushing the blank. Then I would use a screw reel seat of a suitable tube size to slide into position on the blank and glue it in place with Araldite. The Fuji fittings are very good. The fixed ring of the fitting faces the butt end of the rod.

Neither do I much favour the popular Coaster reel fittings – like hose-clips – for clamping a reel to a blank, unless it has a duralumin butt extension or is very thick-walled glass.

All the other rods I have suggested can be made just as easily as the ones outlined – except for the crank-handle baitcaster, since the crank handle is not widely available. I would settle for a factory-made rod, probably one of the Abu-Garcia range.

There are many good, reliable blanks available from which all the listed rods can be made, and I certainly would not discount hollow glass just because graphite and its various mixtures is now the 'in thing'. However, good graphite casting blanks are produced by firms such as Zziplex, Cono-flex, Normark and Century Composites, some of them also making good glass blanks, including tips for boat rods.

There are many good light spinning rods available and it is hardly worthwhile making them at home, unless you have the chance to buy a blank at a giveaway price. Good spinning rods in graphite or a graphite mixture are made by Abu-Garcia, Daiwa, Shakespeare, and Hardy Brothers. These same companies can also be relied upon for suitable reservoir-type fly rods for saltwater use.

Just as there is a very wide selection of suitable rods and blanks for sporting saltwater use, so there is of

reels, both multipliers and fixed-spool reels.

Very different design features are needed for the various types of fishing. For example, surfcasting and spinning multipliers must have lightweight (but fairly strong) spools, so that only the pull of the flying lead or lure keeps them spinning, rather than their own weight, and so that the light spool is able to start to spin easily. Free-running bearings, too, are needed, so that long, smooth casts are possible. A smooth-working drag system, either adjustable with a star-wheel or lever, is desirable when seeking long-running speedsters, like tope and smooth-hounds, though this is not so necessary for cod or bass.

Most of the furthest-casting reels have either centrifugal or magnetic spool-braking systems, which operate fully only when the spool is revolving at peak speeds, and this helps to avoid over-runs, though an 'educated' thumb, to control the revolving spool, is a key factor in good casting. Casting reels need a fairly highly geared recovery rate, so that the lure may be fished quite quickly or that the tackle may be reeled in quickly, to avoid getting snagged on rocks and other seabed projections. Sometimes, too, a rapid recovery rate helps when fighting a fast-swimming fish, like a tope, which will often swim towards the angler and create slack line. Gear ratios of about 4½:1 are about right, though a little more or less will be acceptable.

Reels for boat fishing need very different features. Often the fish have to be hauled up, fighting hard and

When tope fishing from the shore, especially in shallow water, and a fixed-spool reel is used, it must have a free-turning line roller or bollard in the pick-up and a spool capacity of about 400 yd (365.7 m) of 15 lb (6.8 kg) line.

This is the position for the thumb when controlling the spinning spool of a multiplier during the cast. The edge of the ball of the thumb rests on the edge of the spool when the lead is in flight, so avoiding friction-induced line or skin burns.

The lever-drag is simple to use and gives quick, sensitive adjustment while still holding the reel handle.

using their body shapes to resist, helped by the tidal flow perhaps, from very deep water. A very strongly built spool is needed, so that stretched line, recovered under great tension and then contracting on the spool, will not crush the spool, distorting or, at worst, smashing it under pressure.

The spool must have sufficient capacity for the required strength of line needed for the various species, too, and the gearing for most of this type of reel should be no more than about 3:1, because a higher ratio makes it difficult to wind in line against strong pressure. This is especially a requirement when fishing for hard-pulling giants like conger, common skate, halibut and even big cod and ling. A slightly higher ratio can be used, and is often a help, when tackling fast-swimming species that often fight near the surface, particularly the sharks.

Different qualities are required for the fixed-spool reels. Those used for heavy leads, cast from the beach or rocks, need to be robustly built and with big spools and strong pick-up assemblies. The line coming off the front of the spool needs to do so smoothly, and therefore a long spool (measured front to back) is desirable, as well as a fairly wide one. This is a help in reducing the drag of the line over the front lip of the spool as the tackle gets to a point about 80 yards (73 m) from the angler, since the drag over the lip increases as the level of the line on the spool decreases.

Because the act of casting introduces sudden stresses at the moment of line release, fixed-spool reels for heavy shore casting should have a manual line pick-up system instead of the more usual automatic bale-arm system, which tends to be released by the casting action, flicking over and collecting the line. This will cause line breakage or even reel and rod damage.

For light spinning and float-fishing techniques, the fixed-spool reels used may be much smaller and lighter, with higher gear ratios than the 3½–4:1 of the heavier shore models. They may have ordinary automatic pick-up systems to advantage.

Good heavy boat reels for the 20, 30 and 50 lb (9, 13.6 and 22.6 kg) class rods are made by Penn, Daiwa, Shimano, Policansky and Shakespeare, with Abu-Garcia coming into the 20 lb picture with its Ambassadeur 9000 (an older model) and the newer Nine CL. There is a wide price range in good boat reels, with lever-drag models like Daiwa's SLT Tournament series (meant for true blue-water big-game fish in tropical waters but just about justified for our bigger sharks) costing around £500 (for a 30 lb class model) to a more reasonable average of around £80 for a reel to be used for big conger or common skate.

The smaller surfcasting and heavy spinning multipliers are less varied and among the best are Abu-Garcia's Ambassadeur series in models 7000 and 7000C for big fish from the shore, like tope, and the 6500 and 6000 series for lesser fighters and smaller fish – cod, bass, stingrays and so on; Daiwa's Millionaire and Magforce series, Shimano's Triton Speedmaster 11 FSC and the Zebco Quantum. There are other, older surfcasting reels still available, like the Mitchell 602 and 600 models with plastic spools, and, if you can find them, the Penn 150 or 100 models.

This is not a full list of suitable shore-casting and heavy spinning reels, by any means. Expect to pay between £70 and £90 for the best.

Many of these smaller multipliers, which will also double for salmon and pike fishing in freshwater, come equipped with a level-wind system, which re-

The Policansky Monitor Number 2 is a fine reel for heavy shore fish, such as conger and common skate. It will cast 6 oz (170 g) up to 100 yd (91.4 m) but is not a long-distance reel. It is also a good light tackle boat reel.

Some reels come equipped with clamps with which they may be firmly attached to the rod; an Ambassadeur 7000.

An excellent light but inexpensive reel fitting, this Fuji clip is whipped firmly to the handle of the bass rod.

winds the line evenly across the spool. Many casters seeking maximum distances remove the level-wind crossbar and its attached gear and line-spreading loop, replacing the bar with a solid one. Many tackle shops will do the conversion for you. However, I will gladly give up a little distance for the advantage of a level-wind system which, specially for fighting fast-moving fish, avoids the build-up of line that can occur when one's thumb-spreading of the line is forgotten in the excitement of battle. I therefore continue to use my classic Ambassadeurs 6000C and 7000 with their level-wind mechanisms intact.

In some locations, specially in the south and west of Ireland, and in Scotland and the islands, it is possible to cast just a short way from rocks or jetties into very deep water and catch common skate well over 100 lb (45.3 kg). For this, the strongest of the two surfcasting rods, or maybe the uptide boat rod, will suffice, but line of 30 lb (13.6 kg) test, at least, will be required, and this on a very robustly made reel of at least Ambassadeur 9000 or 9000C proportions. The Daiwa LD 50H or Sealine SL250H would also do the job.

Daiwa's Black Giant fixed-spool reel is a rugged shore reel with a manual pick-up for heavy duty work. It has the important revolving roller in the pick-up, which makes line recovery under tension much easier. Shakespeare's Pro Carbon larger models are also good, but have full bale pick-up arms. These may be removed, though, leaving the reel able to do

the heavy work. There are also many fine reels in the Abu-Garcia Cardinal range, and Shimano make a reel, the Custom Lock 7000CL, on which the spool can be locked up when casting.

This last-mentioned feature is an additional block for the flipped pick-up, and also avoids the angler having to tighten up his drag when he casts, to avoid spool slippage. Spool slippage, which occurs under the massive tension on the line at the peak casting movement, is avoided on many reels only by completely tightening the drag.

Mitchell also produce good fixed-spool shore reels and their pedigree and reliability are legendary.

All these companies also make the smaller fixed-spool reels which I suggest for spinning and float fishing, but try to ensure that you buy one with the following features: a smooth drag system, a roller in the pick-up (which should be automatic), a silky recovery and, if possible, corrosion-proof finish.

The smaller fixed-spool reel, for spinning and float fishing, should have two spools, if possible. One should hold 150 yards (137 m) of 3–6 lb (1.3–2.7 kg) nylon monofilament line, to cope with light spinning and light float fishing, the other should hold about 150 yards (137 m) of about 10 lb (4.5 kg) line, for heavier spinning and float fishing. The small spool is for single-handed spinning and for use with the freshwater trotting or Avon-type rod while the larger-capacity one is for use with the salmon/pike spinning rod and more rugged spinning and float fishing. The alternative is to buy two reels, one small, the other of the salmon/pike spinning size.

Left: One of the Shimano range of modern multipliers with lever-drag systems for medium to light boat or heavy shore fishing. This is the Triton Lever Drag and takes 450 yd (411.4 m) of 20 lb (9.0 kg) line. It has a 4.2:1 recovery ratio and costs over £100.

Below: This is the Shimano Triton Speedmaster 2CFS, a superb modern surfcasting reel which takes 330 yd (301.7 m) of 15 lb (6.0 kg) test line. Its 6:1 recovery ratio helps pick up line quickly when a fish runs towards the rod, and keeps the terminal tackle clear of inshore rocks when reeling in. It has a very smooth ball-bearing star-drag system and costs over £90.

The Shimano Biomaster GT 4500 fixed-spool reel is an·up-to-date design with a long graphite spool and a two-speed oscillating system of winding line on the spool, the old crosswind principle. This crosswinding, plus the long spool, which is also slightly cone-shaped, permits very long casts due to lack of buried coils of line. The line-roller in the pick-up is of silicon-carbide for resistance to grooving. The reel holds 273 yd (249.6 m) of 14 lb (6.3 kg) nylon monofilament line. It costs over £70.

Lines

Three types of line are used in the sea: nylon monofilament, braided lines, produced from nylon or Terylene (Dacron in America) and wire. For all shore fishing the monofilament has the advantage. It is much cheaper, less visible to fish, and can take abrasion and knocks without suffering too much damage. It may be easily, very quickly and reliably joined by special knots.

However, nylon monofilament has its faults. It stretches considerably. This is more apparent in the limp, soft types; while the hard, wiry monofilaments stretch least. A monofil that is in between these extremes usually proves best. Stretch hampers the strike of the angler and if there is too much of it the hook may not penetrate the fish's mouth properly; naturally the more line there is between rod tip and fish the more stretch there will be. In addition, monofilament nylon possesses memory, in that it returns to its normal state after being stretched. If that occurs when the line has been rewound on the reel spool under considerable tension (in fighting a big fish, heaving clear of a snag, or winding in a mass of weed), the contracting of each coil imposes tremendous crushing power on the spool, which may become distorted and bind in the frame, or may be literally crushed to pieces! Plastic spools suffer worst from this, but even metal spools can succumb.

In practical terms, so far as the types of angling covered by this book are concerned, the use of monofil can be almost universal, in all tests up to 30 lb (13.6 kg) class – i.e. about 27 lb (12.2 kg) test. Braided nylon suffers from elasticity, too, and is not only more bulky for its test (thus presenting water resistance problems) but it also wears very quickly.

Braided Dacron (American) or Terylene (British) lines are generally used for big-game fishing in tests over 30 lb (13.6 kg). They are comparatively thin, some being thinner than monofilament nylon for their test, but their biggest attribute is their low elasticity. This makes it much easier to strike a hook into a fish and helps avoid damage to the reel spool when winding in line still stressed by a big, strong fish. In British and north-west European waters, however, most fishing techniques for big fish involve fishing a bait on the seabed, and this is where braided Dacron or Terylene lines fail: they do very quickly become weakened by abrasion with sand and rocks etc. In tropical waters, where their use is mainly in trolling for game fish, in the top layers of water, the lines do not come in contact with the seabed and so no abrasion takes place. It is amazing how many British saltwater anglers fail to appreciate that fact.

Braided Dacron or Terylene costs about 2½ times as much as a comparable test of quality nylon monofilament. In 30 lb (13.6 kg) and 50 lb (22.6 kg) class braid is a justifiable expense for conger, the sharks and common skate. However, with a strong reel spool and careful handling, monofilament nylon will do the job almost as well, and the author has reason to distrust braided lines, having lost several big fish, including salmon in freshwater. These lines do appear to break suddenly for no apparent reason.

Finally there is wire line. This is for use only in boat fishing. Both single strand and braided wire lines are available and their use should be confined to fishing in places where there are very strong tides and fairly deep water and where it is otherwise impossible to use sporting tackle. Being very much thinner for its test than either nylon monofilament or braided lines, wire permits the angler to fish reasonable amounts of lead and hold the tackle on, or close to, the bottom. Using nylon monofilament or braided line of similar test would demand two or even three times as much lead. It is very useful to have a spare spool with a boat multiplier with monofilament or braided line loaded to within about ¼ in (6 mm) of its lip and about 100 yd (91.4 m) of wire line wound on top. Wire, especially of the single strand type, which is recommended, takes up very little space on the reel, and it is best wound on over a base so that its coils are kept large to prevent kinks forming too easily. A spool loaded with wire line can make it possible to fish off-

These photographs illustrate how to connect a shooting-taper (shooting-head) flyline to braided monofilament nylon shooting line, which is hollow.

First a needle (this is a flydresser's dubbing needle) is pushed into the end of the braided monofilament (this one is 30 lb [13.6 kg] test) and the needle heated with a flame until the nylon blobs and cannot unravel at the end.

The flyline is inserted into the braided line for about an inch or so. Pushing the braid forward, to concertina it, while pushing in the flyline, is the best way of doing this.

The needle is removed, which leaves the braided line widened, and the hard blob is cut off with a very sharp blade, leaving an open end.

After putting a tiny drop of Superglue on the joint at the point where the inserted flyline ends in the braid (leave the glue to set for about three minutes) the braid is gripped in a fly-tying vice (or held by a helper if you do not own one) and a tight whipping of fine nylon is made over the end of the braid. This forms a Chinese finger trick bond, the braided line biting into the soft vinyl of the flyline coating more deeply with increased tension.

The end of the flyline is cut at an angle, to make a slight taper, which helps to insert it into the braided shooting line. The glue to be used is shown, too – Loctite Superglue, a cyanoacrylate type.

The whipping is finished with a loop to draw the end through, after which the end is trimmed and the whipping lightly coated with Superglue or polyurethane varnish.

shore marks at times when tide flow is at peak, when, without wire, the tackle would either just not get to the seabed or would need to be so heavy to do so as to be not worth the effort. Two hours of extra sport is often possible using wire.

Wire, however, is brittle; it can be difficult to control due to its inherent springiness, and it can be dangerous: wire under tension is one of the most efficient cutting devices known to man and it can shear fingers as easily as cheese! Although the best is stainless steel wire (in the author's opinion it is better than monel metal or phosphor-bronze coated material) it does corrode, and it will break very easily if a kink is allowed to form. Also, the rod must have a large roller tip ring and, if possible, rollers throughout, since if wire is wound through normal rings (the tip one where a sharp angle forms in particular), it will work-harden and soon be weakened.

A bite on wire line, even when fishing at great depths, is a revelation, even more so than with braided Dacron or Terylene. Since the wire does not perceptibly stretch it is highly conductive of fishy movements at the business end to the angler's fingers. Wire cannot be knotted and must be joined, using a loop twisted in the wire and a knot made in the other line – of which more in chapter 8.

There are other lines, such as braided man-made fibres with a core of lead, which are used for trolling elsewhere. However, lines other than those already dealt with have no place in sportfishing in the waters of Britain and the neighbouring countries.

The fly lines needed are ordinary weight-forward floating or sinking freshwater lines, although, when using very big flies, it does pay to use a special type of weight-forward line made for casting big, air-resistant lures: saltwater or bug tapers, as they are called.

Hooks

There is a discussion in later pages about lures to which hooks are already attached or are an integral part; hooks in this chapter are ordinary hooks that are baited.

There are very few major hook-making firms in the world and the sporting sea angler in the waters of Britain and north-west Europe is very well catered for by the world's biggest hook-making concern, Mustad of Oslo in Norway, and by Partridge of Redditch.

From these come the hooks necessary to cope with all the selected sporting species with which this book is concerned, from size 10 (the smallest for grey mullet) up to 10/0 for sharks or the common skate.

For sharks, common skate, congers, halibut and big tope the Mustad Seamaster hook in sizes 6/0 to 10/0

Filing the barb of a Mustad Seamaster hook to a knife edge helps penetration into tough tissue with light rods and lines. The strokes should be made only at this angle to the hook point.

The finished edge on the barb – a way in which big hooks can cut their way in with only a minimum strain.

will be found reliable. It is extremely well made, strong, with a welded ring and forged bend. The finish is corrosion resistant cadmium.

For general shore fishing for bass, cod and smoothhounds, the Mustad No. 79510 in sizes 1/0 to 5/0 is excellent: round shape, fine wire, forged bend with sharp point and moderate barb. It has many fans and many fine captures to its credit. It is not a massive, rigid hook capable of a performance in the mouth of fish with strong crushing powers, but it is possible to take cod up to 30 lb (13.6 kg) with this hook. It also penetrates easily when light tackle is used to draw the hook home rather than punch it in, as with a heavy rod and strong line.

An improvement on the 79510 has been produced since the first edition of this book. Mustad's 79515 is basically the same hook with a straight, tapered eye in place of a turned-down eye. The 79515 lies in a straighter line with the trace or snood when attached with a tucked half-blood knot (knots are dealt with in the next chapter).

Another good hook is the Aberdeen, a long-shank, round-bend type with a straight (ring) eye, and Partridge of Redditch make excellent ones, in bronzed and blued versions. They are good for cod, bass and plaice, flounders, and black and red bream in particular, because they fish a long slim bait – like a strip of squid or fish or worms – very neatly and have good hooking and holding qualities.

For big, heavy fish, like conger, tope, stingray, big pollack and coalfish from a boat, as well as halibut,

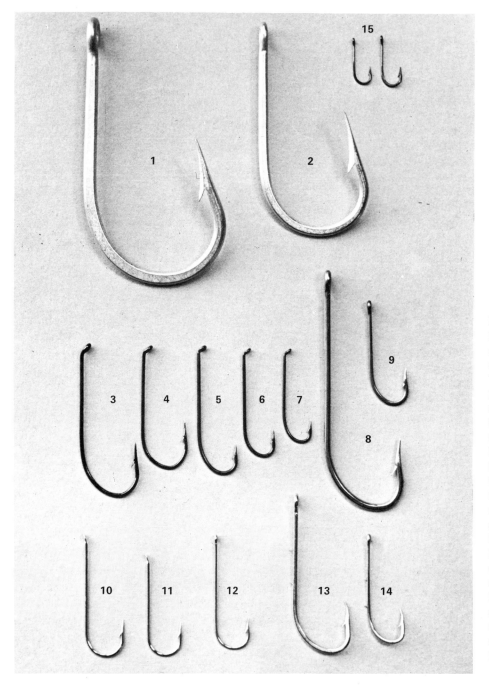

Hooks: Nos. 1 and 2 are Mustad Seamasters for sharks, conger, halibut etc; 3 and 4 are Mustad No. 79510 – a highly regarded hook for bass; Nos. 5, 6 and 7 are Yorkshire Stronghold hooks, excellent for flatfish, ballan wrasse, black bream etc; Nos. 8 and 9 are O'Shaughnessy types; Nos. 10 and 11 are the nickel-plated strong round bend spade ends and the ringed version next to it is a French Cannelle hook; No. 15 shows two sizes of Sundridge Specimen hooks. The two hooks with barbed shanks and incurved (beak) points (Nos. 13 and 14) are not good hookers and should be avoided.

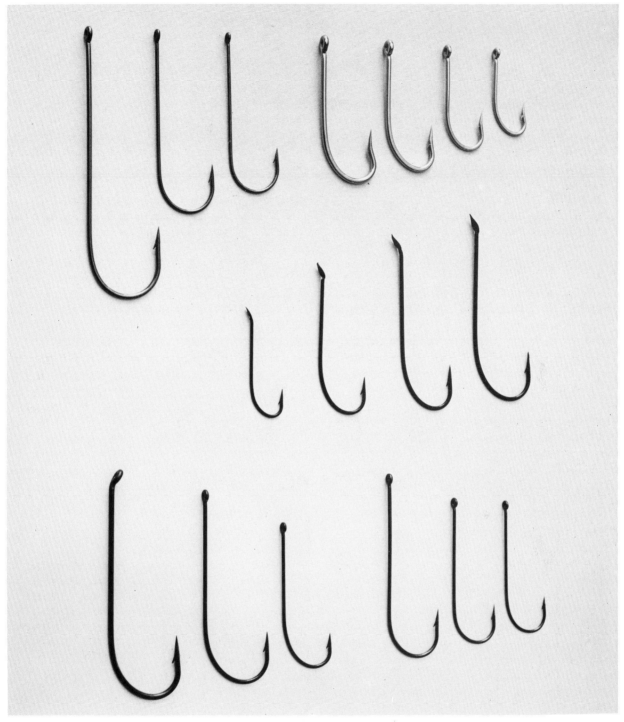

More useful hooks, all made by Partridge of Redditch, the English company which specialises in hand-made, high-quality products. Top left are three Aberdeen bronzed hooks in sizes 6/0, 2/0 and 1/0, suitable, respectively, for cod/bass, codling/school-bass/plaice and plaice/ flounders/black bream. These hooks do not have forged bends. Top right are the company's Sea Prince stainless steel ringed hooks with an O'Shaughnessy-type bend, forged; these are very strong hooks. In the centre are black-Japanned salmon-bend hooks which have a pointed spade-end, which are tied to the trace or snood with a whipping-knot. The spade projecting at an angle retains the bait high on the hook shank. Good all-round hooks for cod, bass, plaice, bream and flounders. Bottom left are Spearpoint hooks which Partridge make for the Breakaway Tackle Development Company, of Ipswich. On the left is the Spearpoint Boat Hook, a 6/0 and very strongly made for big cod, with a turned down eye. The other two are of finer wire and ringed, a 6/0 for cod from the shore (or bass, of course) and a 2/0 for whiting and plaice, flounders and similar size fish. Bottom right are blued fine-wire ringed hooks with lightly forged bends – a useful alternative to Aberdeens, with extra rigidity in the bend.

a very strong hook like the old O'Shaughnessy is required. Mustad, the famous Norwegian company, make good ones, but so do the English company, Partridge of Redditch, and being patriotic, I am a Partridge fan, though I would not be were their hooks not superb. They call their O'Shaughnessy-type stainless-steel hooks Sea Prince.

Partridge also make hooks for the specialist-tackle businesses, and the Breakaway Tackle company, at Ipswich, in Suffolk, is one such business. Their Spearpoint is a black-japanned hook with a small ring and salmon-hook type bend with a very sharp point and small barb. It is made in sizes and wire strengths to suit just about 80 per cent of sea-fishing situations in Britain. A boat-fishing version has an eye slightly turned down, which means that a whipping-knot may be made on the shank with the hook's shank still lying in line with the trace.

No matter what size of hook is used, even the small sizes (1/0 down to size 10, the latter a freshwater hook for mullet) I insist on a wire that will resist opening up under pressure, or breaking. I am not a fan of the very fine-wire hook, since, even when the main quarry may be flounders or plaice, there is a very good chance the bait will be swallowed by a big cod or bass, and it is foolish to risk losing a good fish in that way. Thickish wire hooks may be sharpened sufficiently to do the job required of them – and all hooks should be kept sharp, the bigger ones with a file, the smaller ones with an abrasive stone.

I have never been very enthusiastic about the so-called 'beak' hooks, on which the point curves back in towards the shank. Some of them have barbs, or slices, on the shank's back, facing the eye, which hold a bait up the shank neatly. The incurved point is not a very effective hooker and I recommend for just about all sea-fishing requirements, a round bend or modified sproat or salmon-bend hook, with a forged (flattened) bend which helps the bend resist opening up. A good small hook, in sizes 8 and 10 for mullet, shad and maybe flounders when using freshwater-weight float tackle, which I can recommend is the Partridge sproat forged down-eye model, though there are quite a number of others of a suitable nature.

Always keep a small, high-quality flat file in your kit, for sharpening big hooks, and a flat abrasive stone for smaller ones. Sharpen big, strong hooks, like the Mustad Seamaster and the O'Shaughnessy, by forming a knife-edge on the barb with a file. Such a point cuts into hard-mouthed big fish better than a normal rounded point. When sharpening other hooks, use the stone but mainly work with strokes up against the point of the hook, more on the sides and back of the barb than on the front. A short, sharp point is better than a long, thin sharp one, the latter being very prone to bend or break against a hard spot in a fish's mouth.

Clothing

Time was when sea anglers went out like gipsies, clad in all manner of war-surplus clothing or tattered sweaters and woollen ski-caps. A few still fish thus attired, but many more take advantage of the purpose-designed clothing and footwear available.

Angling at the coast or out at sea, in winter's cold or summer's heat, can be very uncomfortable without proper gear. The shore fisher in summer needs hard-wearing cool trousers, cotton shirt and light woollen sweater with a lightweight hip-length parka with attached hood. For spots where fishing or bait collecting has to be done by being in the water, inexpensive thighboots are the answer – not the expensive trout anglers' type with hobs etc., although when slippery, weed-draped rocks are the base, then hobs do help to get a foothold. For fishing from dry rock ledges, from piers, harbour walls and similar dry spots, canvas baseball boots are good, or if the rocks are rugged and have to be scrambled upon, stout boots that come high on the ankle may save a broken bone. Some of the best rock places are really hard climbs.

In winter, on a shingle cod beach, or on a pier or rock platform, thighboots will tend to be uncomfortable, especially when walking a long way across the beach to reach that special spot. Exposed beaches in a north-east wind and rain are not pleasant places to be in winter unless you are well dressed. The special underclothes providing warmth without bulk and weight can be obtained from such companies as Damart Thermawear and Helly-Hansen. They also provide inner boots that are better than two pairs of heavy woollen socks.

Chest-high trousers worn over knee-length boots with a hip-length lined parka (hooded) are comfortable and afford maximum protection from wind and rain. The best type of waterproof gear is, the

In contrast to the well-wrapped surfcaster of autumn and winter, this summer rock angler is also comfortably attired. Rocks can be hard on the feet without suitable shoes or boots.
Inset: A cold, wet day on the beach can be miserable without adequate protective clothing. Parka with hood covers the tops of thighboots or chest waders.

Jack Austin shows a surf-caught bass and his protective clothing: the waterproof trousers, worn over thighboots, are snugged in at the ankles with rubber bands to prevent waves surging up inside.

at least four inches below the tops of the thighboots.

In all cases, a parka with a detachable lining is a good idea, since it may be used without the lining in summer and with it in the cold weather.

There are some angling situations that demand the use of chest-high waders – for example surfcasting for bass or tope on Atlantic surf beaches in Ireland or West Wales. Avoid any plastic waders of this type, for they will tear and wear at the slightest provocation. Use proper rubber waders, which will still wear and tear but can be satisfactorily patched with a vulcanizing outfit.

A short (waist-length) jacket is useful with chest waders, and when it is necessary to wade into waves that reach near the top of the waders, a belt tight around it at upper waist level will stop water creeping in. The jacket, waterproof nylon or PVC of course, is worn always over the top of the waders.

So far as short Wellington-type boots are concerned, the best ones the author has yet used are Derriboots. They are made from soft plastic with laces to close the tops, and they are light, very comfortable, warm in winter, cool in summer and have a good sole for grip on many surfaces.

Finally a word on hand protection. In winter the cold can be so intense on the coast or at sea that exposure of the hands, especially when it is snowing or raining as well, can make them useless. They become frozen and senseless. To avoid this it pays to rub some protective cream or grease on and then wear lined leather mittens, leaving the fingers free for baiting up, tying knots etc. Knitted woollen mittens are warm, but they can prove a terrible nuisance since hooks constantly catch in them and are difficult to extricate. A small hand towel can be very useful to wipe the hands dry after baiting up or unhooking a fish. Dry hands never feel so cold nor so painful as wet hands do.

Having now dealt with major items of tackle and the types of clothing suited to the various aspects of sportfishing at sea, it is necessary to discuss how to use the tackle within the many varied situations of shore and boat fishing. The other necessary items of gear, including gaffs, nets, and bits of terminal tackle, will be dealt with as they arise in the following chapters.

author feels, made from PVC-coated nylon with a lining of nylon and Terylene-filled gap. Such gear is light, absolutely proof against wind-driven rain, and warm. It is also remarkably hard-wearing. At the present time no clothing tested has reached the standard of the Angler Superjacket, and trousers and one-piece suits made by the Manchester firm of Henri-Lloyd.

On boats, and whenever there is no need to wade, the best waterproof outfit is the parka and bib-type trousers, the latter coming over calf-length boots so that water is drained off completely – trousers that are too short funnel water into one's boots!

If wading is necessary in winter cold and rain, then the parka will need to be long enough to reach

3 How to use the tackle: basic techniques

Shore fishing

Surfcasting in its purest sense involves projecting the baited hook from an open beach into the breaking waves. To do this it is necessary to add sufficient weight to the tackle to carry the bait out and to hold it in position on the seabed.

In other parts of the world, notably on both American seaboards, surfcasting also involves casting heavy artificial lures, then reeling them in again. In the waters of north-western Europe and Britain, however, there are few fish that respond to such technique.

The amount of weight to be cast in surfcasting will vary, with a few exceptions, from as little as 2 oz (56.6 g) to as much as 6 oz (170 g).

Surfcasting varies considerably in that on the wild Atlantic storm beaches characteristic of south-west Ireland and west Wales one is often wading waist-deep in surf and casting 50–100 yd (45.7–91.4 m) into incoming rollers where the water, over hard sand, is only 2–3 ft (0.6–0.9 m) deep. The quarry will be mainly bass or tope, should the beach be one where they come close into the shoreline. If bass, the lighter surf rod will be used; the heavier outfit will be used for casting a big bait on a big hook for tope. Or the casting may be done from the dry shingle of a steep beach in Kent, East Anglia, or Dorset where the water is deeper – as deep as 50 ft (15 m) in places – and where the surface of the sea may be quite calm, though a strong tidal current may be travelling along the beach. In winter, the quarry will be cod, big cod running up to 30 lb (13.6 kg) perhaps; in the summer months the species sought may be tope, congers, various rays, flatfish, smooth-hounds, bass, and in a few areas, black bream.

These two different types of beach – the flat, sandy

This photograph catches the caster in the phase just as he begins to apply full power. The reel is a Mitchell 602 AP.

Atlantic storm beach with its lines of white surf rolling in, and the steep shingle beach running down to sandy or muddy ground – need very widely varying approaches from the angling viewpoint. In the first instance, the wild rolling surf is, perhaps paradoxically, very much less of a problem to the angler wishing to hold his baited tackle out there than are the usually less turbulent waves on the steep-to shingle beach. Atlantic storm beaches are generally easy to fish with a lead of 2–3 oz (56.6–85 g) since there is usually little lateral tidal flow to put pressure on the line and thus drag the lead and baited hook in a downtide arc towards dry land. On the other hand, steep beaches in the North Sea and English Channel usually have strong tidal flows and it is sometimes necessary to use 6 oz (170 g) of lead to hold out. The storm beach waves coming straight into the beach, run up the angler's slim line and give no such problems.

To project the baited hook and necessary lead to the chosen fishing position a long flexible rod is used as the prime instrument. When firmly held by the hands and swept through an arc at an accelerating speed, it acts as both a lever and a spring to catapult the tackle up and out. It has been found by trial and error that for all shore angling purposes (sporting angling, that is) the optimum rod length is about 11½ ft (3.5 m).

Although it is not really accurate to discuss the lead and terminal tackle being cast in terms of ballistics, since a bullet, for example, is in free flight while a fishing lead is tailed by the line (and slowed down by having to pull a baited hook, trace etc. behind it, adding to air drag), there is some common ground. When a bullet is shot, the less time it spends in flight the less time gravity has to pull on it and drag it towards the ground.

In tournament casting, only a streamlined, bomb-shaped lead is on the end of the line and casters aiming for long distances try to cast the lead as fast as they can: 'tip speed' is a term often heard on the tournament field.

Both the bullet and the fishing lead go farther when projected at high speed but air resistance also acts against both. If two bullets are fired at the same velocity, but one is twice the weight of the other, the heavier bullet will travel further because the energy it possesses makes it harder to stop. Similarly, if a lead of 3 oz (85 g) and another of 6 oz (170 g) are cast at the same speed and both are cast upwards at the same elevation, the heavier led will travel much further. In competitive casting, the standardised 5¼ oz (150 g) lead will always travel further than a 3 oz (85 g) lead, cast by the same person.

In actual fishing, however, it is not possible always to cast the streamlined lead at high speed, thus gaining long distances, because its weight and shape are hampered by its having to drag the wind-resistant bait and hook etc behind it. In general terms, a slim, streamlined bait – such as a firm lugworm, big ragworm or a strip of squid – will cast much further than, for example, the tail half of a 12 oz (22 g) mackerel, a whole Californian squid or a crab 3 in (7.7 cm) across the shell. Also, the angler will find he needs to cast the bulky bait higher, to compensate for its lower speed, to get any reasonable distance.

There are numerous styles of casting and many produce excellent results. Some involve mounting the reel high on the butt of the rod, say 30 or even 40 in (76–101 cm) from the extremity, while others involve the reel being fitted only 10 in (25.4 cm) or so from the extremity. Some right handed casters control the reel with the right (upper) hand while others use the left hand to control the reel at the bottom of the handle. Most casting is done from a position facing the sea, but one or two famous casters on the East Coast of England attain record distances casting with their backs to the sea! The important point is to be able consistently to put the lead and bait where it is required, not only long or short distances out but also accurate laterally. For this reason the writer does not favour the back-to-the-sea style; not forgetting that on a storm beach an incoming wave can hit the caster in the back and tumble him over and into trouble.

For many reasons the free-spool multiplier is the author's recommendation for surfcasting: it is not difficult to use once the basics are understood and a multiplier is a better and more reliable reel on which to play big fish; it also casts further than a fixed-spool reel for most people. However, some anglers will never be competent with a multiplier and others favour a fixed-spool reel, and, provided a really good, strong model is chosen, such reels will do the job reasonably well.

Casting with the multiplier is done by first putting the spool into the free position by means of a button or lever, then, keeping the thumb of the top hand (with the reel mounted as the author suggests, about 23–30 in (58.4–76 cm) above the butt extremity), the rod is swung to the right side (for a right-handed caster) and back, the tip pointing either immediately behind the caster or even slightly to his left side (when facing the sea). It is then brought forward, round and up, the right hand pushing and the left hand (for a right-handed caster) pulling the butt down. The action is smooth but has an increasing speed as the moment of release comes, at which point the thumb is lifted from the spool and the rod whips over to project the lead and tackle up and out. The light spool of the reel has line pulled from it and if there is any tendency for the spool to revolve faster than line is being pulled off, a light dab with the thumb on the left side of the spool – not on the line, since that will be damaged by friction-induced heat, as well as burning the ball of the thumb – will slow it down to the correct speed.

Any casting movement that involves both hands being above the head when holding the rod at the start of the cast is wrong and quite useless. Not only the arms but the shoulders, trunk and legs are used to put the correct smooth effort into a casting movement. Short, quick movements are incorrect and can never attain adequate distances for surfcasting.

It is important that the reel spool is loaded to within about 1/16 in (1.5 mm) with relatively thin line so that the pull of the flying lead is on the periphery of the spool flanges, at which point less pull is needed to make the spool revolve than at a lower point. Also, each turn of the spool yields more line when it is loaded than it does when the coils become smaller as the spool empties. Thin line remains higher on the spool for longer than does thick line, of course, which is another good reason for using thin line.

Some multipliers have devices that wind the line back on to the spool evenly, others do not, and the angler must spread the line across the spool using either the ball of his thumb or by allowing the line to run through his thumb and forefinger. Closely wound coils are a further help in long, smooth casts without over-runs, since each coil that comes off the spool is roughly the same size. Crosswinding produces coils of unequal size and they can cause trouble.

Level-wind mechanisms on the Ambassadeur range work perfectly and there is no great advantage in removing them, as some anglers do, in the hope of increasing casting range by reducing a small amount of gear friction, except, perhaps, in cod fishing. The advantages of having the line rewound in close turns far outweigh any small amount of friction, and when fishing after dark, or in the excitement of playing a big fish, it is nice to be able to forget the line coming on to the reel and concentrate on the fishing.

Multipliers should be kept scrupulously clean and lightly oiled so that they run smoothly. The best of them have spindles ground and polished to a mirror finish that run in well fitted brass or phosphor bronze bearings or in ball races. If the steel spindles on any reel are not really smooth they should be polished with 400 mesh silicon carbide paper, then fine steel wool, revolving the spindle in a folded piece of paper (abrasive) or pad of steel wool. Such treatment often works wonders. Use only fine machine oil on the

bearings and a molybdenum disulphide grease on the gear teeth. Protect the reel always after use, washing (freshwater of course) then drying it, followed by a spray of WD40 or similar product.

Fixed-spool reels work quite differently from the multiplier. The drum of the latter revolves to yield line during the cast – and when the line is being rewound – while the drum or spool of the fixed-spool reel remains stationary during the cast and during the recovery: the only time the spool revolves is when a big fish pulls against the pressure of the drag or braking system.

So, line comes off the front of the spool in coils, and as the level of the line falls in the spool, the coils have to climb over the front of the spool, increasingly rubbing harder on the top of the lip. Again, fine line helps to minimise this friction – quite apart from doing the same to the friction through the rings of the rod – by remaining at a higher level for a longer period.

When the tackle has come to rest on the seabed, the pick-up arm is activated on most fixed-spool reels by a forward turn of the handle. In actual fact there is really no need for an automatic full bale pick-up on reels used for surfcasting, and the best reels have simply a wide roller-bearing in a hook-type affair into which the line is placed by hand after the cast. This set-up is much stronger than a bale arm.

In surf fishing the reel has to take a few knocks and at one time or another some sand is going to get into the works. When this happens wash it out thoroughly in the sea, then wash the whole reel, inside and out, in warm freshwater when you get home. Oil it when all is dry.

Casting with a fixed-spool reel and 2–3 oz (56.6–85 g) of lead is fairly simple: the reel is mounted high up the rod handle, and the reel stand is held between the middle and index fingers of the upper hand, the index hooking the line where it comes off the spool and holding it firmly. In the lighter freshwater situation the forefinger often holds the line against the lip of the spool, but when casting 2 oz (56.6 g) or so, the pressure is too great and the line will slip from under the finger. In fact, there is some difficulty in holding the line under the crooked forefinger when casting with power for long range with leads of 5 oz (141.7 g) or more. Some anglers use a leather finger-stall to help, which also avoids soreness caused by the line whipping off the pad of the finger. There is also a device on the market called a Thumbutton which is whipped tightly to the rod at a point level with the reel spool but on the opposite side of the rod. The line is caught between two faces and held there by thumb pressure on a button. The thumb pressure is eased at the point of maximum velocity in the cast and the line is released perfectly, even being held when punching hard with a lead of 6 oz (170 g).

Playing a fish with a fixed-spool reel is done in the same way as with a multiplier: the clutch is preset to the strain that will bend the rod sufficiently but will slip at a pressure less than the test of the line being used. Any additional strain is put on the fish by pressing the forefinger of the hand holding the rod or the thumb or forefinger of the reeling hand against the lip of the spool's front.

Fixed-spool reels for heavy fishing must have an anti-reverse mechanism which prevents the handle and flyer from being pulled round by a fish taking line from the spool when the drag is hard on. This should always be in operation, even when the rod is being fished in a rest.

Because line is pulled off a fixed-spool reel round the pick-up quite severe friction is in operation at the point of contact with the line. It is therefore of vital importance, as stressed in previous pages, that the line passes over a roller which turns very freely, working like the pulley on the top of a crane. Keep the roller lubricated regularly with a little light machine oil or a dry lubricant such as molybdenum disulphide.

While there are many advantages in using fine lines for shore fishing (and boat fishing, of course) the light test lines will not take the shock of a cast with a heavy lead when seeking maximum range. It is possible to cast a 2 oz (56.6 g) lead 80 yd (73.1 m) or so on the bass rod using 12 lb (5.4 kg) test line, but it must be done smoothly. If longer ranges are necessary – and *always* when using 15 lb (6.8 kg) main line with leads of 4 oz (113.3 g) or more on the big casting rod – it is essential to join a casting leader to the main line.

This casting leader is a length of nylon of a stronger test than the main line which is long enough to pass from the reel through the rod rings with about 8 ft (2.4 m) hanging from the tip ring, and make at least three turns round the spool of the reel. Thus the leader takes the shock of casting, and once the leader has passed through the rings the finer line is dragged behind it. Leaders are also useful for protecting the fragile reel line from seabed abrasion and for dragging fish by brute force ashore through heavy surf – in which case the leader should be extended to about 12 yd (10.9 m).

Joining the leader to the reel line demands a smooth knot and many different knots are used. The main problem is that of getting the turns of heavy nylon to snug down with the turns of the lighter, more flexible nylon. For example, in cod or tope

shore fishing with line of approximately 15 lb (6.8 kg) test the leader will need to be about 35 lb (15.8 kg) test when casting 5–6 oz (141.7–170 g) leads 130 yd (118 m) or more. Some anglers who can really zip a 6 oz lead 150 yd (137 m) use 50 lb (22.6 kg) leaders! For 12 lb (5.4 kg) test line or thereabouts and 2–3 oz (56.6–85 kg) leads, a 20 lb (9 kg) leader will permit casting to ranges of 100 yd (91.4 m).

The author has always used a blood knot to join leaders to reel lines and has never had any reason to change. It is, however, very important to make about six turns round the heavy material with the light, and only three turns round the light with the heavy. As always, moisten the turns with saliva before pulling up, and help the coils of the heavy leader to bed down by pulling on the end of the leader nylon as the knot is tightened up, by pulling the main line and leader firmly apart.

Another reliable knot is as follows. Tie an overhand knot in the end of the leader line, but do not pull

Forming the blood knot to connect a thin reel line to a heavy casting leader. Approximately six turns are made with the reel line round the leader, and only about three turns round the reel line with the heavy leader. This, when moistened with saliva, may be drawn up into a fairly neat knot, and when the ends have been trimmed off flush with the coils of the knot the junction passes easily through the rod rings. As it is used the ends will snug down and bed the coils even more.

Alternative line-to-leader junction. An overhand knot is tied near the end of the leader material and the reel line passed through before the overhand knot is tightened. Then the reel line is taken about six times round the leader and the end turned back.

The end is then made into a circle, the coils made unwound again by forming a whipping knot round the leader with the reel line, and the turns held by the finger of one hand while the whipping is snugged down by pulling alternately on the reel line at both sides. Then the knot is pulled up against the overhand knot.

it up tight. Now pass the end of the reel line into the front of the overhand knot and make six turns loosely round the leader material with the reel line. Holding the leader line in the right hand (if you are right handed) take the reel line back and form a loop, lying the free end along the leader line. Now, hold all firmly and whip over the free end of the reel line with the reel line loop, and as you do so the turns you originally made will unroll to leave you with a whipping knot of fine line round the leader line. Tighten by pulling on both ends of the reel line, then pull the whipping knot hard up to the overhand knot and tighten the overhand knot in the leader line firmly before trimming all ends flush.

This knot is very popular with tournament casters and is a little less bulky than the bastardised blood knot. They appear to be just as good and it is a matter of choice as to which of them one uses.

The subject of knots brings us to terminal tackle rigs, of which sea anglers in the UK use scores. However, there is need for only two basic rigs for proper surfcasting and shore fishing on the bottom in

general: the fixed nylon paternoster and the running paternoster.

Prime considerations for choice of terminal rigs for shore fishing are that they should cast well and present the bait properly without any tendency to tangle. This means that the lead weight, whenever possible, must be at the end of the line when the tackle is suspended from the rod tip and must lead the tackle in flight.

The fixed nylon paternoster serves perfectly well when it is necessary to have the gear in a state that will cast a long way and remain tangle-free while it is fishing. This applies in situations where fish sought are unlikely to be put off, or are able to drop the baited hook if they do become alarmed by any tension in the nylon linking them to the main line and the anchored lead. This rig is fine for cod, for bass in wild surf, and for some flounder fishing. The running version is excellent for quieter waters where the fish takes the bait, swims away with it and is brought up short: for bass among the rocks in shallow water or in estuaries, for conger or tope from the shore, and for

Above: A fixed nylon paternoster for shore casting. Note that the distance between hook and loops is less than it is between loops and the lead. This ensures a clean flight, with the lead leading the air-resistant bait.

Right above: A more refined fixed paternoster. With the swivel running between two stop-knots and the pieces of plastic tube (or small beads) snood twisting is avoided.

Right: The running paternoster. Note once again that the length of line to the lead is more than the length of the hook trace, which gives a smooth flight and prevents tangling.

smooth-hounds. The fixed version can have a short snood or hook link – as little as 4 in (10 cm) – or a long one – as long as 6 ft (1.8 m). If the hook is kept sharp – as all hooks should be – the fish takes the bait, swims away with it and is brought up suddenly by the anchored lead. The point of the hook catches in the skin of the mouth, the fish panics, lunges away, and the hook sinks deeper. The angler sees the rod tip movement or feels the pull on the line if he is holding the rod, and pulls home the barb.

However, there are times when fish are not quite so

swivel for several feet, depending on the slackness of the line from lead to rod tip, and the fish is likely to swallow the bait as it begins to move away. The signal of the bite is seen or felt and the strike made in the normal way. Not only bass but tope, smooth-hounds, rays and conger are usually best attacked with the running paternoster.

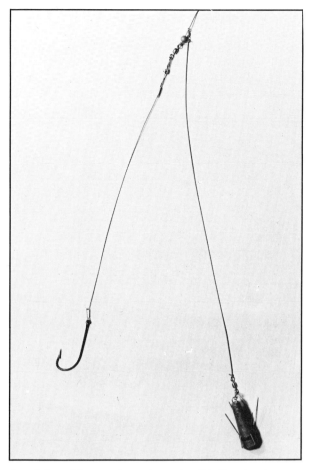

A variation of the running paternoster, this time for shore fishing for tope, conger, common skate and other 'toothy critturs'. The hook trace may be quickly detached from the link-swivel and a new one fitted.

ready to be fooled. A bass hunting at leisure among the weedy rocks for crabs and small fish, for example, will often inspect a bait for a while before gently picking it up and tasting and feeling it. Should the fish at this stage feel any untoward resistance it is likely to drop the bait. But with the running paternoster the hook link may be pulled freely through the eye of the

1. Making a blood loop for a paternoster begins with a circle formed by twisting the line around itself (without using an end) or by using an end and tying six overhand knots, one after the other. A gap is then made in the centre of the twists . . .
2. . . . and the untwisted side of the circle pushed through . . .
3. . . . at which time one's teeth come into play to hold the end of the loop – use the canine inside the loop, do not bite the nylon – while the two ends are pulled to tighten the knot. Keep the loop quite small.
4. A small, neat blood loop for the hook trace loop.

Many anglers no doubt use a normal running leger, the lead on a link-swivel or (worse) on a Clements boom or a Kilmore clip, and are wondering why the running paternoster is being praised while the straight leger, with the lead running directly on the main line and not on a dropper lead link, is being ignored. Well, the reason is that the running paternoster not only casts with the lead in front of the rest of the rig, but it also permits the fish more freedom to take the bait gently. Small swivels are less obvious than Clements booms and the like; they are also much cheaper!

Simplicity is the key to good terminal tackle. If something does not do a useful job on the rig, then it should not be used.

With the fixed nylon paternoster the length of snood is usually best kept to less than 1 ft (30.48 cm) where the distance between its point of attachment on the standing part of the line is about 2 ft; only rarely is it necessary to change this proportion. And generally speaking, similar proportions of hook link and lead link serve well with the running version.

There are many leads made for surf fishing, and most of them are unnecessary. There is no good reason nowadays to use any shape other than the elongated pear or bomb shape, with free-swinging

anchor wires or without. If the water being fished is not too boisterous the ordinary bomb lead will be fine, as it will if you want to allow the tackle slowly to rove about the seabed. If, however, you want to cast far and hold the bait in one position then use an anchored lead known as a breakaway lead.

This lead has been largely instrumental in helping British sea anglers who wish to use lighter tackle to do so, because its adjustable anchor wires collapse at a light pull and trail inoperative behind

Breakaway leads made by the Breakaway Tackle Development Company. The middle one, with the old bead system of holding the anchor wires in the active position in recesses moulded into the lead, has been used for two tides. Note distortion of lead caused by reeling in over pebbles. On the left is the long-tail Breakaway with a more modern system of plastic rollers to hold the wires, and a very rigid attachment ring to the trace. These are damaged less easily by contact with shingle beaches. Right is another version of the lead, intended for uptide casting from a boat. This one is said to grip the seabed more tightly, but can be used for shore fishing, too, in very rough seas or strong tides.

For long-distance casts with lug, rag or soft shellfish baits, a relay clip on the terminal rig keeps the baited hook lying close to the main part of the trace. This clip is made by the Breakaway Tackle Development Company, is plastic and is threaded on the trace and held firmly in place by a piece cut from the tubing supplied. The sphere on the hook snood is a split shot (it can be a bead with Superglue dripped into the hole to fix it in place on the nylon) which prevents the bait being pushed up the snood too far in flight. The hook is held by the relay clip's hook when the standing part of the trace is under tension. When the lead touches the seabed, that tension is released, and so is the baited hook.

as the lead is wound in along the bottom. The old type of wired lead has its wires set at a right angle to the lead's axis, moulded in, so that they have to be pulled from the sea-bed by brute force, and once pulled free often hook in again on the way in. These leads, which, incredibly, many anglers still use, demand heavy lines and strong rods.

The breakaway or break-out lead was perfected by two of the old *Angling* magazine contributors, the late Ian Gillespie and Nigel Forrest, following a campaign by that publication for more sporting tackle in the sea. Many weird systems were produced by readers and contributors.

Commercial production of these release leads came via the Breakaway Tackle company, and initially the wire anchors were held in the gripping position by depressions in the lead into which plastic beads, mounted on the wires, located. Some anglers still like this design. Then came a lead with a plastic collar around it and let in near the front. In the collar were slots into which the wires could be clipped, to keep them in position.

Finally has come a similar arrangement but with plastic-tube rollers replacing the beads on the wire. They are, of course, cheaper than the beads, but do the same job, and the four slots into which the plastic rollers locate hold the wire more firmly than the small, semi-circular recesses on the bead version.

No sporting shore angler should be without such leads. So, on an Atlantic surf beach, for bass or whatever, the fixed nylon paternoster with a 2–3 oz (56.6–85 g) breakaway lead is cast out, the hook carrying lug, razorfish or clam, and the slack line taken up. The light rod is held and bites are felt for by hand, through the rod or through the line.

If it's tope from the shore, or big stingrays, maybe, then the heavier rod might be used. For tope or conger the running paternoster rig is made up with a wire trace connecting the hook to the link swivel at the end of the casting leader. The bait, such as mackerel or small pouting is cast way out, the breakaway lead pulled into the bottom, and the rod set up on a rest so that its tip is high. The reel is set so that a taking fish can pull line off against a slight check and so give audible warnings as well as the visual one of the rod tip's movements.

Again, when fishing among rocky ground, for bass or conger, the running paternoster is used. For bass the rod is held so that bites of a shy nature may be detected and the correct action taken; for conger the rod is rested, as for tope or rays.

These methods are basic and are at present only being touched upon. They will be dealt with again later.

A rectangular dropnet with a tubular alloy frame and deep, strong net of nylon cord. Rectangular nets do not roll along rocks and breakwaters when a fish is being guided into the rim.

Another shore fishing situation is the pier, stone breakwater, bridge, rocky promontory or similar seaward projection. Strangely, though it would seem that such places would offer better chances of good fishing than the shoreline itself, such is seldom the case. Such projections are usually in areas of high population or with industry, so that pollution and disturbance weigh against the right habitat for good fish. However, some of the above mentioned spots do produce good fishing for cod, bass, rays, mullet, mackerel, conger, flounders and others on our sporting list. One of the big advantages of a good pier or projection is that not only can legering be tried but float fishing, spinning and driftlining as well.

Before going on to deal briefly with the basics of float fishing, spinning and driftlining, it must be pointed out that no sporting angler should venture on to any projection high off the water without carrying a big dropnet which can be lowered to the water to lift fish up. With fish weighing over 30 lb (16.6 kg) (congers for instance), a gaff on several screw-connected sweep's canes or similar, sufficient to reach the water at the lowest time of the tide, should be carried.

For float-fishing from some form of projection, the fixed-spool reel is generally first choice since casting long distances with reasonably light end tackle is easy. However, should there be no need to cast, just lower the tackle down to the water and allow it to wash around the piles of the pier, by the weedy walls of the breakwater or down the side of the rivermouth shorings, then a centrepin reel will do the job.

Sliding floats will be called for at times to fish at depths much more than the length of the rod, and these may be of balsa wood, plastic moulded, or roughly made from odd pieces of polystyrene to which is tied a small swivel through which the line can run. Sliding floats with holes lengthwise through their centres are favoured, but those with eyes fitted top and bottom are all right too. It is cheaper to make such floats at home from balsa wood of about 1 in (2.54 cm) square. This is cut into suitable lengths and drilled centrally lengthwise to take a plastic tube about ⅛ in (3 mm) in diameter which is glued in. The float can be roughly shaped by rasp or file, then finished with varying grades of glasspaper. Several coats of paint must be put on to waterproof the body and the top is best painted with fluorescent orange over a white base.

A slim torpedo shape seems to work best and offers less resistance to a taking fish. Make or buy a selection of floats that will support lead bullets or barrel leads of ¼–1 oz (7–28 g). There are a number of ways to stop the float on the line at the required depth and yet still permit the stop to travel from the reel and through the rings of the rod without any impediment. But perhaps the best is a length of elastic band about ⅜ in (1 cm) tied into the line at the selected point with a clove hitch or similar knot that will pull out once the elastic is removed.

Freelining is simply dropping a baited hook into the water from the end of a pier or other projection and letting it waft about in the surges below or be taken away by the tide. A very small lead may be used to help control the bait but it is not sufficient to cause it to sink quickly to the bottom. This can be very effective on a pier for bass and pollack, bites being felt by holding the line below the butt ring of the rod.

Spinning can be practised from open beaches as well as from rocky promontories, piers etc, but it seldom works well in water less than about 5 ft (1.5 m) deep, and 15 ft (4.5 m) is usually better. Species that may be taken this way include bass, mackerel, garfish, pollack, coalfish and big ballan wrasse.

Open steep-to shingle beaches are usually better than sandy shallow beaches, and rocky coasts are better than both. Estuaries also provide good opportunities for spinning.

Sometimes a heavy spoon, such as a 1 oz (28 g) Toby, 1 oz Koster, big German Sprat (Condor spoon) or an artificial sand-eel (Red Gill) kept down by up to 2 oz (57 g) of lead – the eel, that is – is necessary to get both range and depth. At other times the salmon-type

rod and 8–12 lb (3.6–5.4 kg) test line necessary for this work can be changed for the single-handed rod and baits weighing only ½ oz (15 g), which may be cast adequate distances with the fixed-spool reel and line of about 5 lb (2.26 kg) test. Whenever this is possible the real meaning of sportfishing is apparent, especially when a 5 lb (2.26 kg) bass, a 1½ lb (0.6 kg) mackerel or a 6 lb (2.7 kg) pollack grabs the lure.

Last of the shore techniques to be mentioned is fly fishing – which is also very useful when in a small boat, or an uncluttered large one. It will be dealt with in depth in chapter 11. The only point to note at this stage is that fly fishing on this side of the Atlantic is very little done (in saltwater) and it is usually only successful in very clear water conditions and from June to mid-October.

Boat fishing

Fishing from a boat with sporting tackle may be done in various ways, some of them are very similar to the shore fishing techniques: for example, legering a bait on the bottom from an anchored boat, spinning, fly fishing, driftlining, float fishing. In addition there are some other ways to show the bait or lure to the fish which include trolling a lure or natural bait (fish) behind a moving boat, drifting with the wind or tide (or both, which is not so good) with the baits either being worked on sandy bottoms, jigged over rocks or wrecks (lures etc.) or with fish baits on float tackle, usually for sharks and tope.

Boat fishing tactics for the light tackle angler can be extremely interesting and exciting, since there is plenty of opportunity for experiment. Yet the average sea angler, who uses cumbersome tackle, drops a vast hunk of lead and indifferent bait over the side of some evil smelling, unsuitable hulk on a place as barren of fish as the moon's surface, leaving it there for crabs to munch while the lazy boatman settles down for a snooze.

The knots used for making up shore tackle are also used for boat fishing, but there are one or two other knots and attachments which must be adopted since the pressures on the sporting gear when fighting big fish from a boat are sustained and the gear must be 100 per cent reliable.

Certainly one of the most reliable knots used by sportfishers (although it is strictly a hitch rather than a knot) is the Bimini hitch, 20-times-around knot, Bimini twist or hangman's jam. It may be used in monofilament nylon or braided Dacron or Terylene lines, being easier to tie in the latter. Not only does the Bimini produce a super-strong end loop, to which many types of terminal rig can be attached, but it also

1, 2. One way of forming a Bimini twist, hitch or twenty-times-around knot with a short loop. There should be 20 turns made (1) before the turns are made back to the starting point (2).

3, 4. When the original turns have been covered, always keeping plenty of tension on the whole job, a hitch is taken round one side of the loop which has been formed (photo 4).

5, 6. When the first hitch has been tightened, another one is made round the opposite side of the loop. These lock all the turns, but a final knot is made to prevent the last hitch from coming undone.

7. The completed Bimini. It is not a knot since no part is holding any other in the actual twists, only the twists are locked by the final hitches. This produces almost one hundred per cent of the line's full test. For making a long loop for the doubled line for shark fishing, a helper is needed to take the place of the nail and wooden dowel.

Bimini tyer.

produces the doubled line used when after big fish, such as sharks. The double portion is usually about 15 ft (4.5 m) long so that it can resist abrasion on the fish better than single line, and it may also be used by the boatman or a fellow angler to haul the beaten fish to the side of the boat for gaffing or tailing.

For producing Biminis with short loops one can make and use an ingenious little tool invented by an angler named Brian Barber and first shown to the angling public in the March 1976 issue of *Angling* magazine. Many anglers have since acclaimed it as a godsend.

Whenever what the Americans call 'toothy critturs' are the quarry, it is necessary to include in the tackle something which prevents the fish biting or wearing through the line above the hook, or, in the case of sharks, prevents the rough hide of the fish rubbing through the line during a prolonged battle.

The usual way of combating fish with sharp, powerful teeth is to use a wire trace to connect the hook (or lure) to the rest of the line, usually via a link swivel. There are many types of wire used for traces, including solid stainless-steel piano wire, twisted multistrand wire, the same but covered with a nylon jacket, and braided multistrand. While the piano wire is much used in tropical and subtropical waters for trolling for gamefish, it is not much favoured on this side of the Atlantic. Here few species in the cold or temperate waters will react to a trolled bait or lure – species, that is, which demand heavy wire traces.

It is suggested that only twisted multistrand trace wire is used. If nylon-covered wire is used there is a risk of the fish's teeth wearing a cut through the nylon by its teeth continually sawing over one small part of the wire, which will often shear. Without a covering the wire is sufficiently smooth and hard to resist this happening, though once in a while a fish will bite through even 300 lb (136 kg) test wire!

Trace wire for the fish and fishing described in this

1. Making a wire trace involves first threading a metal ferrule on, passing the end back to form a loop, then bending the end again and pulling it back into the ferrule . . .
2. . . . crimping pliers crush the ferrule tightly to the wire.
3. Crimp firmly and evenly.
4. The finished loop.
For attaching hook to wire, pass a ferrule up the wire, thread on hook and tie two overhand knots before pushing the wire through the ferrule again. Tuck it back, then crimp firmly.

The finished trace with the equipment necessary to make it.

Pincers make good wire cutters, but this little tool made by the Sargent company of Newhaven, Connecticut, USA, is even better and can do most of the other work an angler has to do in making up tackle.

book from 40 lb (18.1 kg) test to 300 lb (136 kg) test is required (Berkley's is very reliable). The 300 lb material is only used for the last 18 in (45 cm) of shark traces (the hook link) to prevent the big fish from biting through; wire of about 175 lb (79.3 kg) test may be used for the rest of a shark trace. It is not strength with which one is concerned here, simply something bite-proof and wear-proof; and even 300 lb wire is only about 1½ mm thick.

To join the twisted wire securely to hooks, swivels and other rings, and to form loops, it is necessary to have a pair of crimping pliers, some metal sleeves and some wire cutters. Again, Berkley produce excellent crimping pliers and the brass or silvery sleeves in the correct sizes for each diameter of wire.

Another very useful tool for the light tackle boat angler is a pair of those special pliers that incorporate wire cutter, hook bender and straightener. A good one is made by the Sargent company of New Haven, Connecticut, USA and no self-respecting game-boat skipper or mate would be seen dead without one! Built on the powerful double-hinge principle, this tool is rarely found in a tackle shop on this side of the Atlantic.

It will be seen in the photographs that the ends of all wire trace joints are doubled over, then pushed back into the sleeves before crimping so there is no sharp end projecting. This not only stops water-borne debris catching on the trace, but it avoids very nasty cuts on one's hands when the trace is being used to haul a big fish, like a tope or shark, to the waiting tailer or gaff.

Accessories

On the shore it is not necessary to carry a vast box or bag and a mountain of gear weighing some 20 lb (9 kg), as so many sea anglers do. Of course, if the trip is an extended one and hundreds of miles from home, then a lot of gear may have to be put into the car just in case. However, on any actual fishing session ashore, even when fishing part of a tide for (say) tope, and another part for bass, if the two reels and other bits and pieces cannot be carried in a small haversack and weigh less than about 6 lb (2.7 kg), you are taking too much gear!

Apart from a small compartment box containing a few spare link swivels, swivels, hooks, a file or flat stone for sharpening hooks, a reel of elasticated thread (for tying on baits to the hook), one needs a sharp lock-blade knife or sheath knife (no more than a 5 in (12.6 cm) blade), spools of nylon for traces and leaders, spare wire traces, spare leads and, if fishing at night, a small headlamp or torch. A gaff or tailer and a net has sometimes to be considered.

On a boat more gear has to be carried and there is little doubt that a proper box of tough plastic with cantilever trays and drawers helps make life easier by storing everything one is likely to need, even on an extended trip a long way from home. This means, of course, carrying one or two tools for making up traces, repairing reels, even spare rings for rods and the thread and quick-drying varnish with which to make a temporary but strong job.

The best of the plastic tackle boxes for boat anglers is the Plano company's range, especially those made from ABS and polypropylene, which are tough enough to withstand the rough and tumble of offshore sea angling. There are others, but many have been found lacking, with weaknesses in the basic material or the locks, hinges and handle attachments – a box that accidentally opens and spills several reels and all a man's gear into the gap between boat and quay is calculated to bring even the mildest person to the point of derangement and is no bargain at all!

Perhaps at this stage the author should state that in mentioning brand names he is not favouring any one company but is stating his personal preferences after many years of using and field-testing a great deal of fishing tackle and accessories. He has no connection,

Good knives must be of stainless steel and keep a sharp edge. The slim knife is by Normark, the lock-blade by CK and the multi-tool knife is by Victorinox.

in any financial way, with any maker of tackle or accessories.

So, the following items should go into this big tackle box and always be kept there and any losses made good, so that at all times there are enough items to permit one to go fishing for just about any fish that swims in British waters: swivels and link swivels, sizes 10 to 4/0; hooks, sizes 2 to 10/0; crimping sleeves, crimping pliers, wire cutters; wire; sharp lock-blade or sheath knife; butt pad (for cushioning the rod butt in the stomach when fighting big fish); a set of files and flat sharpening stone; running booms, plastic beads (in case that swivel will not stop a running tackle above the hook); spools of spare lines for making up traces etc; elasticated cotton for tying baits firmly to hooks; mackerel feathers for catching bait for bigger fish, Red Gill eels in several colours, including red, blue and black; a plastic box of bomb-shaped leads from ½–2 oz (14–57 g); a box of heavy spoons (Toby, Koster, Condor); a plastic bottle of reel oil; a coil of commercial longline nylon (about 100 lb (45.3 kg) test); floats and at least two dozen balloons (for shark floats); spare tip rings, intermediate rings; whipping thread and fast-drying varnish; fast-curing epoxy-resin adhesive (all for emergency repairs at sea); spare reel clamps, reel spanners, some reel

Above: open D swivels, excellent but expensive.

Above: open box, diamond-eye and Berkley-McMahon swivels.

Left: big Berkley swivels, the one on the right finished matt black.

Above: Mustad lead or trace clips.
Below: spiral clip does same job.

Above: Berkley link-swivels – very strong.

Left: a home-made lead clip from stainless steel wire.

Useful swivels, links and clips.

spares (spools, nuts, washers and screws); polarised spectacles; baiting needles (6 in and 10 in) (15.24 and 25.4 cm) and a small box containing some aspirin or similar, antiseptic plasters, and a tube of sunburn cream.

In addition, you will pack your reels into the main compartment of the box, plus any afterthoughts you may have for any specific trip. Any heavy leads in the range 4 oz–3 lb (113.3 g–1.3 kg) should be carried separately in a small canvas drawstring bag.

One of the author's favourite items, which goes on every fishing trip, freshwater or saltwater, is a Victorinox Swiss anglers' knife with superb stainless-steel blades, screwdrivers, scissors, reamer, can opener, corkscrew, bottle opener, tweezers and toothpick. It is invaluable at times.

4 Baits: natural and artificial

Without good, fresh and suitable bait, a very skilled angler with the best tackle, a good boat and a knowledgeable skipper over a good mark can draw a blank; with good bait and indifferent gear another angler could succeed – at least in getting fish to take his baited hook. The skill to beat them is another ballgame, as the Americans say. And it's exactly the same when shore fishing.

Bait may be bought, dug, netted, collected; some is easy to come by, some is gained only by either a great deal of very hard work or paying a lot of money for somebody else, a professional digger or collector, to do the work.

Most of the baits used by boat anglers are fish or fishlike: mackerel, herrings, sand-eels, whiting, pouting, pollack, coalfish, pilchards and the tentacled cephalopods, cuttlefish, squid and octopus. All these may be used whole, as fillets, or cut into strips. If used whole, the most likely fish baits selected would be small pollack, coalfish, whiting, mackerel or herring, weighing between ½–1 lb (226–453 g).

Shore anglers also use fish baits, whole or in strips or chunks, for the larger predators, like conger, tope, pollack, bass, rays and even common skate. But most baits used by shore anglers are either dug or netted or picked up. They include marine worms, shellfish (such as razorfish, piddocks, cockles, clams, and mussels), various kinds of crabs, prawns, shrimps and small fish from among the rock-pools, like blennies, rockling and gunnel (butterfish).

Mackerel used for bait – they are also used minced-up as a smelly, oily attractor when shark fishing – may be caught on traces of feathers; feathers will also produce the big sand-eel (greater launce) at times on off-shore marks. The feathers are usually white cockerel hackles whipped to the eye or spade end of the shank of a long shanked stainless steel or cadmium plated hook, approximate size 1/0, and set about 15 in (38 cm) apart on short snoods. A lead of suitable weight – 4 oz to 1 lb (113.3–453 g) – is used on the end of the feather trace to search the water with a sink-and-lift motion, from near bottom to just subsurface.

Whiting should be used very fresh. They, too, may sometimes be feathered when the shoals are thick, but any caught on bait can be transferred to the big hook during a mixed fishing session.

Bait collecting is a fascinating and educational pursuit. Here the target is a dozen or so soft and peeler crabs, for bass fishing in the same location when the tide floods in.

Occasionally squid and cuttlefish may be caught on lumps of fish when they follow up the bait to the boat. Sometimes they get hooked, but the best way is to put a net quickly into the water behind them and scoop them up as the bait is lifted out. They will squirt their ink in alarm at this stage, so keep them in the water, trapped against the boat's hull, until the ink has stopped squirting!

Sand-eels are generally netted in fine seines in estuaries, or raked from the soft sand as the water leaves the shoreline, using a blunt instrument rather like a bill-hook, called a vingler. Sand-eels are very popular as bait in Devon and Cornwall, where they thrive. They are used alive or dead, but must be fresh.

Most fish baits go soft and smelly once they are dead, and quite apart from the fact that most large predatory fish generally prefer fresh fish they become difficult to retain on the hook if not fresh. This is a problem more of the shore angler, who has to cast his bait, while the boat man usually simply lowers his gently over the side.

Pirks are very effective for many species, including cod like this one, caught of Guernsey, but only the smaller pirks are of much use with light tackle.

Buying baits from fishmongers can be hazardous, as one is hardly ever able to buy fish that is really fresh; it may be sold for human consumption, but often the tope, conger or bass will turn up its nose! If mackerel look greenish-blue rather than dark blue, they are fresh enough. If herring or sprats or the rarer pilchards have a fair number of scales still

Wading in a shallow Cornish estuary Mike Osborne uses a vingler to scrape for sand-eels. The flat, blunt blade has a hooked end in which the sand-eels are caught. Considerable skill and speed is needed to grab the sand-eel in the hook of the vingler before it wriggles free and burrows back into the loose sand.

Close-up of the vingler and the sand-eel it has caught.

The spotted smoothhound may be one of the smaller members of the shark family, but it is highly rated as a fighting fish. This one accepted a crab bait from the shore in a spot where bass and congers might also be caught.

This tope will live to fight another day because no gaff has been used. The angler's companion is lifting the fish aboard the boat by gripping the wrist of the tail and the dorsal fin.

The blue shark is perhaps the poorest fighter, size-for-size, among the British species but it is a surprisingly beautifully-shaped shark, as the picture shows.

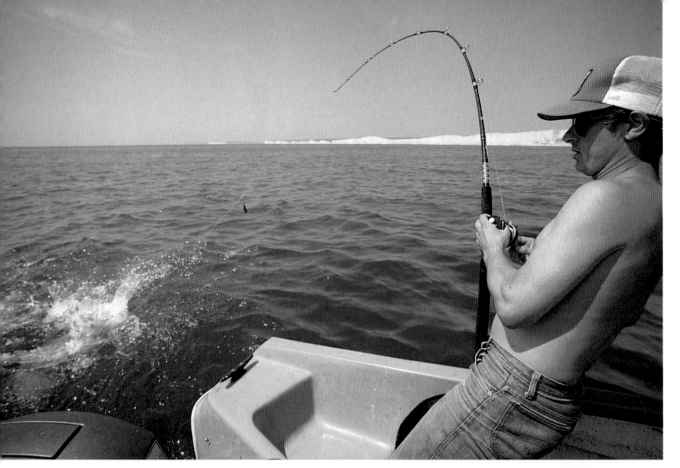

A tope hooked off the Sussex coast makes a final dash away from the boat, but the angler's flexible rod and modern multiplier reel should cope with the strain on the fragile line.

Below: Tope fishing from the shore usually entails long walks along the cliff tops, not to mention hair-raising climbs down the cliffs to reach rocky platforms near the water. This party is heading for a favourite haunt in Cornwall.

Right: Robin Potter shows his massive British record rod-caught conger weighing 109 lb 6 oz (49.4 kg), caught off Plymouth – south east of the Eddystone Reef – in 1976.

Conger eels, especially those caught over wrecks or reefs well offshore, can be massive creatures, fighting strongly from bottom to top. Their undulating, backward movements impose a great strain on the tackle and the angler. On this boat the fish box is nearly full and the system usually involves the skipper taking most of the catch for sale. Interestingly, conger flesh is used in the production of fish-paste.

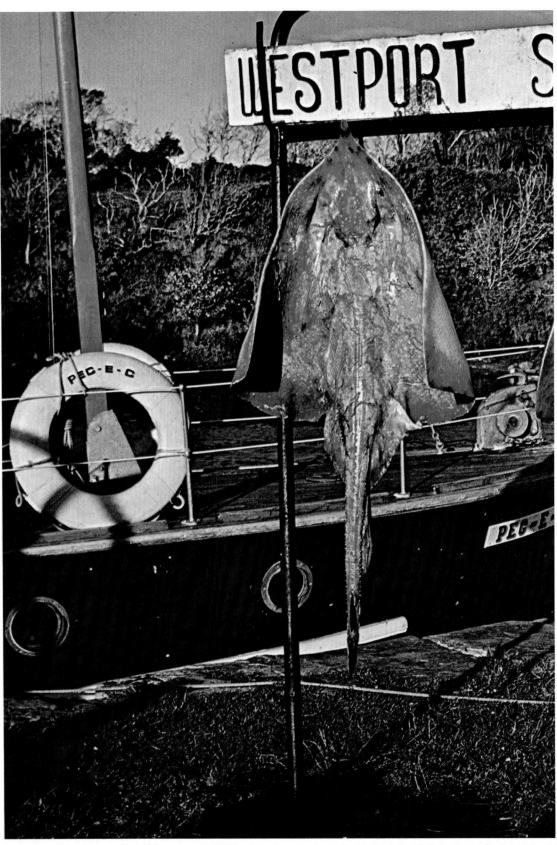

Dead common skate exhibited on a gantry in Westport, County Mayo, Ireland, makes a sorry picture; it would have been far better to set it free at sea, for it weighed 60 lb (27.2 kg) – way off record size.

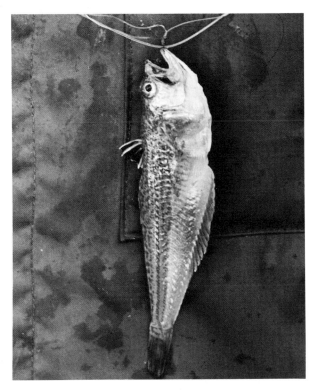

A fish to beware of. It may be caught from the shore on sandy bottoms, or encountered when bait digging or collecting. It is the lesser weaver; its dorsal spines, which are black, inject venom. Weavers are best held down by a booted foot and the head severed before the hook is cut free. Throw the body into the sea, or bury it deeply.

Filleting the side from a mackerel as a conger or tope bait is accomplished by cutting from behind the gill covers with the blade of the sharp knife held flat against the backbone.

Gaper clams are dug from muddy estuarine beaches and are fairly plentiful in Ireland. They are excellent bait for big bass in the surf, and outsized flounders are also fond of them.

adhering to them, they are suitable. Some fishmongers sell squid and octopus; they often have frozen packs of small Californian squids and these make very good baits and may be stored in the freezer at home and used on sudden trips.

Small whiting and pouting may often be caught on bits of worm or herring, from piers, rocky shores or from the boat. They may be kept a few hours in ice and then used as baits for big fish, or used immediately. Some anglers like to fish these small fish alive to lure predators, but it really is not necessary.

So much for the fishy baits, then.

On the sandy/muddy mixture shores, especially near estuaries, lugworms are often found in dense beds, although in recent years professional diggers have reduced some of the more accessible beds by supplying too many worms to anglers who usually have at least half of what they take fishing left over and often wasted at the end of the day.

Lugworms are quite expensive to buy. There are two main types, the big adult worms, either black, darkish brown or maybe reddish, from 6 in

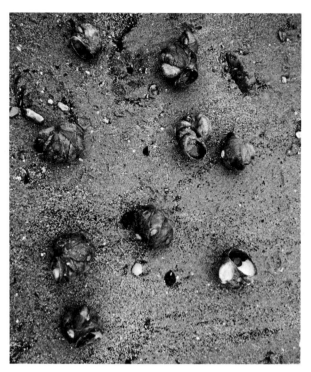

Storms often wash up slipper limpets, which may be collected in a leisurely manner. Good baits in bunches for bass and flounders, as well as wrasse and cod at times.

Superb baits: razorfish enclosing some prime lugworms. For cod and bass these are most reliable when fished on to sand.

(15.2 cm) to 1 ft (0.30 m) long, and the tiny red 'blowers', which may be only 2–3 in (5–7.5 cm) long. Usually the big worms are dug nearer to the low water mark while the 'blowers' can be dug close to the area of beach that is only just exposed on short (neap) tides.

There are also two ways of digging them. The big lug usually burrow deep into the muddy sand. Sometimes they are in firm sand, in which holes may be dug which do not collapse too quickly. In this case a narrow-bladed lug spade is used, each curly cast on the surface being dug up and the worm's burrow followed down by constantly cutting across it. This can be very hard work and though the rewards are big worms, it may take well over an hour to dig 50 of them.

In other areas the sand may be wetter and looser, with more mud. Here the lug may well be closer together in vast beds and a simple trench is dug in the thickest areas of casts using a flat-tined fork. Usually it will be necessary to dig down about 18 in (45.7 cm).

One or two areas exist, some in Scotland, where vast lugworms 18 in (45.7 cm) long or more may be lifted by hand from soft mud. Such places are rarely found, however, and the finders keep them secret!

In the past couple of years, bait-pumps have become quite popular as a method of getting lugworms out of the mud-sand mixtures in which they burrow. Rather like a king-size cycle pump, they work by sucking up the sand in which the worm has burrowed, but they do not work in all types of lugworm habitat. They are best in fairly soft sand/mud mixtures, specially on beaches where the worms tend to burrow straight down.

The technique is fairly straightforward, if rather strenuous. The open end of the pump's tube is located over a worm cast and the handle, which has been first pushed into the pump barrel, is slowly lifted. This will sink the pump into the sand, though some downward manual pressure is often required. When the pump barrel is down as far as it will go, the handle is lifted. This takes some doing at times. If you are lucky, the worm will be expelled with a downward push on the pump handle, along with the sand in which it has been burrowing. But life is often not that simple, and several attempts may be needed before the worm comes to hand. It pays to look down the hole left by withdrawing the pump, to try to establish

Top: A straight, narrow blade with a sharp edge is used for mature lugworms in firm sand or sand/mud mixtures. The spade will cut across the cast and expose the burrow.

The digger has seen the worm's tail, taken a slice of sand from behind it to expose the firm body, and is now feeling for it with his finger. Pulling the worm's sand-filled tail instead of gripping the firm body will cause the tail to break off.

Centre: Success! Up comes a juicy lugworm. The worm is squeezed on to the sand to kill and gut it. This way the worm remains in good condition for several days if wrapped separately in newspaper.

Right: Mature black lugworms like these are a lot of effort to dig and must be carefully treated to remain in firm, fresh

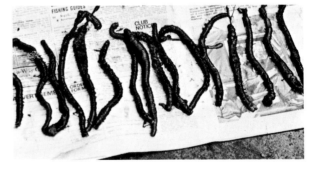

condition for several days, if necessary. Place them in newspaper and roll up the paper so each worm is kept separated from any other.

Baiting up with mature lugworms should be done from the tail end after the sand-filled tail has been removed. This way the worm's tail-end holds on to the hook eye well.

Below: The sea mouse, often washed ashore after gales, is a good cod bait, but must be tied to the hook at both ends with shirring elastic, since, if the body is punctured, it deflates into a shapeless mass.

Short snoods and big black lugworms can be cast a long way to cod without coming adrift. The worms must lie straight on the hook to streamline the tackle in flight.

The razorfish's muscular 'foot' anchors itself in its burrow. This one has just been pulled clear after dropping salt down the hole, which caused the razorfish to surface.

one entails killing the worms first, in the second they are kept alive. Big adult worms are best killed by nipping off the head, then squeezing the entrails out towards the head end. Wash the worms in seawater, dry them in newspaper, then wrap them in dry and preferably old newspaper, each worm being kept separated from the others. The paper should be changed after a few hours and the worms wrapped again. Keep them cool (in a refrigerator, but not frozen) and they will remain in good condition for up to a week.

The smaller, softer 'blowers' must usually be kept alive since they become jelly-like and decompose rapidly after death. This is achieved by first washing them in seawater, then drying and either wrapping them in tens in folds of newspaper, or laying them in damp (not wet) seaweed or in vermiculite chips in a cardboard box. The vermiculite chip method, incidentally, is also used for big ragworms; alternatively, the ragworms are wrapped in newspaper, again kept apart from each other.

All worm baits should be stored in a cool place. Do not try to deep-freeze worms; they become soft and

When a crab is found being carried beneath another (usually larger) crab, the carried crab is certainly either a peeler or a soft crab. Gloves prevent painful scratches from barnacles and mussels.

if the worm's burrow has turned off at an angle. This needs to be done quickly, before the sand collapses to obliterate the burrow.

If the burrow has turned off, try another pump along the line of the worm's change of direction. It can take several attempts before the worm is caught – or not, as the case may be.

Like a lug spade, a pump is not infallible, and just as competency with the spade is required to obtain useful numbers of worms, so it is with the pump. The spade is more versatile, but the pump is comforting to have since thrusting a hand into freezing sand to pull up a dug-out lugworm is pure agony.

Various types of ragworm also make good baits, including the giant king ragworm, often attaining 18 in (46 cm) in length and nearly ¾ in (2 cm) in thickness; smaller red ragworms 2½–4 in (6.5–10 cm) long, and white ragworms, 3–5 in (7.8–13 cm). Estuaries, areas of shell-grit, fine shingle mixed with sand, even sandy/stony ground will produce king ragworms, though these areas are limited. Red ragworms are often found in lug-inhabited areas while digging lugworms, as are white ragworms, though the latter prefer coarser sand. Forks are best for rag digging.

To keep lugworms there are two main methods:

useless when defrosted.

What else can be dug from sandy shores? Razorfish for a start, though they are less numerous than they once were. The cold 1963 winter killed off many of the colonies. These are excellent baits for bass, plaice, flounders, cod and they are usually found in beds on sandy banks near the low water mark. They too live in burrows in the sand, usually driving almost verti-

A peeler crab is prepared for the hook. First the back shell or carapace is lifted clear, then the belly shell and legs are peeled.

Below: This crab has just crawled clear of its old shell, now lying open. It is as soft as a jelly, and had the angler not found it, the crab would have hidden under a rock or weed until the new shell hardened. Now it will hopefully catch the angler a bass.

cally. They may be dug with a lug spade or lifted out, once the burrows have been located, by pouring salt down the hole, which makes them surface in a few minutes. Another method involves inserting a metal rod with an arrowhead-shaped tip down the hole. The idea is that the razorfish clamps its shell together as it feels the tip go by and is then lifted out as it becomes wedged by the barbs.

In any method the shellfish has first to be located, and this is done by spotting clean holes in the sand, which are sometimes round and sometimes keyhole shaped. Often there are the marks of a jet of water imprinted in the sand beside the hole. If one stamps about on a razorfish bed the creatures become alarmed by the vibrations and shoot jets of water into the air, thus giving away their positions.

Simply keep razorfish in a plastic bucket after washing them in seawater; covered with a damp bit of sacking and kept cool they will keep alive for nearly a week. Some tackle dealers deep freeze them for stock, but they, like lugworms, also become very soft when defrosted and are not very good baits.

In bait-inhabited areas it pays to walk the shore after a big onshore gale because often razorfish, lug, slipper limpets, queen cockles, cockles, whelks, hermit crabs and other useful baits are washed up on the shore, especially by the highest tide.

Hermit crabs live in empty whelk shells and may be caught in a fish-baited dropnet or sometimes picked up in tide-pools at low water. They make very good baits for many fish, including bass, cod, smooth-hounds, rays, plaice and flounders.

The other crabs that make excellent baits are those that grow by changing their old shells for bigger ones every so often – common shore crabs, edible crabs and velvet swimming crabs are among the most used. Immediately a crab has cast its old tight shell it is soft and rubbery, the back and rest of the body gradually hardening into a new shell. It is then a very good bait

and known as soft crab or a 'softie'. Before the shell is cast it looks dead and may seem to be loose fitting where it joins the V-shaped underside at the back-end. A thumbnail inserted will often lift the whole back shell off: the crab is a 'peeler' and again an excellent bait. Before use, however, it is necessary to peel the dead, hard shell from the claws, legs and underside. Failure to do this will surely result in the hook point being protected by the shell when you strike a bite.

Always keep crabs alive, if possible in a small, damp sack or wooden or plastic box or bucket, since they decompose quickly when dead. It helps to keep them covered with some damp weed. Always keep soft crabs separated from peelers, or else the soft ones will be eaten by the others or become soft and useless from constant nipping.

Sand-eels may be kept alive all day in a cooler-box with ice – this apparent miracle was publicised by a well-known Cornish angler, Mike Osborne.

A small-meshed dropnet baited with some old bits of smelly fish such as kipper and left in deep, weedy rockpools at low water or suspended down by the side of a concrete harbour wall or rocks, will produce prawns. These may be kept alive in damp weed in a cool place for an hour or so and fished alive on float tackle for bass and pollack.

Mussels may be collected from the shore, especially from rocks near the low water area on spring tides, when the bigger ones are revealed. They are good for cod, plaice, flounder and will even catch bass when nothing else is available. Keep them in a small damp sack, again in a cool place.

In some areas where the shore has soft rock, such as chalk, old peat-beds or rotting timbers, the boring

Small harbour ragworms dug from a muddy creek are put to dry out on an old towel. They keep in better condition when dry.

bivalve, known as the piddock, may be found. These, like many other forms of shellfish, were hard hit by the big freeze of the 1963 winter, since they often live in colonies high up the beach. Recently, however, there have been signs of a come-back and piddocks of a decent size make excellent baits for plaice, flounders, cod and bass. They may be dug out with a lug spade, a hunk of peat lifted clear and broken up to remove the soft-shelled piddocks, or by levering away lumps of chalk or soft rock. The wood, peat, chalk or even firm clay, in which piddock colonies are found, appear like Gruyère cheese on the surface, and when the holey areas are knocked, jets of water will emerge from the disturbed piddocks.

While searching rocky shores at low water for crabs one often finds small fish and eels in the pools, under rocks. Most of these, alive or dead, will make good baits for bass, congers and rays. Incidentally, in May and June and less frequently later on, one often comes across one crab carrying another beneath. The one being carried will be a hen crab and she will either be a softie or a peeler. Pick up the cock, which will try to pinch you, and sneak the hen away. It's a bit tough on the crabs' love-life, but the life on the shore is tough for all creatures, most of which eat others and are in turn eaten.

Although many other creatures of the shore make good baits, there are only two more that really must not be left out: sea-slaters and harbour ragworms or mudworms. Sea-slaters, which are like big woodlice, live in the splash zone high on the shore, among the cracks of sea defences, in rock crevices, along old, cracked concrete piers. They may often be grabbed as they scuttle around and be put into a plastic baitbox with a perforated lid. They are excellent for float-fishing for bass, and in estuaries seatrout certainly take them when they can.

The little ragworms are found in oozy, evil smelling mud in estuaries, saltwater creeks back in the marshes, or on exposed mudbanks in extensive harbours. They are normally about 1½–2½ in (4–6 cm) long, but sometimes colonies of bigger ones up to 3 in (8 cm) may be discovered. They leave the mud honeycombed with burrows, and a small handfork is a good tool for extracting them. This is a filthy and sometimes dangerous job as it is easy to sink thigh-deep in the ooze. Always take great care when after these worms. Keep them cool in a plastic or wooden box and covered with a seawater damped flannel cloth. They are excellent when floatfished for mullet, bass and flounders, and they sometimes accidentally (!) lure seatrout in estuaries. They will keep well for about two days. Do not put any green or yellowish worms in with the red ones or else all will perish.

A small squid, freely available in some fishmongers or deep-freeze stores. The head has been cut off and the transparent 'pen' removed.

The body has been slit open and spread flat on the wooden board before being cut into strips.

To bait a big hook (for bass or conger, for example) push the point through the complete body at the pointed end and bring it out again.

The head of the squid makes a good bait, complete with tentacles, for bass, cod, conger and skate.

Now push the hook down into the body cavity and bring it out through the side, pulling the point of the body above the eye of the hook.

Pinch the body tightly and wind firmly with shirring elastic.

Pull the elastic to break it off. No knot is necessary, the material locks itself. This bait will cast a long way without breaking up, since it is streamlined and supported by the hook eye.

Hook them by the head, and for bass use a bunch of up to a dozen, always on a fine wire hook.

Cutting bait and baiting up

It is easy to spoil good bait due to bad preparation or bad presentation. There are good and bad, right and wrong ways to bait hooks with various baits.

Always cut fish and squid-type baits on a softwood board, using a *very* sharp knife with a thinnish blade. If you can't shave your forearm with the knife it is too blunt! Such fish as mackerel, whiting and herring should be held by the head, then cut with the blade held flat and against the backbone, sliding the knife towards the tail. Turn the fish over to take off the other fillet.

If the fillets need to be cut into strips, lay the fillets skin side down on the board. It is much easier to cut neat pieces that way.

Usually it is best to mount whole fish, tail-first, up the trace, the hook being lodged near the head, as most predators turn their prey to swallow it head-first. One exception is the sand-eel, which is always presented with the hook point facing forward, whether the bait is fished dead or alive. Also, when using small live fish, such as whiting, pouting, various rock-pool fish or elvers (baby eels) they should be lightly hooked through the top lip.

There is seldom need to conceal the hook in the

bait, as, generally, fish in the sea – and in freshwater for that matter – do not appear to be aware of hooks, on lures or in a bait. The size of hook should of course match the size of bait. It is also necessary to choose a hook that, when baited, will have its point and barb clear of the bait, to avoid the bait deflecting the hook point from the mouth of the fish on the strike.

Big adult lugworms are best baited head-down: it is at the head end that the scent-laden fluids ooze out, and if the hook point is in that area it is quickly engulfed by the fish. There is also the very important fact that a lugworm's tail end is firm and tends to grip the hook eye and knot more than does the head end, so it casts better, lying straight and streamlined for its passage out to the fish when hurled by the surfcaster. Blower lug, however, are usually so small and so soft that several, up to a dozen for big cod, may be needed on the hook. As these blowers are usually kept alive, they remain soft and are best baited from the head end, the point being carefully inserted into the sucker-like mouth and the worm slid up the hook and on to the trace; this is repeated as often as necessary to achieve the correct bait size. For sole and dab, perhaps, one worm would do on a small hook.

King ragworms are baited from the head, the hook being inserted through the mouth and the worm slid up the hook shank: it should be remembered that the eye of the hook and the knot with which it is attached to the trace should be used whenever possible to hold a bait in a neat position on the hook. For big fish, like bass, a whole big worm will be fine; pieces of worm may be used for smaller fish. Red and white ragworm used singly or in bunches for short casting or float fishing, may be nicked lightly through the head end; when a firmer hooking is required, for surfcasting to 50 yd (45.7 m) or more, then the hook should be inserted into the mouth and the worm pulled up above the eye. Small harbour ragworms (mudworms) are simply nicked through the head, used in bunches on fine wire hooks.

An innovation called a bait clip is a useful addition to the terminal tackle when a fixed paternoster rig is being used to try to catch fish at great distances from the beach or pier-head. The bait clip is a hook-shaped device, of plastic or wire, slid on to the standing part of the rig and fixed in position with a stop knot below which is a short length of plastic or rubber tube.

The position of the bait clip must be arranged so that when the snood holding the hook is pulled down, the hook will just engage with the hook of the bait clip under some tension. A small bead of fresh-water split shot is clamped on the snood after the worm is slid up it; the bead or shot prevents the worm being forced up the snood when the tackle is in flight, specially at the moment of peak speed when the cast is made.

The clip holds the baited hook close to the main part of the terminal tackle and in a straight line, thus streamlining the tackle in flight and preventing the baited snood or snoods flapping in the air and setting up air resistance which slows down the flying rig and shortens range.

For most types of fishing, bait clips – or relay clips as they are sometimes known – are not really necessary, but when cod, especially, or any other fish at times, are known to be well out from the angler's stance – over (say) 140 yards (128 m) – a bait-clip rig can make all the difference between success and failure. They increase distance and keep the bait intact, despite the stresses of the cast.

The baited hook is held in the clip under line tension, but when the lead touches the seabed, that tension eases and the hook or hooks should fall out of the clip or clips and fish naturally.

Razorfish are best threaded on the hook from the firm, foot end, the foot holding on to the eye better than the other end. Piddocks, cockles, slipper limpets, mussels and clams need be hooked twice through the hardest part one can find on their body, the soft parts being wrapped round the shank or bend of the hook.

Prawns and shrimps are best fished alive on float tackle, and they are hooked by passing the point once through the second segment up from the tail, from the underside, so that the hook protrudes from the back. Fish usually fold the crustacean in its natural curve to swallow it, perhaps to avoid a stab from the sharp spikes on the head of a prawn.

Fished alive, the sand-eel can be hooked in a number of ways, all of which are aimed at keeping the creature alive for as long as possible. At the same time the hook should be in as good a position as possible to hook the taking fish. However, some of the methods of hooking a live sand-eel are extremely inhumane and unnecessary. Two methods that work well are a simple lip hook job: attached from the inside to the outside of the top lip; and the other by passing the hook carefully into the mouth, out of one gill cover, then nicking it just under the skin a little way back of the gill cover.

Live sand-eels are delicate creatures and the above methods of baiting them will not permit any jerky, long distance casts. Instead, swing out the tackle – be it float, leger or driftline.

Freshly killed sand-eels are a different proposition. (It is best to keep them alive on ice in the cooler-box, then kill them just before baiting up.) One can insert the hook through the mouth and then bring it out halfway along the body. Alternatively two hooks can be used: one some two inches behind the other, so that one is in the bait's mouth, the other somewhere along the body. An excellent way of using a dead sand-eel on a one-hook rig involves inserting the hook into the bait's mouth and then out behind the gills, followed by forming a circle of nylon with a half-hitch ahead of the eel's head, then slipping it over the snout, pulling tight simultaneously. This forms a simple hitch of the nylon on the firm snout and, when a fish takes and is hooked, pulls free so that the trace is unknotted and at full strength. This method permits very long casts without the delicate little fish tearing free.

Large sand-eels may be cut in two equal pieces and used as legering bait as above.

Soft and peeler crabs are sometimes quite a problem when baiting. When long casts are not essential both soft and peeler crabs may be hooked by passing the hook through the back, out at the underside, and out through the back again. Naturally, one needs to choose the right hook size for the size of the crab.

However, often it is necessary to cast 50 to 100 yd (45.7–91.4 m), and crabs baited as above will tear off the hook. So, with a soft crab, bait as above but tie at

A big sand-eel being mounted on a hook to wire for shore tope. It is secured round the nose with nylon to keep it in position when long distance casting. With a nylon trace, a half hitch may be made in the trace, which is then slipped over the nose and drawn down to the hook. It pulls out when a fish is hooked.

least two legs up the trace above the hook, using elasticated thread (shirring elastic) from a draper's store. This material can be wound for several turns and tightened, at which point it locks and needs no knot. Do not pull it too tight or it will cut through the soft crab and prove useless. With soft crabs bigger than about 2½ in (6.5 cm) across the shell, it may be best to cut them in half with a sharp knife before use. Then, stick the hook through the shell side, put it back through and bring it out again through the shell, then wind shirring elastic round the whole bait and hook; fish don't care about a 'packaged' crab so long as the juices remain.

Peeler crabs are a somewhat tougher bait than soft crabs, though soft crabs vary in consistency depending on the degree of hardening following the shedding of the old shell: newly shed soft crabs have the consistency of soft jelly; better are those that feel rubbery. The crabs that have hardened to become what anglers term 'cracklebacks' or 'crispies' are

The most famous and most effective of all saltwater lures: the Red Gill, superb for bass, pollack, coalfish and big ballan wrasse.

usable, but are very second-rate baits and do come off the hook easily when cast.

But back to peeler crabs. The shell and the two lobes that are left on each flank just above the legs must be removed; then, the belly segments of shell must be taken off with the thumbnail until the whole crab including claws and legs has been peeled. Push the hook through from one side of the back, out through the belly, then in again, so that the point protrudes from the back – which is where, normally, a bass tries to grab a crab. Tie two legs up the trace with the shirring elastic.

Much nonsense has been talked in the past about presenting crab bait 'naturally'. A bunch of soft legs is a killing bait, so is a mushy parcel strapped to a hook, made up of bits and pieces of various crabs; it is the succulent smell and taste of the bait, not its appearance, that makes bass (and other fish) go crazy for crab.

What of hardback crabs? Some anglers have undoubtedly caught bass on them when forced to use them since nothing better was available; but really small hardback crabs are useful only for ballan wrasse in general, though cod will sometimes take them. This is one of sea angling's mysteries: why fish are found to have eaten large numbers of hardback crabs yet consistently refuse to take one on the hook.

All equipment used for digging or other methods of obtaining sea baits must be kept free of rust and corrosion, or else it will become useless. A lug spade or flat-tined fork or a bait pump should be washed in freshwater after use, then dried and wiped with thick oil or grease. A rusty tool makes for hard work as it is difficult to move through sand or mud rather than slicing through. Any net frames used for prawns, hermit crabs or little rockfish should be made from galvanised wire – they need be only enlarged versions of children's toy nets. Both handles and dropnets are easily made at home for less than half the price of shop-bought ones.

Artificial baits

There are many artificial baits that will catch sea fish in British and north-west European waters, but in the field of sportfishing some of them, the author feels, are undesirable, in that they do not necessarily hook fish fairly in the mouth. The heavy lures that will *not* be listed in the following pages are pirks or jigs, some of which weigh as much as 2 lb (900 g).

There are four metal spoon-type lures that have long proved their worth for the sea angler fishing for sport: the ABU Toby, the same company's Koster, the Condor spoon (often called the German sprat) and small bar-spoons such as Mepps, Veltic, Celta, Droppen, Reflex and some others of similar design.

For bass, pollack and mackerel the first three lures are all excellent, from as light as ⅝ oz (18 g) up to just over an ounce (30 g). The bar-spoons are good for very light tackle fishing for school bass, mackerel, garfish, grey mullet (thick-lipped) and – whisper it – seatrout in estuaries, which sometimes get caught accidentally when after other species.

Silver is by far the better colour of the two for most saltwater metal lures.

There are a number of rubber or soft plastic lures available, all of which are eclipsed by the astounding success of Alex Ingram's Red Gill sand-eels. Used in all available sizes, they consistently catch bass, pollack, coalfish, cod and big ballan wrasse. Lures that are made in the same way as the flies of the freshwater angler – from hair and feathers, tinsel etc – are also excellent saltwater lures for the sportfisher, not only for catching mackerel for bait but for bass, pollack, coalfish, garfish, thick-lipped grey mullet – even sharks.

Saltwater flies are generally made to simulate small fish on which predators feed. Various patterns will be dealt with later.

Have no truck with any of the artificial baits that are said to smell or taste 'like the real thing' and which are cast and allowed to fish on the bottom. Such baits as artificial lugworms, crabs and small squid do not catch fish by being so fished and are a waste of money.

PART TWO

The fish and the fishing

Previous page: From shallow, sandy beaches like this one in Ireland big tope may be caught by casting fish baits. Hooked in the shallows, perhaps only a foot or so (30.4 cm) deep, the tope will make runs for the deeper water, taking up to 200 yd (182.8 m) of line – very exciting! The angler must have patience, though, for this is a waiting game, ambushing the few fish that come inshore so far.

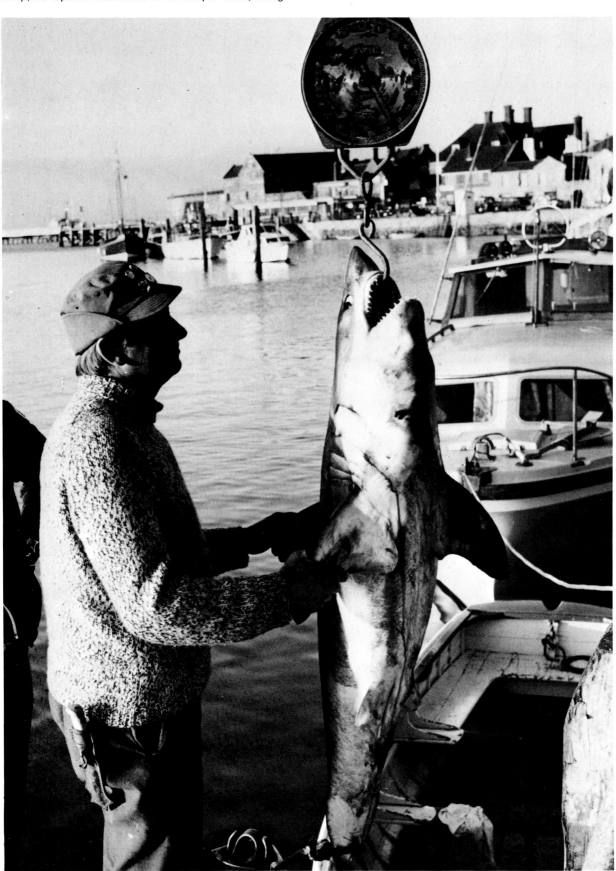

5 The sportfisher's sharks

There are four sharks of interest to the sporting angler in British and north-west European waters: blue, porbeagle, thresher and mako and they are caught in the greatest numbers in that order.

Very few anglers specifically fish for mako and thresher sharks in the waters of the British Isles and neighbouring Europe, since the small number of sharks does not justify the effort and cost. Cornwall offers the best chance of a mako, and perhaps the best port to go from is Falmouth. Looe is also a good bet, and it was from this famous shark-fishing port (where blues are the main catch) that the biggest British mako, a fish of 500 lb (226.7 kg), was taken by Mrs Joyce Yallop in 1971.

Threshers are probably not as rare as the mako. The scimitar-shaped tail of the thresher is sighted at many points round the coast. Unlike the other sharks, which the novice may have difficulty in identifying at a distance while the fish is swimming in the water, the scimitar-shaped tail of the thresher is quite unmistakable and anybody who sees one or more of these tall, sword-like tails thrashing the sea to foam as the fish circle rapidly round a panic-stricken shoal of mackerel, can be sure that the sharks are threshers. The sharks herd the bait-fish into a tight knot and then rush in to feed on them.

There is no particular place one could depend on having a good chance of thresher shark, and it is less easy to advise on than the mako. Perhaps the waters off the Isle of Wight, where porbeagles are fished, would be as good a place as any. The British record of 323 lb (146.5 kg) was caught off Portsmouth in 1982, six miles south of the Nab Tower. Since threshers have occasionally been hooked in other places, while bottom fishing near rocky outcrops, reefs and headlands – usually in turbulent water – it is now a commonly held view that the best chance of hooking a thresher shark in Britain and its environs would be to fish a big bait near the bottom in such places. Also some form of groundbait attraction working at that level would help. This method is used mainly for this species of shark; indeed, it is a peculiar way to tackle a fish that, on the few occasions it is seen, is actively herding mackerel on the surface!

More blue sharks are caught than any of the other sharks in British waters. The bulk of the catch comes from the West Country ports of Devon and Cornwall – Mevagissey, Looe, Fowey, Falmouth, Plymouth and

Left: This Isle of Wight porbeagle, being steadied by the author, was boated in very little time on 10 lb (4.5 kg) test line by Vince Lister. It weighed 63 lb (28.5 kg) and missed a world 12 lb (5.4 kg) class record by 4 lb (1.8 kg).

Right: This 252 lb (114.3 kg) porbeagle shark was hooked only half a mile out to sea off the cliffs at Crackington Haven, on Cornwall's Atlantic coast.

Penzance, all having good reputations. The north coast of Cornwall also produces blues, though the charter-boats are in general not as readily available or specialised as the others.

The west and south-west coasts of the Irish Republic are good blue shark waters, too, the best known ports being Kinsale, Dungarvan, Courtmacsherry, Cahirciveen, Dingle, Tralee, Kilkee, and up to Westport, the Clew Bay and Achill areas being particularly good.

Blue sharks do not usually attain big weights in British and north-west European waters, 50 lb (22.6 kg) or so being about average. The rod-caught British record is a fish of 218 lb (98.8 kg). Because the majority are taken on heavy tackle, often hired out by the charter-boats to tourists, the blue shark has a reputation for being a non-fighter. That the blue has not the dash and strength of the porbeagle, size for size, is indisputable, but when taken on lightish tackle the blue can be given the title of sportfish.

The porbeagle is the best of the British and north-west European sharks so far as the sporting angler is concerned. It grows to a good size and it is a strong and tenacious fighter. The British record is a fish of 465 lb (210.9 kg) caught from Padstow, Cornwall, in 1976.

Porbeagles are much more tolerant of cold water than are the blue, mako and thresher sharks and in fact they have figured in late autumn and winter catches of herring in the southern North Sea; Scandinavian boats longline for them in the North Sea, and fish are known to swim in the waters off the Scottish coasts, the area of the Mull of Galloway having produced actual hook-ups.

Among the best locations for porbeagle fishing are the Isle of Wight grounds, the West Country ports already listed for blue shark fishing, the north Devon coast between Bude and Ilfracombe, especially the turbulent water off Hartland Point, and Carmarthen Bay across the other side of the outer edge of the Bristol Channel in South Wales. In the Irish Republic porbeagles are taken on the parts of the west coast where boats and skippers have the expertise: the Clare and Galway coasts host many fish, which often come so close inshore where steep cliffs fall to deep water that they are caught from the cliffs. Later in the year, in September and October, the fish appear in large numbers off Achill – although in the past few years the numbers of fish taken have fallen.

The smooth-hound is a beautiful fish: this one is the spotted variety, *Mustelus asterias*, just about to be slid back into the sea after unhooking.

Those, then, are the four main quarries for the sportfisher bearing the name shark. However, there are other members of the shark family that are of equal interest, if not more, in spite of the fact that they do not attain such weights. These are the tope, which averages about 25 lb (11.3 kg) but often reaches 40 lb (18 kg), and the two species of smooth-hound: the unspotted variety, *Mustelus mustelus*, and the spotted variety, *Mustelus asterias*. The one without spots certainly reaches weights of over 30 lb (13.6 kg), though a good one is reckoned to weigh 15 lb (6.8 kg), and the spotted one 20 lb (9 kg), though a good one weighs half that.

Both tope and smooth-hounds are, size for size, the equal of any of the true sharks in these waters so far as fighting ability is concerned. When hooked in shallow water, as they often are, they show turns of speed and lengths of run that would make the mako and porbeagle seem tame. Of course, they need to be fished with matching sporting tackle, and these fish are regularly caught at depths of 3–30 ft (0.9–9 m). In water that is more than, say, 40 ft (12 m) deep, these mini-sharks do not perform very well as a rule.

The beauty of tope and 'smoothies', as anglers describe them, is that they are often taken by casting from the shore – from beaches and from projections over deepish water – and thus they produce excellent sport on the long, light casting rod without having the bother and expense of going afloat.

Tope are distributed all round the British and Irish coasts, being particularly numerous in the bays of extensive estuaries, usually over sandy or gravelly seabeds. However, there are comparatively few places where shore fishing proves worthwhile. Locations worth trying include the western side of Kent's Dungeness promontory; Selsey Bill; Park and Lepe Beaches in the Solent; Dorset's Chesil Bank; various steep beaches and rocks in Devon and Cornwall, especially the north coast of Cornwall, from St Ives to Trevose Head; the Gower Peninsula and Carmarthen Bay in South Wales; Cardigan Bay and the Lleyn Peninsula up to and including the tope-inhabited waters of Anglesey and the Menai Strait; plus south and south-west coasts of the Irish Republic, especially west Cork and the Dingle Peninsula.

Smooth-hounds are strange fish in that they

Tope are streamlined sharks and capable of terrific speed and long runs. This one is held by angling writer Ian Gillespie.

Right: Two gaffs are used to haul a big porbeagle aboard off the north Cornish coast. Those teeth are sharp!

appear to change location for no good reason, turning up in widely different environments. They do have a penchant for very large estuaries – perhaps they favour the less saline water? – and the area from The Wash down to the south side of the Thames Estuary, then again from Selsey through the Solent to Durlston Head, is a regular producer of these fish. Anglesey is also worth a try. In Ireland reports of smooth-hounds are few, but that may be due to the fact that some anglers may not recognise the difference between the unspotted smooth-hound and the tope. The only reliable reports of smooth-hounds in Irish waters have been from Tralee Bay in Co. Kerry.

Seasons for sharks usually begin about the end of May and last until mid-September, both dates being dependent on long-term weather conditions. Although little work has yet been done on the idea, there seems little doubt that porbeagle sharks could be caught right up until Christmas, especially in the southern North Sea (East Anglian herring grounds) – provided the sea conditions at that time of year permitted boats to get out regularly.

For tope and smooth-hounds seasons vary more widely, depending on area. May and June are usually best, especially on shallow water inshore marks, but after the end of June 'smoothies' seem to move to deeper water. Tope can be taken well into October, especially in the south-west of Britain and Ireland. In some of the Welsh estuaries of the Gower, for instance, tope are often taken from the shore in shallow water in April.

Light tackle and sharks

With light tackle and big sharks it must be remembered that one either spends a lot of money on booking a boat for one or two people, or else, if three or four anglers are required to share the expense to make the trip economical, then before fishing begins, there should be a draw to find out who takes the first fish, who the second and so on, regardless of whose tackle the fish comes to take. Also, it should be decided before booking the boat what tackle will be used – 12, 20, 30 or 50 lb IGFA – and each angler must ensure that the rod, reel and line he takes with him is satisfactory to the other anglers who may have to use it.

The basic shark fishing technique has been so well written about these past few years that it would be mere repetition to go deeply into the matter. However, most of the written lore is based on the use of heavy or comparatively heavy tackle, eg IGFA 50 lb and 80 lb (22.6 and 36.2 kg), and fishing from boats of

30–40 ft (9.1–12.1 m) in groups of three to six anglers. Ideally, light tackle shark fishing should be carried out, whenever wind and water conditions are favourable, from a fast and manoeuvrable boat of between 20 and 27 ft (6 and 8.2 m), so that the angler is given every advantage to play his fish safely on his light tackle. Ideally the skipper of the boat should keep the angler facing his fish over the stern end of the gunwale.

Whether the quarry is a blue or a porbeagle, or even the rarer mako and thresher, the following basic system applies, although suitable variations can be suggested later.

Sharks hunt by scent, even the big-eyed porbeagle being attracted to the boat in the same way as the slit-eyed blue – by chumming, as the Americans and most other English-speaking nations have it, or the use of rubby-dubby in Britain. The basis of the scent trail is oily minced and/or chopped fish, such as mackerel, herrings, anchovies, pilchards, sprats, and even pouting and whiting, which are less oily. The fish need not be fresh; indeed oily fish that have spent a day in the sun and smell quite high make excellent rubby-dubby.

Some charter-boat skippers do the job properly, which is hard work; others simply prepare one onion sack of the evil concoction, then sit back and await results, while having a sleep. There is no doubt that the number of sharks attracted to the boat is in direct proportion to the amount of work put, by both skipper and anglers, into laying a good trail. And obviously, anglers who want a real oil-slick and particle curtain in the water must help the skipper. One onion sack over the gunwale is not enough. Far better to have three sacks, one over the bow, one amidships, the other over the stern. Each bag, which should just be dipping into the water each time the boat rolls, so that oil and particles of fish are washed out continuously, should contain about 8 lb (3.6 kg) of minced fish mixed with about three double handfuls of bran. The bran helps to release oil slowly, particles drifting away on the surface and fluttering below it. Use strong nylon sash cord to suspend each bag.

In addition, it pays to chop up on a board some 20 bait-fish into tiny cubes – like canned pineapple – and have them going over the side, say, three every five minutes. These pieces sink and will bring up any sharks, porbeagles in particular, that might otherwise

Right: An average size tope taken from a trawler. Fish of this size are excellent sport on 12 and 20 lb (5.4 and 9 kg) outfits, though 30 lb (13.6 kg) may have to be used where tidal streams are strong.

Doubled line is best either whipped for about ¼ in (6 mm) every foot (30.4 cm) or, as in this case, held by soft plastic tube.

miss a scent trail only on the surface. Always beware of putting over too much diced fish or having pieces larger than suggested, otherwise there is a chance of feeding a following shark, while the plan is to excite the fish's appetite and bring it near the boat.

So, once the boat has been positioned to begin the drift – preferably wind-driven across the tidal flow so as to lay a broad trail, if this can be arranged – the first job should be to put over the three rubby bags and begin to feed over the pieces. Both mincing for the rubby bags and dicing for the deeper attraction should

be done on the way out to the mark or, better, before leaving port.

Let us assume an ideal fishing expedition: there are two anglers and a skipper aboard the boat. The boat is a 23-footer (7 m), so there is ample room. There has been agreement that both rods will be 30 lb (13.6 kg) IGFA, each lever-drag reel loaded to within ⅛ in (3 mm) of the lip of the spool with monofilament of about 26–28 lb (11.8–12.7 kg) test or the more expensive IGFA-rated line. As has already been said, the length of line should be in the region of 500–600 yd (457.1–548.6 m) long for this type of fishing.

Traces are 15 ft (4.5 m) long and of plain multi-strand stainless-steel wire of about 175 lb (79.3 kg) test, to each end of which is attached a strong link-swivel, preferably of the American Berkley type. Hooks are attached to about 18 in (45 cm) of 300 lb (136 kg) test wire, the free end of which is looped. (Details such as attachment of swivel or hooks to wire are dealt with in chapter 3.)

A Bimini hitch is formed in the end of the reel line, so that the loop forms the last 15 ft (4.5 m) of the line,

A typical light tackle shark trace: 15 ft (4.5 m) long; this includes the hook trace for IGFA record application purposes. This one is 15 ft long with an additional 18 in (45 cm) hook trace. Both the line/trace and trace/hook link junctions are of the quick release type, formed with Berkley swivels.

this being double the strength of the rest of the line. (The Bimini hitch is also dealt with in chapter 3.) Besides being an insurance factor against any wear to which the last few feet of line might be subjected should the shark's rough skin come in contact with it, it is also an aid to bringing the shark to the gaff once it has been subdued. When a couple of turns of the doubled line – which should be whipped together, or held by plastic tubing every foot (30.4 cm) – have been got round the spool, it is possible to increase the safe maximum pressure to get the fish within reach.

The main part of the trace is not just to stop the shark's rough hide from rubbing through the reel line, but to give added strength so that once the skipper or a companion can grab hold of the wire below the top swivel, he can afford to pull firmly to bring the shark to the side of the boat and the gaff. The last bit of heavy wire to the hook is to prevent the shark's teeth from severing connection with the angler. Once in a while a shark will manage to bite through even 300 lb (136 kg) test wire! This piece of wire that carries the hook is looped at the free end (see chapter 3).

To the end of the doubled reel line (it is in fact a very long loop) is tied either a plain strong swivel or a strong welded steel ring. A tucked half blood knot is used for this junction. The ring or swivel forms a speedy attachment point for the link-swivel at the top of the trace.

This main part of the trace may be formed of heavy nylon, as used by commercial longline fishermen. This can be bought from chandlers and commercial fishing supply shops in test of about 400 lb (181.4 kg) and is fixed by crimping metal sleeves in the same way as wire. It is said that it is less visible in the water and does not put off a shark from taking the bait. However, the fact remains that a large number of sharks do take baits with wire traces above them, and the visibility aspect is probably a theoretical point that has little bearing on the actual fishing.

The bait used is a large mackerel. A baiting needle

is inserted just behind the gill cover and brought out at the extreme root of the tail. The actual tail fin is removed first, with a sharp knife, which stops any tendency for the bait to spin and tangle the trace as it moves through the water behind the boat. The loop in the hook link is now inserted in the hook of the baiting needle and the wire drawn through and out of the tail root. The hook is pulled into the body cavity, so that just the bend and barb lie clear of the bait's flank. Clip the loop of the link to the link-swivel on the trace.

Let the bait overboard now, and measure off by the span between chin and hand a distance of about 15 ft (4.5 m) of the reel line. Hold the line at the selected point and then, bending the line over the tip of a matchstick, push the line and match halfway into a piece of suitable plastic tube about ½ in (1 cm) long. Tie the balloon by its neck to the free end of the tube with thin string. Alternatively, one can make up float

To make a tucked half blood knot pass end of nylon through hook or swivel ring (eye). Make at least five turns with the end around the standing part.

Now pass the end through the hole between hook or swivel and the beginning of the twisted section of nylon and then through the open loop caused by bridging the gap between the end of the twisted part and the gap between the twists and the eye.

Tighten knot, after moistening turns with saliva or water, by pulling on hook (swivel) and the main part of the nylon. Trim end to ⅛ in (3.17 mm).

links in advance, using a small paper stapler, as shown.

When a shark takes, or certainly when the strike is made, the line forces the match from the tube and the balloon is ejected. On light tackle one does not want any 'passengers' on the line when a shark rushes off.

Allow the balloon to float away from the boat some 25 yd (22.8 m) before leaning the rod securely against the gunwale in such a way that the line may run freely from the reel and with the reel in free spool with the audible ratchet engaged. Or else, if the wind or tidal flow is such that the line is not held on the ratchet, leave the reel in gear but with minimum drag that will just hold the line from being pulled off.

The second rod is made up in the same way, except that the fishing depth is increased to about 50 ft (15 m), and a balloon of a different colour to the first one used is attached to the line. This selection of different colours avoids confusion when the baits are fishing. This deeper rig is let out further from the boat than the first one, about 35–40 yd (32–36 m), so that fish coming up from the deeps towards the trail emanating from the boat may run into it; fish coming closer to the boat nearer the surface are likely to find the bait at a shallower depth.

Once the rods are out keep the diced fish going overboard, and every few minutes give the rubby bags a jerk so that bits of fish flow away. It is essential to

The author's shark and tope quick-release balloon float set-up. The line or cord from the balloon may be tied or stapled to the piece of plastic tube, stripped from electrical wire.

The reel line is bent under tension over the end of a matchstick, which is then pushed into the tube to hold the line in place at the predetermined fishing depth.

This is how the balloon fishes. When a fish takes, the match is pulled out by the tightening line and the balloon released from the line.

retain an unbroken oil-slick on the surface and a rain of tiny pieces of fish sinking through the water. Also, ensure that the area around the rods is free of any junk causing obstruction. Stow all gear securely out of the way, but keep a fighting butt socket (belly pad) within easy reach so that it may be instantly strapped round the angler who takes the rod.

Change the contents of the rubby bags with new minced fish and bran every hour; use the washed-out material to feed over the side in palm-size helpings.

Quite often the fin of a shark will be seen coming up the rubby trail. A pair of binoculars makes the waiting interesting in this respect – although often the first sign of a fish will be the balloon travelling along the surface in jerks, then quickly submerging.

At times a shark, especially porbeagles, will come up to the balloons and bunt them several times; if this happens it is almost certain that the fish will then submerge and take a bait.

As the float goes down and breaks away the check on the reel will begin to sound: the regularity of the clicks is an initial indication of how fast the shark is travelling with the bait held in its mouth. The angler should pick up the rod and knock the lever or button into free-spool (no click), keeping sufficient thumb pressure on the spool of line to prevent any tendency for an over-run to occur. Some fish will take 20 yd (18 m), stop, then rush off again; others will go for 100 yd (91 m), stop, then go off again more slowly; and still others will go off and not stop at all. And, unfortunately, some will move away with the bait, then drop it. Some come back for a second bite, others go away for good. It is worthwhile, if the bait is dropped, to begin to wind in line fairly slowly – but with a very light drag on the reel. The fish may be tempted to have a bite at a bait moving away as if alive. If the bait is taken on the move, free-spool immediately and let line go against thumb pressure. The other line is quickly reeled in.

If the fish goes a short way, stops, then rushes off again, allow 40 yd (36 m) or so of line to go, then put the reel in gear and let the rod take the strain, pulling the hook into the fish's mouth. Do not, as anglers using heavy gear do, attempt to strike hard several times. The light rod tip will not sink a hook of shark size properly, but a constant firm pressure will *drag* it in past the barb – provided it is properly sharpened to a knife edge at the back of the barb.

A point here about the drag setting. It should be such that the rod can be pulled into about a quarter-circle before any line is yielded. This is tested with the butt of the rod and the end of the line roughly at right angles. With a lever-drag reel the drag is preset at this tension or, if there is no setting equipment or markings on the drag system – as with a Policansky – stick a piece of tape on the edge of the sideplate. Using this as a guide, the drag can always be returned to the pre-set safe position if it has been moved to allow a fish to run off line, against the ratchet only, while fishing.

Of course, preset drags are a problem on any star-drag reel, since there is no sure way of being able to back off pressure, then return the wheel to its former preset situation. The only safe way is to preset the star-drag and leave it at that position. For a 30 lb (13.6 kg) class outfit the setting should be such that the rod will lift a dead weight of about 6 lb (2.7 kg) bent into a quarter-circle when held with the butt horizontal – and the drag will just yield line when the rod is given a jerk. That may seem a very light pull to pit against a shark of 80–200 lb (36.2–90.7 kg), but it is the sustained pressure that weakens the fish, and the rod and reel drag must be allowed to do their work.

Vince Lister in action against a porbeagle shark with light tackle.

Once the fish is hooked – or believed to be hooked, for often the shark will 'come unstuck' after 5–10 minutes, during which the rod was under maximum safe pressure and one felt the fish could not just be holding the bait – get the butt into the belly pad and keep the rod bent into a quarter circle. Usually a shark of over 80 lb (36.2 kg), especially a porbeagle, will more than help in this respect, either by a long run away from the boat, or by sounding, which can be a problem when light tackle is used. It is usual for sharks hooked on 30 lb or less tackle to fight near the surface, perhaps because there is no alarmingly strong pressure being imposed on their movements. The idea is to keep the fish moving, making it swim against sustained light and safe strain which, it is hoped, will confuse the fish and eventually tire it sufficiently for it to be brought to the boat.

The skipper must keep the engine running during the fight, ensuring the angler is kept facing his fish from the gunwales near the stern. This can mean that the boat will be pivoting from the stern, or moving away from the fish if it tries to run under the boat or go deep. A fish can resist a strong pull from directly above, as anglers who fish with 50–120 lb (22.6–

Some groin protectors (or belly-pads as they are also called) have no crossbar to take the slot of the rod butt. This is an American protector that has proved ideal for the job.

A small porbeagle is held by the trace close to the boat. It is obviously not a record and is to be released without risking internal damage by lifting using long-handled wire cutters to snip the hook off close to the eye (*inset*).

54.4 kg) test lines will know, but when the pull is from a shallow angle, there is a far better chance of the fish being lifted by the water pressure due to its body shape, even if the pressure is very modest.

Beware of temptation to add manual pressure to the line or the sides of the reel spool during the fight; a sudden spurt by the fish is almost sure to result in a break. Patience and that quality anglers (and horsey types) call 'hands' is the name of the game.

Some sharks, particularly male porbeagles, or a mako, will make a very long run or runs away from the boat – perhaps as far as 500 yd (457 m). If this happens the boat should travel towards the fish at a speed sufficient to shorten the line and with which the angler is capable of keeping up by recovering line. A large, fast-swimming fish can easily break a line by taking off several hundred yards, then turning, so as to create a big loop in the line. Water drag on this loop will break the line, even when there is apparently little extra pressure coming through to the rod.

When the fish begins to tire, and comes within a few yards of the boat, the boatman should keep the angler facing the fish as it swims, circling the boat due to the pressure exerted by the tackle. Line is gradually shortened by pumping, which means raising the rod tip slowly and smoothly to the vertical position, then lowering it again more quickly, winding the resulting slack line quickly on to the reel. The angler must always be ready for a sudden lunge by the fish and be prepared to yield line.

Now the skipper, or another experienced angler, must put on a pair of leather, heavy cotton or plastic gloves (industrial type) and prepare to get a firm grip on the top of the trace below the swivel joining reel line to trace. There must never be any attempt to wind the trace round a hand as fingers, or even a hand, could be lost that way, should a fish of even 150 lb (68 kg) make a frantic lunge.

If the fish is not wanted for weighing ashore, ie if it is obviously not a potential line-class record, it is best to let it go. This is best achieved by the trace being held firmy so that the fish is tethered close to the boat, when one person can lean over and cut off the hook as near to the fish's mouth as is possible. Long-han-

dled wire cutters are used for this purpose. A fish will usually survive with a hook in its mouth or throat, provided the point has not pierced any vital organs or blood vessels, and often it will be able to rub out the hook or in some other way get rid of the hook. It is amazing how fish can do this, and proof has several times been obtained when hook-caught sharks have been put into aquaria, and the hook has been found on the floor of the tank next day.

If the fish is to be killed for weighing then it must be gaffed aboard, and if it is a really large fish, it may be necessary to tail-rope it as well.

A tope thrashes the surface as it is brought near the boat. These Welsh anglers use a tailer instead of a gaff, so they can return the fish to the water without gaff damage.

Chris O'Hara with his first shark, taken on 25 lb (11.3 kg) test line and 30 lb (13.6 kg) class rod on the Isle of Wight grounds. The fish weighed 85 lb (38.5 kg).

A proper flying gaff must be used, one that has a head with a ring welded to it and which is a loose fit on the shaft. The hook is held in place by winding the rope that is tied or lashed to the ring in the head several times round the shaft, then, holding the rope firmly against the shaft. The gaff is pulled in firmly, perhaps near the pectoral fins (under the belly) or near the vent area. The rope is allowed to pull free and the gaff head comes off leaving the fish held by the rope. The free end of the rope must be firmly hitched to a stern post or some other strong anchorage in the boat.

The shark is likely to thrash around now. The angler must keep out of the way of whoever is gaffing the fish but must back off his drag just in case the fish comes off the gaff and rushes away again in a frenzy. However, if there is only the angler and his companion to get the fish aboard – the skipper being perhaps occupied with keeping the boat steady against tricky seas – he should quickly unclip the top trace swivel and lay the rod down out of the way before hauling on the gaff rope or putting on a tail rope.

Any fish of great size is best tailed as well as gaffed. The tailer should be made from about 9 ft (2.7 m) of Bowden brake cable or rigging wire with either a ring crimped to the end or a loop formed by crimping. The free end is put through the ring or loop and the other end looped for attachment to several yards of 1000 lb (456 kg) nylon rope. A wire noose can be manipulated under water and over the shark's tail, when the tail may be lifted above the water. At once the fish loses its motive power and is much more manageable.

Once the shark is inboard, beware of its teeth and flailing tail and body. One man must hold the tail while several hard blows with a heavy club or hammer are administered just ahead of the eyes. Beware of missing the fish and crashing the hammer through the deckboards or hull! It has happened. (It is doubtful if a shark, once hauled into a boat, will live if returned to the water since internal organs tend to be ruptured once the water support is absent.)

Immediately the shark is dead, the boat should be sluiced down and scrubbed to get rid of blood and slime, since it is very easy to slip and injure oneself on a slimy deck. In addition, the angler who gets the next fish needs a sure footing to play his fish.

Mention of standing to fight the shark may surprise those anglers who have always thought sharks were fought from a swivel-chair. A swivel-chair can be a great aid to a heavy tackle angler, but the light tackle man, though he may use the chair, will usually find it easier to stand up and fight, since he is not exerting great pressure and can be more active on his feet to deal with sudden moves of the fish.

Never try to remove the hook from a dead shark; 'dead' sharks have a habit of biting off people's fingers! Let the hook remain where it is for at least two hours, if possible. Cut out the hooks back on land, and even then do it carefully.

This may make boating a shark on light tackle sound easy, and indeed it is not very difficult. All that one needs is common sense and an understanding of the tackle and its capabilities. The author knows several anglers who had never fished shark before and who have subdued fish of up to 182 lb (82.5 kg) on line of 26 lb (11.7 kg) test without too much difficulty, even when using a star-drag reel, which is much less protective of the line than a lever-drag reel.

One important point to remember is that when a fish has taken a lot of line from the reel, the level of the line having fallen considerably, the amount of resistance from the drag will increase because the line is being pulled from a point nearer to the axis of the spool – in the same way that a big heavy car without power steering is fitted with a big steering wheel while a little wheel handles the requirements of the mini. So, if a fish goes off with 300 yards (274 m) of line in a rush ease off the drag a little. This is easy on the lever-drag reel, and the lever may be returned to the preset spot when line is being regained, but it has to be a hit and miss affair on the star-drag reel ... you pays your money and you takes your chance!

Sharks will take a bait well down in the water at times, especially in the areas of reefs and overfalls, and at such times it may be just as effective, or easier, to fish the bait without any float to support it at a pre-determined depth. A bomb lead may be suspended from the line/trace junction swivel with soft copper or brass wire (which will release the lead when a strike is made) if necessary, to get the bait well down, and line is measured off in the same way as when using the float. Always take care when lowering the bait overboard as quite often a shark will grab it immediately, and woe betide anybody whose hands are fouled in the trace.

Fishing depths of up to 60 ft (18.29 m) may be tried in deep water areas, but porbeagle sharks will come inshore into very shallow water – even as little as 20 ft (6.09 m) – and take a bait. Blue sharks and mako sharks, however, are usually encountered over deep water, although threshers turn up in a few feet of water at odd times during hot summers, often to

Mackerel rigged for trolling

frighten holidaymakers by swimming round the piers of resorts like Newhaven in Sussex or Folkestone in Kent.

Trolling is not a method much used this side of the Atlantic, but it does catch porbeagle sharks, as several anglers proved in an exploratory trip to Ireland's west coast a few years ago. The fact that the fish will follow the bait visibly on the surface for a while before taking it is a big plus in favour of trolling, but for ground coverage it has little advantage, except that when porbeagles are known to be in a very precise small area it is possible to cross and recross the ground continuously, whereas a drifting boat cannot be precisely put over the ground.

The only special tackle needed to troll for the porbeagle is at the hook end. The same type of wire trace is used, of course, to protect the line from the shark's teeth and its rough hide, and the swivels used should be oiled so they turn freely. The bait is usually a dead mackerel with the hook set just behind the head and low down so that it keels the bait in its natural swimming position; the egg-shaped lead is either suspended on the solid wire loop beneath the bait's

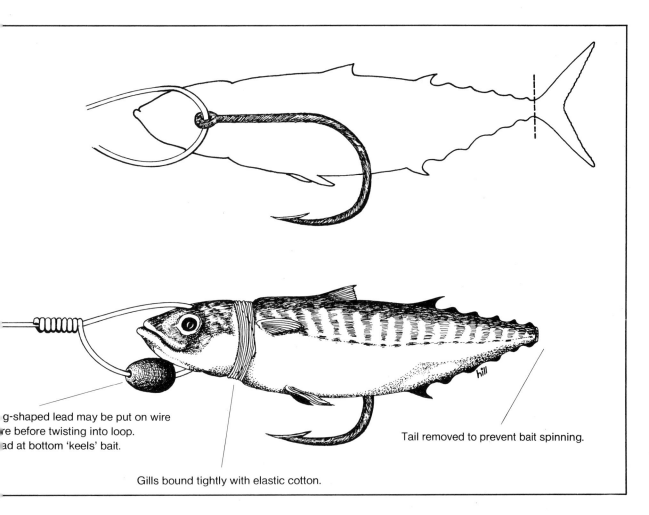

g-shaped lead may be put on wire
re before twisting into loop.
ad at bottom 'keels' bait.

Gills bound tightly with elastic cotton.

Tail removed to prevent bait spinning.

The mount is made of single strand stainless steel (piano) wire. The hook is pushed in position first, then the wire is pushed down through mackerel's skull, through eye of hook, out of 'chin' and then twisted to form a loop. This anchors hook to bait and stops damage when trolling.

chin, as in the diagram, or threaded on the wire 6 in (15 cm) ahead of the bait to act as a further stabiliser, as well as to get the bait down a little.

A trolled bait must not spin but simply wriggle enticingly on an even keel as it is towed behind the boat. Speeds of 2–3 knots have proved about right and one big advantage of hooking sharks on a trolled bait is that usually the hook is lodged in the corner of the mouth rather than down the throat, which results in a far more lively fight and the chance to put fish back alive and unharmed. With the hook just inside the mouth, it is possible for two or more anglers to hold the fish against the boat while the hook is cut out with a sharp knife and freed with long-handled pliers.

Finally, a thought on trolling baits: a grey mullet makes an excellent tough bait and a 2 lb (0.9 kg) fish would doubtless prove ideal, though the thought may not be very acceptable to conservationists. A half-dozen mullet baits per day, however, would not be unreasonable and they certainly outlast mackerel.

Porbeagle sharks are catchable from the shore in some places, such as Ireland's rugged West Coast, Kerry and Clare being two notable places where they have been contacted. In parts of west Wales and in north Cornwall porbeagles will undoubtedly be taken from the rocks, once anglers dedicate themselves to the problems involved. Indeed, in Clare a fair number of fish have been taken by the well-known specialist Jack Shine, who had fish of nearly 100 lb (45.3 kg) on line of 19 lb (8.6 kg) test and over 140 lb (61 kg) on 31 lb (14 kg) test!

The author was present when two anglers, bringing in a mackerel and a pollack on spinning tackle, had them taken by porbeagles on the same day. This happened about 16 years ago on the Dingle Peninsula in Kerry, and other sharks were seen a few yards from the rocks, too. The sharks that grabbed the hooked

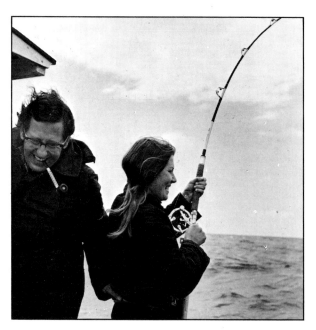

Beginners have some hair-raising moments when first fighting sharks on light tackle, but usually come out on top. Vince Lister holds on to Diane Bellingham as she gleefully bends into a 100 lb (45.3 kg) porbeagle which she eventually boated on 25 lb (11.3 kg) test line.

fish were well over 100 lb (45.3 kg), and in the same area, in Ventry Bay, only about 12 ft (3.6 m) deep, a massive porbeagle, estimated to weigh well over 400 lb (181.4 kg), was watched for more than an hour by the author and some friends using binoculars. It slowly cruised up and down some 200 yd (180 m) out before it finally went down.

Late July to late September is the period when porbeagles may be expected to be close in to rocky, deep shores, and calm sea conditions and an offshore breeze to blow the balloon and bait out is desirable. A heavy surfcasting rod and the 30 lb (13.6 kg) IGFA reel should suffice, with the usual shark trace and belly pad. Of course, a long-handled gaff to reach the fish and drag it up to the rocks is needed and at least one man got over this by having a set of drain-cleaning rods (like sweep's canes) at hand, which he screwed together to make the necessary length.

The tope is a true shark and is caught in the waters under discussion to weights of 70 lb (31.7 kg) or so. A good fish is over 30 lb (13.6 kg) and anything above 50 lb (22.6 kg) is exceptional.

Tope are sleek, streamlined sharks and they tend to bottom-feed to a greater extent than the other sharks so far discussed. They eat flatfish, crabs, cuttlefish and squids but will also swim near the surface voraciously to attack mackerel or herring shoals. They also swim into water barely deep enough to cover their dorsal fins and quarter the sand for such fish as bass, flounder and mullet.

As a light tackle fish the tope is among the best, and the shallower the water in which one can find it, the better the fight. Indeed, tope weighing 30–40 lb (13.6–18.1 kg) are taken in 2–4 ft (60 cm–1.2 m) from shallow, sandy beaches and will frequently dash out towards deeper water and take 300 yd (274.3 m) of fine line, sometimes even leaping clear of the water.

Boat fishing for tope can be done using either the 12 lb class (5.4 kg) or 20 lb class (9 kg) outfits as a rule; only rarely will 30 lb class (13.6 kg) have to be used, such as when fishing for very large tope known to inhabit a strong tidal current.

It is usual to leger a bait for tope, both from boat and shore. However, tope can be caught using the drifting boat and rubby-dubby tactics as for the other larger sharks. First, though, legering from an anchored boat.

The tackle is made up as follows: the 4/0 to 6/0 forged hook is attached by ferrule and crimping to about 1 yd (90 cm) of 40–50 lb (18.1–22.6 kg) cabled wire, a loop being crimped to the other end. Then 6 ft of about 60 lb (27.2 kg) nylon monofilament is fitted with a size 1 link-swivel at each end, preferably the strong Berkley type. One swivel clips to the hook link loop, the other to a ring or swivel at the end of the reel line. The heavy nylon is resistant to rubbing by the tope's sandpaper-like hide and is unobtrusive.

On the line (before the trace is clipped to it) goes a small Clements boom or Ashmore's Sea-Boom to take the lead, and if it is preferred, a small plastic bead which will rest on the swivel that connects line to heavy nylon trace, although the swivel or ring will stop it anyway.

Baiting is done in exactly the same way as for the bigger sharks, except that mackerel of 8–10 in (20–25 cm) or other fish, are more suitable. At times when tope are finicky and drop the whole fish after a short run, it often pays to substitute a whole side fillet from a large mackerel. This bait is hooked through the tail end, then once more about halfway along the bait, after which the tail end is pulled above the hook eye and secured with shirring elastic.

The tackle is let slowly over the side and allowed to touch bottom, streaming downtide. The lead must just hold the bait firmly on the bottom and this can mean leads varying from perhaps 4 oz (113.3 g) up to more than 1 lb (453 g). Some anglers like the bait to be a long way from the lead so that it is wafted freely in the currents. To do this a piece of plastic tube and a matchstick, used as for the shark balloon float release, is used at perhaps 20 ft (6 m) from the swivel joining trace to line. The lead is held above it and then gently

These two cod being boated by gaffing took artificial
squids fished on droppers or snoods over deep water.

A winter cod angler is overtaken by an incoming wave having grabbed his fish by the gills to carry it up the beach to safety. With really big fish a companion is an advantage to either gaff or gill it, with the angler farther up the beach and in control of his tackle.

Gaffed! Not the best place to set the point, but sometimes with a strong tide, light tackle and a skin hook-hold, there is no second chance should the fish suddenly go berserk.

Left: Rocky coves on the Atlantic seaboard can provide interesting fishing for a variety of species, including small coalfish and fairly large pollack. This spot looks like it could yield conger, ballan wrasse and mullet as well.

Right: Deep-water pollack, caught two at a time, can often be a tackle-busting combination. One hook or lure is usually sufficient for the sport fisherman. Netting the fish is better than gaffing since they can then be returned alive, hopefully to fight another day.

Below: This bass fell to a bait of peeler crab fished among the rocks, but was only lip-hooked. The large mouth of this fish enables it to engulf large food items with ease.

When casting into the surf for bass – as well as other fish –
it is often necessary to hold the rod high, so as to keep the
line clear of the closest breakers in which there is often
floating weed which can foul the tackle and drag it inshore.
This angler is fishing a beach near Porthleven, where plaice
and rays, as well as bass, are commonly caught.

Two fine bass caught from an outboard-powered small boat, not far off the chalk cliffs of Sussex. Bass are among the handsomest species found in British inshore waters – but regrettably have been much reduced in numbers by commercial fishing because they are so highly regarded as food fish.

let down into the water. A jerk will free it and the lead is pulled up to the usual stop, which will permit fish to be brought close to the boat for tailing aboard.

There is, incidentally, no good reason to gaff and kill a tope, apart from any that may be of record size and wanted for setting up as trophies. A salmon tailer, or a smaller version of the big shark tailer, is fine for both boat and shore use. In fact, from a boat low enough to reach into the water, or from a shelving beach, there is need for neither tailer nor gaff. It is an easy matter to grab the wrist of the tope's tail with one hand and the dorsal fin with the other and lift it gently. Better still, remove the hook or cut the wire trace, while the fish is held by the boat or while in shallow water. The same internal injuries can be caused by hauling them from the water as with big sharks.

This is the cone-shaped mackerel bait for such fish as shore tope. Its shape and shirring elastic support permits long casts to be made with relative ease.

But back to the boat fishing.

When a fish takes the bait the rod tip will usually nod once or twice, then will curve over as line is pulled rapidly from the reel, which has been put in free spool with the audible ratchet on, or if the tide is strong, with the drag lightly on to prevent line pulling off, and the ratchet on. While waiting for a run the rod should be held or may be leant against the gunwale so that line can run freely.

A tope will usually run between 30 and 50 yd (27.4 and 45.7 m), then stop briefly. Then it will move off again, more slowly. The usual advice is to strike as the fish moves off after that pause, but it does result in a lot of tope being hooked in the throat. It works reasonably well to pull into the fish when the first run has taken 25 yd (22.8 m) of line, though some runs will be missed, which is the price paid for trying to hook the fish in the lip.

Fightwise, a lip-hooked fish performs far better than one that is deeply hooked, plus the fact that lip-hooking permits an almost guaranteed live return of a fish.

As with the bigger sharks, fight the tope by keeping the rod bent into a quarter-circle. Allow the fish to run against drag pressure; when the run slows or stops, regain line by pumping. A belly pad makes boat fishing for tope more comfortable, since a 40 lb (18.1 kg) fish on the 12 lb (5.4 kg) outfit may take 15 minutes or so to beat, and the rod butt can be very uncomfortable against the lower stomach when the fish makes a sudden dive or rush.

Float fishing may be carried out from an anchored boat or, better, from a slowly drifting boat, which covers a lot more ground, in exactly the same way as for the bigger sharks, except that the bait should be just above the seabed, which is arranged by careful siting of the balloon on the line. Also, float fishing may produce better results if a whole side fillet of fish is used rather than a whole fish.

The tope season runs, usually, between mid-May and early October, but when shore fishing, the best chances may come as early as April in some areas and through to the end of May; then will follow a dull period until mid-August and through September, when the fish move inshore again. That is not to say, however, that shore fishing for tope in the intervening months is wasted effort.

Shore tope fishing may usually be divided into two types: casting from an open sand or shingle beach, especially into the deep channel of a wide estuary, to fish the bait in, say, 3–20 ft (1–6 m) of water; and casting from a rocky outcrop or a ledge low down a cliff face into deeper and perhaps more flowing water – 15–40 ft (4.5–12 m).

Tackle arrangements must be changed to meet the different conditions, and the main problem to be overcome is that of casting a relatively big and heavy bait a sufficient distance. Distance is not always a problem: in some places a gentle lob of 40 yd (36.4 m) will place the bait where a patrolling tope will find it; but at others, notably the shallow and sandy beach that has little incline, it may be necessary to punch out at least 80 yd (73.1 m), maybe 120 yd (109.7 m).

Blue shark fishing with light tackle: the fish is gaffed aboard, having regurgitated its stomach during the battle, the angler ready to yield line should the fish struggle free; gloved hands hold the trace preparatory to removing the hook or the trace; and finally the angler shows his fish, which would not have survived had it been returned, due to ejecting its stomach.

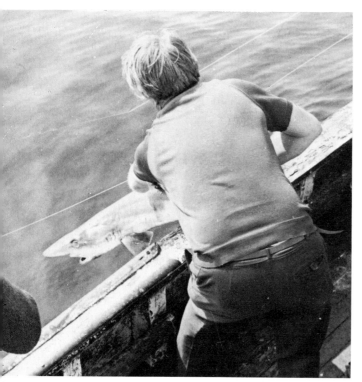

When the angler can reach the water from a boat with a deck low to the waterline, no gaff is necessary for securing a played-out tope. Here the author lifts one aboard for a friend by gripping the wrist of the tail and the dorsal fin.

A long hook trace makes a bad casting set-up, especially when the hook carries about 4 in (10 cm) of the tail end of a mackerel or herring. And more especially when the trace is of wire.

Here is the suggested terminal tackle that has worked very well for a number of keen shore tope hunters. The hook, size 3/0–5/0, is crimped to 18 in (45.7 cm) of the same wire suggested for boat fishing, a loop being formed at the opposite end. To the end of the reel line, which must be at least 250 yd (228 m) of 15 lb (6.8 kg) and better still 400 yd (365.7 m), is knotted a casting leader of about 45 lb (20.4 kg) nylon. The reel line is doubled for a few inches before forming the knot if a blood knot is used. And to the 45 lb casting leader is knotted 6 ft (1.8 m) of 60 lb (27.2 kg) nylon. Moisten the knots with saliva before pulling up tight.

On to the end of the 60 lb nylon is slid a size 1/0 link-swivel, which can be followed by a plastic bead before a second link-swivel is tied to the end of the 60 lb material. The hook trace loop is clipped to the link of the swivel. The lead weight, usually a bomb-shaped or pyramidal model, is clipped to the link-swivel running on the line. If a bomb lead is used it is

best not to use one with anchor wires, whether of fixed or breakaway type, since wires can tangle the trace in flight. To hold the tackle out when tidal currents are strong a pyramid lead will be found suitable, provided the seabed is of sand, sand and mud or very fine shingle, and that the leading edges of the lead are sharp. The base of the pyramid lead, an American design, digs into the seabed when pulled by the rod and line.

Depending on the location, the bait can be a piece cut from a fresh mackerel, garfish or herring, a whole whiting or pouting, about 4 in (10 cm) long, or a big sand-eel, so far as fish-baits go; many anglers fail to realise that tope, particularly when on their inshore raids, are very partial to soft or peeler crabs.

It is essential to mount the bait so that it permits a long cast to be made, at the same time being retained on the hook without tearing. This is not too difficult and simply means trying to achieve as streamlined a bait as possible.

The tail end of a mackerel is shaped like the nose-cone of a rocket, and provided the narrow end travels first, it will cast surprisingly well. That also goes for a tail end of herring, but ideally both baits must be fresh and firm, a bit of a problem with herring. One way out with the herring involves first mounting the tail-ends on hooks, complete with wire traces, then freezing them at home in packets, each one individually. The frozen baits may be taken fishing in a wide-necked vacuum flask and, of course, will permit

The pyramid lead is suitable for most shore tope fishing, as well as conger etc. A pyramid takes a good hold on sandy or sand/mud bottoms by digging in its sharp base edges.

fierce, long casts since they are almost solid ice! The only disadvantage is that the bait will remain frozen in the water for rather a long time.

When mounting a big sand-eel or a small whiting or other whole small fish for shore tope, pass the hook point first through the open mouth, then bring it out about halfway along the body. The mouth should be pulled up above the hook eye and there bound tightly to the trace with elastic cotton. The tail-end baits should also be bound at their slim ends in a similar position.

Sometimes, when maximum distance is called for, and only a sand-eel gives really good range out of the baits so far discussed, it may be necessary to reduce the desirable size of the bait and use a long, slim strip cut from a mackerel or herring or garfish. Then, cut from the tail end of the fish a strip about 5 in (13 cm) long by about 1 in (2.54 cm) and put the hook (this should be reduced to 2/0 or 3/0) in through the centre near the tail end and bring it out about an inch further on, then put it through once more, pull it above the hook eye and tie it with the usual elastic cotton.

The lead weight is stopped, of course, 18 in (45 cm) from the baited hook when the cast is made, and this fairly short link is a great help to long casts, though it might be imagined that it presents a disadvantage so far as bait presentation is concerned. However, although it is an asset in a boat to have plenty of bait movement in the tide, in practice the short hook link works perfectly well from the shore.

It is usual to rest the rod since shore tope fishing can often involve long waits; in fact, it must be faced that several sessions may pass without any signs of tope being present, which is indeed probably the case. However, when a fish does come across the bait the blank sessions will soon be forgotten, provided that the fish is hooked and is of a reasonable size. On rocks the rod may be rested on a fishing bag or damp hand-cloth to protect the varnish and whippings from damage by abrasion or knocks. The reel must be positioned on top with the free spool lever in the 'free' position and the ratchet on. Again, tidal conditions may make it necessary to leave the reel in gear and have just a very light drag on.

From the open beach a monopod rest is best, the reel again in free spool, ratchet on if possible. Have the monopod angled so that the rod is pointing in the general direction of the bait and at an angle of about 45 degrees from the vertical.

This is a thresher shark, also called a thrasher. Note the long upper tail lobe.

There are several ways in which a shore tope can announce its presence at the bait, the most exciting being a sudden scream from the reel and the rod bending over as yard after yard of line streams out to sea. However, shore tope can be very gentle, and a gentle nodding of the rod tip may be the first indications of a customer. The nods will end soon and line will begin to run out, slowly at first, perhaps, then faster as the fish gains impetus. It is probable that fish rush off like this because they fear another fish might grab their find, though sometimes, if the fish feels heavy resistance from the tackle, it may be due to fear.

When the run is under way, then, pick up the rod, gently, and equally gently thumb the spool to prevent any over-running of line. The fish may be struck in mid-run or after it pauses to move off again. Since shore baits are relatively small, the mid-run strike will often connect.

The word strike should not be interpreted as a full-blooded backward stroke with the rod, perhaps combined with a backward run. Instead it is best to knock the reel into gear (the drag must have been set to pull the rod into its quarter-circle before yield-ing), wait for the rod tip to become heavy as the fish's weight is felt, then simply hold everything firmly for a second or so until the rod takes on its fighting curve and the drag begins to whine.

At this point the fish will probably race off with 80–200 yd (73.1–182.8 m) of line. Make no attempt to do anything about it but keep the rod bent into its quarter-circle. In fact, if the fish begins to feel heavier with 150 yd (137 m) of line out, back off drag pressure a little, as explained earlier. When line level on the reel gets low, remember, it takes more pull to turn the spool.

A shore tope, especially from a shallow surf beach of sand, will often run along the beach once its first mad dash out to sea has been thwarted. It then pays to follow the fish, keeping as parallel to it as possible. Use any waves coming on to the beach to bring the fish close in – but be ready for mad rushes once the fish is in a foot or so of water: tope get very alarmed in such a situation and are intent on reaching the far horizon!

From a rocky stand above the water, securing a beaten tope is more difficult than from a flat beach, of course, and is a two-man job. In fact, when fishing

Even when the gaff has to be used, it can be so placed that the fish is relatively undamaged. The point can be placed under the jaw or into a pectoral fin, taking care to keep well clear of the delicate gills area.

That much-pictured shore-caught Cornish tope again. This shot illustrates the cramped and tricky conditions under which it is often necessary to fish. Here there was little chance to use anything but the gaff.

from places which involve climbing down cliffs, or walking across mudflats and the like, never, ever, go alone. Tragedies occur that way.

In the shallows it is easy to straddle the fish as it lies on its belly, one knee either side just behind the head, and pull open the mouth by gripping its nose. The hook may then be cut or pulled out and the fish returned to the sea, or if the hook is deep, the wire trace cut as close to the hook as possible. If it is desirable to nick the flesh in the back of the mouth to remove the hook, be sure to use something to gag the fish with first, say a block of wood, bottle etc. A tope

A large unspotted smooth-hound, *Mustelus mustelus*, taken in Essex.

can give a nasty bite. On the rocks get the fish back into the water as soon as possible and remember the internal damage that can be caused to sharks once removed from the supporting water; treat the fish gently.

Once in a while, from boat or shore, a tope that has given a good fight will suddenly begin to come in rolling around. This is usually caused by the fish rolling itself up in the trace, which is the reason for the 60 lb, then 45 lb (27.2 and 20.4 kg) nylon links attached to the reel line: a tope's skin is like sandpaper.

Last of the sporting shark species in this chapter, but certainly not the least so far as fighting ability is concerned, are the spotted and the non-spotted smooth-hounds.

The main difference between fishing for smooth-hounds and fishing for tope is that no wire trace is needed. Unlike the other sharks mentioned, the smooth-hound has no razor-sharp teeth for cutting and ripping but has flat, grinding teeth, which marks it as an eater of worms and crustacea rather than a grabber of fish.

Other books on sea angling contain very few mentions of smooth-hounds, probably because for so long they had been confused with tope. Apart from the teeth, the smooth-hound can easily be distinguished from the tope since its dorsal fin is set almost directly above the pectoral fins, whereas the tope's dorsal is set well behind the pectorals. Also, the tail of the tope is deeply indented; that of the smooth-hound is far less so and has a very tiny lower lobe, while the tope's lower lobe is almost as long as the upper.

Smooth-hounds of both kinds are found in shallow, wide estuaries, and along open beaches. They seem to like areas of sandbanks, even when the depth is two or three feet (60–91 cm), venturing to the shallows as the tide floods and leaving for the gullies just before the water leaves the banks.

There are two boat fishing methods: one involves

Using a baitcaster like this to play a fish can be very tiring on the wrist; even modest species, like plaice or black bream, can feel like giants. Some anglers like the agony!

If a large fish is hooked and the fight lasts a long time, this is the best method of using the baitcaster. The right thumb can stop winding to brake the spool if necessary, and the line is wound back level automatically on the Ambassadeur 5000 and 6000 series reels. The butt is supported by the lower abdomen.

The head of this spotted smooth-hound, *Mustelus asterias*, is beautifully streamlined and illustrates how the fish can produce such fast, long runs for its relatively small size.

using the little freshwater baitcasting rod (when conditions are suitable – shallow, slow-moving water about 20 ft (6 m) deep), or the 12 lb (5.4 kg) boat outfit both fished downtide from the boat; or the bass surfcasting outfit (which is for casting away from the boat) or maybe even the salmon-type spinning rod. The reason for using a casting set-up is that in very shallow and clear water the shadow of a boat and the vibrations caused by water against the hull and by anglers in it can undoubtedly put shy fish off the feed or frighten them from the area.

With the baitcaster or 12 lb (5.4 kg) outfit one simply lets the tackle over the side, especially when fishing at low water times in the systems of gullies with which most good smooth-hound grounds are laced. The tackle rig is simple: the trace is approximately 6 ft (1.8 m) of monofilament nylon of about 15–20 lb (6.8–9.0 kg) test to which a forged O'Shaughnessy hook, about 1/0 to 3/0 is tied with a tucked half blood knot. The bait is usually soft or peeler crab or king ragworm, used whole. Smooth-hounds will also accept razorfish and, less frequently, lugworm. But crab and ragworm are by far the best.

The trace is made up as a running leger, as for shore tope fishing, using link-swivels for both lead and trace attachment. The bead stop is again optional.

Nearly all smooth-hound bites are fast and take yards of line from the reel with a rush. So, fish with the reel out of gear and the ratchet on, and be ready to grab the rod should you rest it against the gunwale. In fact, it is best to hold the rod. When using the bait-caster the fight can be very exciting – and punishing on the wrist if you decide to fight single handed, rather than hold the rod ahead of the reel and rest the butt against your body.

To secure smooth-hounds a big landing net is very useful, although the tope tailer will do. The net must be very large (a circular one about a yard across (1 m)) and strong and about 4 ft (1.2 m) deep. The Canadian Stag brand salmon net is absolutely first class.

When using the bass casting rod or the salmon and pike spinning rod to cast away from the boat when anchored on shallow banks, the same terminal tackle is used, except that the running lead is a breakaway type. The cast is made from the side of the boat, uptide and out, and line is permitted to spill from the reel until it forms a big bow in the tide. This bow drags the anchor wires into the seabed and holds the tackle in position well away from the boat, even in strong currents which sometimes run over shallow banks.

The bowed line also affects the way in which the bite is registered. Instead of the reel screaming as line is pulled off by the fish the rod tip is likely to jump back from its tensioned position, and then the line will drop slack and spill downtide. The fish has taken the bait and dislodged the lead's anchor wires, causing it to tumble downtide as the fish moves off with the bait. Pick up the rod, wind in the slack as fast as possible, and wait until the fish is felt as a heavy, moving weight before pulling in the hook. Of course,

Just a final reminder about those shark teeth. This is only a small specimen, a porbeagle, but those teeth can do a lot of damage to a hand or leg!

when fishing with the casting rod in the shallows when there is no tidal flow to worry about, an ordinary bomb-shaped lead may be used to hold bottom; in which case the bite will be a fast, audible check run with the rod bending and nodding.

From the shore the bass rod will usually be found ideal with its matching line and reel. In fact, if the cast does not have to go much more than 40 yd (36 m), then the salmon type rod and reel with its 10 lb test (4.5 kg) line will provide some excitement.

Smooth-hounds fight very hard indeed; in fact they are thought by some light tackle anglers who regularly hunt them to be the hardest fighting saltwater fish of all.

The author's first encounter with a smooth-hound, which just happened to be the spotted variety, occurred while bass fishing in the surf on a Kent shingle/sand beach with peeler crab. The first fish took off on a long run, stripping 60 yd (55 m) of line, out to sea, then ran up and down the beach just behind the surf line for five minutes or so before being beached. The visions of a new name on the record bass spot were destroyed when the mini-shark, at first thought to be a tope, came ashore. It weighed only 9 lb (4 kg) but had fought much harder than its weight, as anglers say.

An unspotted smooth-hound of 35 lb (15.8 kg), or a spotted one of 25 lb (11.3 kg), on the kind of tackle suggested here will prove to be a memorable encounter.

6 The conger eel

The conger is a fish of legends, the malevolent haunter of dark wrecks and reefs, whose bite is terrible to see, a severer of fingers and of thick wire traces. And surely few other fish can look so fierce as they come to the gaff, spinning, lashing the water, mouth snapping, exerting tremendous strength against the tackle.

So, how, one might ask, can this monster be taken on light tackle – up to 30 lb class? The answer is, by skill and with sound, good quality matched tackle. And with confidence, of course.

Conger eels no doubt reach incredible weights: 200 lb (over 90 kg) is on the cards and the current British rod-caught record at the time of writing is held by a fish of 109 lb 6 oz (49.6 kg) from a Devon port, though it was taken well out.

However, many big congers are taken, even from the rubble and entanglement of deep water wrecks, on lines of no more than 30 lb test (13.6 kg). One of the clever anglers who has set a standard for light tackle conger fishing – and who has made those who have for years insisted that 80 lb (36.2 kg) test is 'light for conger' look a little silly – is Ray Rush of the British Light Tackle Club. He has taken many big congers on 30 lb class tackle, topped by a fish of 80¼ lb (36.4 kg)!

However, since congers are pulling fish, rather than fast swimmers, and it can take a lot of hauling to get a very big one away from its rock or wreck habitat, there are special situations where a 50 lb (22.6 kg) class line and matching rod and reel can be required. Such a situation is where very big fish have previously been lost on a mark, specially when that mark is over very deep water and the seabed is very rough or fouled by pieces of wreckage.

Once again it is necessary to examine the separate aspects of shore and boat fishing for congers, and to explain how it is that massive, strong eels of the above mentioned sizes may be vanquished on such comparatively light tackle.

Like fishing for sharks, boat fishing for conger usually begins about May, but it usually ends in late October, not because the fish are not available in our wat-

The rock-hoppers' heaven. The author has just won an encounter with a conger of about 15 lb (6.8 kg) hooked on legered mackerel in this rocky depression. The fish has been gaffed using big hooks on a rope.

131

ers at any other times, but mainly because the winter weather conditions make long hauls out to West Country wrecks impossible or dangerous.

Although the Devon and Cornish coastline tends to produce the biggest congers, mainly due to the specialised wreck boats operating with Decca navigational aids and the skill of the skippers, there are also large congers taken from the coasts of Dorset, Hampshire, Sussex and Kent. Excellent congers are also taken in Scottish waters, especially on the west coast.

Boat fishing for conger can be over inshore rocky marks or rough ground, or way out to sea in very deep water into wrecks. Inshore conger fishing can be done from small boats, though anything much less than 14 ft (4.2 m) is a little limited when sharing the space with 6 ft (1.8 m) of lashing eel! Wreck fishing is usually carried out from boats of 40 ft (12 m) or more and the use of Decca is necessary to locate and anchor over far-off wrecks. Often the fishing is limited to · neap tides and to the two or three hours or so either side of high and low water, due to the difficulty of fishing in very deep and fast water.

The 30 lb (13.6 kg) IGFA rod with matching line and reel, is quite capable, in skilled hands, of subduing any amount of 50–60 lb (22.6–27.2 kg) congers, and, as has been proved, much heavier specimens on occasions. It is well to remember, though, that it is a very different matter bringing a big conger to the boat from the bottom in 30–40-odd fathoms (55–78 m) of water, than beating a porbeagle or mako shark twice as heavy on the same outfit. Sharks fight by swimming and can be exhausted by being encouraged to do so; congers do not make long runs when hooked in deep water from a boat; they hang back with powerful, sinuous body undulations, moving backwards in direct combat with the pull of the rod. Usually, once in a cleft in a rock or among the debris of a wreck, the fish will be almost impossible to extricate . . . and so the light tackle tactic is based on not letting the conger ever get into his holt.

Constant heavy pressure will be brought to bear on the tackle in combat with a 50 lb (22.6 kg) plus conger, and for this reason a line of Dacron or Terylene is advisable rather than nylon, which stretches and then recovers, and in so doing can crush very strong metal reel spools. In spite of the fact that many conger-addict wreck anglers do not like to see fellow anglers using braided lines (they reckon that braids are bowed more by tide and drift leads to tangle with other gear) the use of braid for light tackle fishing is advisable for big conger, not just to protect the reel but for other important reasons, sensitivity being one of them.

While fishing in deep flowing water, the signals of a fish at the bait are largely nullified by the stretch in nylon monofilament of 30 lb (13.6 kg) class. It is generally not until the eel has emerged from the wreck or reef, pouched the bait and begun to move back into its lair that the bite is telegraphed up the line to the angler. And that may be too late – at least, too late with light tackle to be able to haul out the fish.

The light tackle man must fish in a different way. His success rate depends on knowing when a conger first touches the bait, so that he can lure the fish from its lair. This is done by slowly recovering line once a bite is felt. The eel will more often than not slide out of its hole or crack to retain the bait, and, if care is taken not to reel too quickly, nor jerk the bait, the eel will come several yards off the bottom with the bait in its mouth.

Then comes the crunch. The eel suddenly feels insecure; something is wrong. Dive it must! Which it does, and then is brought up against the rod tip, and the hook point pierces the soft jaw.

Now is the time for action. The rod is kept at its maximum curve and the eel pumped off the bottom if it will come. If it pulls so hard that there is a risk of line breakage, the drag must be allowed to give a little line; not too much, but just enough at the peak of each lunge to avoid the sudden snatch that spells disaster. For this reason, and the fact that with conger there is no mass of line stripped from the reel, it is best to set the drag a little lighter than for shark, and add any necessary extra pressure by thumb pressure on the spool of line.

Terminal tackle needs no great finesse. Since the braided Dacron or Terylene stretches little a short length of heavy monofil – about 40 lb (18.1 kg) test – is attached to the Dacron by means of a strong Berkley barrel swivel. The Dacron is doubled for about 4 in (10 cm) and the tucked half blood knot tied in the doubled end for added security. The heavy monofil is tied with the same knot to the other ring of the swivel. On the nylon runs a Clements boom or a big link swivel to take the lead, with another strong link swivel at the very end to take the hook trace. The hook can be a strong forged type, sizes 6/0 to 10/0, crimped in the usual way to about 2 ft (60 cm) of wire, about 100 lb (45.3 kg) test. The usual loop is formed at the other end to fit to the link swivel.

This rig, with leads between 10 oz (283 g) and 2 lb (900 g) should cope with most offshore conger fishing from a boat. It is appreciated that many anglers will scoff at such comment, but the fact remains that many conger of 50–80 lb (22.6–36.2 kg) have been beaten on such 'fragile' gear. However, in deference to the power of a big conger this is one of the few times in this book that it will be agreed that, at times, a 50 lb (22.6 kg) IGFA outfit may be appropriate. This is not an admission that 30 lb class is insufficient but that many of us lack the skill to use it on such monsters.

Quite apart from these very big congers that live in wrecks and reefs way offshore in deep water, there are many others up to about 50 lb (22.6 kg) or so within half a mile (0.8 km) of most rocky shores and in water no more than 20 ft (6 m) deep. Often the eels of such areas, especially where the rocks are interspersed with patches of sand or mud, can be taken on 12–20 lb (5.4–9 kg) after dark when they leave the rocks to hunt the open patches. Simple leger tackle, made up in the same way as for offshore congers, is in order, but the wire may be reduced to about 50 lb (22.6 kg) test.

Hooked on this light tackle in open ground the congers on the shallows will often fight harder than the bigger offshore specimens, making long, quite fast runs instead of simply hanging back and undulating.

A really large conger is an awesome creature. This 88¾-pounder (40.2 kg) shown by Bernard Williams came from the West Country. Fish of just over 80 lb (36.2 kg) have been caught on 30 lb (13.6 kg) class tackle!

Of course, to take matters to a logical conclusion, there is great sport in challenging eels that may run between 10 and 40 lb (4.5 and 18 kg) or so with the bass surfcasting outfit from the shore; or, if the conditions warrant it – such as jagged masses of weed-draped rocks, an old harbour wall laced with conger-inhabited crevices or similar – then the big surfcasting rod and the 20 lb (or even 30 lb) class boat reel – such as Ambassadeurs 9000 or 7000 – will be called into action.

Nylon monofilament lines of 15–18 lb (6.8–8 kg) have been used to land conger of 50 lb (22.6 kg) from rocky shores, and there is no good reason why this should not be a regular occurrence. There is great magic in being out on a warm summer or early autumn night, the water lapping, and hearing the gentle ticking of the ratchet as a conger picks up the bait and slowly moves off with it. The rod may be rested in a monopod on the beach or laid down, reel up, on rocks or a stone pier.

Warm and settled summer weather is the best for conger fishing, especially when it is muggy. Sport seldom is good when there is a strong wind blowing, in this case particularly if that wind is onshore.

It is important, when casting into rocky or rough ground, not to drag or allow the tide to drag the

tackle across the seabed once it has been cast, otherwise the lead or hook will without doubt become snagged.

Playing shore conger on a bass rod and light line is – or should be – a delicate affair. It is no good merely hanging on like grim death and not yielding any line at all; similarly it is senseless to let the eel have free rein so that it can get into a rocky crevice or hole, there to stay with its tail locking it firmly in position. One keeps that important quarter-circle of bend in the rod and takes a turn or two with the reel whenever that curve straightens a little and the eel yields ground.

Too many British anglers want to see their hooked fish too early in the fight, so they haul hard. And many of them get broken more times than they like to remember. It is not often that a fish breaks an angler's line; it is more often the angler's mistake or a fault in the tackle that does so.

The author's first encounter with conger on bass tackle from the shore occurred one night in a rocky Sussex estuary. Bass were the quarry and the bait was a whole side of fresh mackerel legered in only 3 ft (91 cm) of water with 12 lb (5.4 kg) test line and no wire trace, of course. The two congers caught weighed 18 lb and 22 lb (8.1 and 9.9 kg) and they each fought for about 30 minutes, making runs of 30 yd (27.4 m) or so repeatedly.

Another memorable conger weighed about 25 lb (11.3 kg), but it was beaten on a 7 ft (2.1 m) seatrout spinning rod, fixed-spool reel and 8 lb (3.6 kg) monofil, when the author was fishing for plaice from a dinghy on a sandy patch among the rocks. That fish

A useful set-up for conger from the boat: a running leger using an Ashmore Sea-boom. Alternative running booms are the double-eyed Clements and the single-eyed Kilmore. Again, the wire trace is ready for quick release via the Berkley link-swivel.

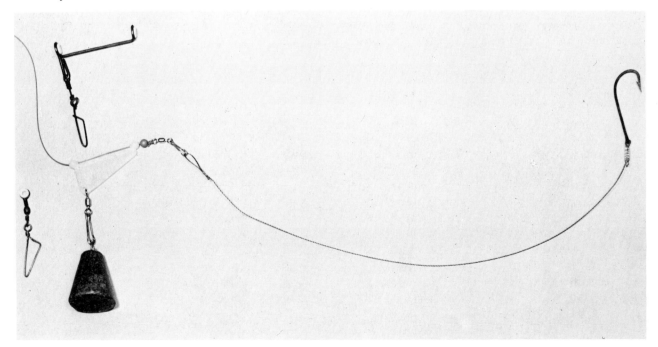

took only about 15 minutes to bring to the boat, but was a very satisfactory exercise in patience and tackle manipulation!

There is only one practical way of bringing a conger into a boat or on to a beach or rocks, and that is with a sharp, strong gaff. The best type is a simple cadmium plated and tinned lash-on hook (Mustad make good ones) strongly whipped to a broomstick or similar handle about 4 ft (1.2 m) long. The tang of the gaff shaft is first located in a hole drilled in the wooden handle, the whipping being done with strong nylon or Terylene thread, and well varnished, or with copper or brass wire, which may be carefully covered with solder.

The stroke with the gaff should be made just back of the head and the movement continued in a smooth arc to bring the fish into the boat or on to the beach or rocks. From high rocks, a harbour wall or pier three 12/0 big game hooks brazed back to back to form a triangle and attached to a strong nylon rope with about 1 lb (453 g) of lead pipe on the rope just above it, will bring congers to the platform. The triangle of hooks is lowered in position, the eel held as quietly as possible, and the rope given a sharp jerk to penetrate the fish.

There is no need when boat fishing to go to any lengths to present the bait cleverly. Half a mackerel (cut across the body), a whole one or similar lumps of herring, pouting, whiting, pilchard or squid and cuttlefish are all good baits. In addition, crab is good used from the shore.

On the boat simply hook the bait by putting the hook through one end and bringing it back through the bait so that the point is well clear. When a longish cast must be made from the shore, then baits as for tope fishing from the shore should be used for streamlining and security.

Finally a word of warning: conger have powerful jaws and sharp cutting teeth. Do not be tempted to extricate a deep hook unless either the eel has been still and out of the water for at least an hour or you have long-handled pliers with which to work. Since this is a book on sportfishing and not 'meat fishing', it hardly seems appropriate to advise on quick and humane ways to kill fish. Nevertheless, congers are difficult to unhook and return safely, even fish of under 20 lb (9 kg), because they are so slippery and immensely strong out of water. If it can be done, then do it using pliers. But if the fish must be killed (and conger steaks or fish cakes make good eating) hit the eel hard and several times with a heavy priest across the tail, just behind the vent. The conger's important

This huge conger of 104 lb 6 oz (47.1 kg) is thought to have come closest to the British record fish of 109 lb 6 oz (49 kg 609 g) caught in 1976.

'works' are located there and it will soon succumb. A knife with a pointed, sharp and strong rigid blade should be driven through the eel's spine just behind the head, which will irrevocably disconnect the 'sharp end' from the 'works' and make it fairly safe. Even so, anybody who puts his fingers near a conger's jaws, even a 'dead' conger, risks a nasty injury.

A sack should be used to hold congers in a small boat or on shore, the neck being securely tied with strong cord; on a big charter-boat the eels are usually stowed in the fish-hold immediately on being caught.

7 Skates and stingray

The skates under discussion here are not the fish so described in the fish-and-chip shops. There are only three true skates swimming in the waters with which this book is concerned: the common skate (*Raja batis*), the white skate (*Raja alba*) and the long-nosed skate (*Raja oxyrinchus*). Of these, the common skate, sometimes called the grey skate, is by far the most common – true to its name. It forms at least 95 per cent of rod-caught skate captures. There has been no true long-nosed skate verified on rod and line to the author's knowledge, although most years some white skate are caught from Ireland's west coast, especially in the Clew Bay area, in Galway and Tralee Bays.

The so-called fish-and-chip shop 'skate' is in fact a ray, usually the thornback (*Raja clavata*) although other rays are not rejected when they turn up, of course!

So far as the angler, and more particularly the sportfisher, is concerned it is wise to forget the other two skates and concentrate on the common one: the white skate may turn up once in a lifetime, by chance, and the same tackle and techniques will be suitable.

It is obvious that many anglers will raise their eyebrows – if they are gentlemen, and utter profanities if they are not – by the very inclusion of common skate in a light-tackle book. However, although many still cling to the idea that skate fishing with anything less than 80 lb (36.2 kg) test line is madness – and that 100 lb (45.3 kg) 'string' is better – one cannot help but defend the sportfishing idea by gleefully pointing out that Robin Macpherson's former British record skate of 226½ lb (102.7 kg) was beaten in 55 minuters with 40 lb (18.1 kg) test line on a small Mitchell surfcasting reel and a cheap Japanese rod that a sportfisher would ridicule.

Also, more than a few enthusiasts regularly boat common skate of over 100 lb (45.3 kg) on lines of about 30 lb (13.6 kg) test, and it is a fact that from a few deep-water piers in the country, mainly in Scotland and in south-west Ireland, skate of around this weight are taken on strong casting outfits. In fact, one angler of the author's acquaintance vanquished a common of 106 lb (48 kg) with such tackle, including line of 19 lb (8.6 kg) test from Fenit Pier in County Kerry. The battle took four and a half hours!

The trouble is, most anglers who do seek common skate seek big skate, and that means fish well over 100 lb (45.3 kg). So, they use heavy gear, just in case they do encounter a true leviathan, for fish of more than 400 lb (181.4 kg) have been landed by commercial fishing boats. They also tend to fish only in those areas where common skate are known to live but, of necessity, where there are suitable boats and skippers. The small skate they catch are then regarded as tiddlers, whereas the light tackle angler could have some fun with them – fish of 30–70 lb (13.6–31.7 kg) or so.

Where are the skate grounds? They may lie in many as yet undiscovered areas, but the ones that regularly produce fish include the famous Orkney and Shetland grounds, Ullapool, Stornoway, Mull, to name a few of the Scottish ones; the deep water off the Isle of Wight, off the Devon and Cornish coasts (where little angling is done, but where commercials catch them by accident), and the south and south-west coasts of Ireland, the hot-spots being famous names: Ballycotton, Dungarvan, Youghal, Cobh, Kinsale, Baltimore, Kenmare River, Valentia Island and Cahirciveen, Tralee Bay, then right up the west coast (Clew Bay is famous but has been overfished and has declined) as far as Sligo.

As already stated, there may be many more excellent grounds, especially off the north-west and northern coasts of Northern Ireland, the western isles of Scotland and between Shetland and the Faroes.

So far as the light tackle man is concerned, however, the existing skate areas will afford plenty of sport, since the 30 lb (13.6 kg) outfit reaches its lifting limit of skate of about 80 lb (36.2 kg). One has to remember that skate do not usually fight by making long tiring runs and by swimming; they tend to use their vast wings as foils so that tide keeps them 'glued' to the bottom; and even if the tackle will lift them a few feet they are very capable of regaining the seabed with a few slow, powerful wingbeats. In any really

One of the best feats of light tackle angling ever achieved, in the author's opinion: Frank Avery with his 106 lb (48 kg) common skate from Ireland's Fenit Pier. He fought the fish for 4½ hours on line of 19 lb (8.6 kg) test! The reel was a lightweight bass surfcasting model.

strong tidal stream, the 30 lb (13.6 kg) outfit will be quite incapable of lifting the fish or stopping a dive.

However, since the 226½ lb (102.7 kg) fish was beaten on 40 lb (18.1 kg) line, it is obvious that there are ways to do the apparently impossible.

This is what usually happens: big skate, which

favour areas of sand and mud surrounded by rough stretches of marly ground, tend to lie firmly on the seabed when the tide is flowing strongly. When the run eases, at high or low water, the fish heave themselves off the bottom and feed a little before settling in a new position as the tide begins to strengthen in flow from the opposite direction, so that their heads face the flow which keeps them on the seabed. It is therefore at slack water – specially on neap tides – that any light tackle skate fishing should be done. In fact, any skate fishing, whatever the tackle!

Naturally, once a skate is hooked on 30 lb (13.6 kg) tackle, time is of the essence: if the fight extends into the period when the tidal run picks up again there may be little hope of a successful conclusion so far as the angler is concerned. As with the really big conger, it must be admitted here that once the optimum period has passed, or if the fish in the locality do feed into the tidal run period (as is sometimes the case) the 50 lb (22.6 kg) outfit must be brought into use. The actual line test will be in the region of 45–47 lb (20.4–21.3 kg).

One of the main reasons why British anglers do tend to use very heavy tackle, whether for skate, conger, tope or shark, is because few know how to play a big fish and are impatient to see what it is they have hooked. So, they pressure the fish to get it near enough to have a look at it – and that leads to tackle breakages.

The 30 lb (13.6 kg) outfit is used, then, with either Dacron, Terylene or nylon monofilament line, the braids being safer since they stand less chance of crushing the reel when the coils are rewound under high tension. The whole outfit, terminal tackle included, is almost the same as that for conger, except that the hook trace itself must be about 4 ft (1.2 m) to avoid the line being rubbed on the skate's rough leading wing edges, and may be reduced to 60 lb (27.2 kg).

The first signal of a skate at the bait is often a shiver running up the line – probably caused by the skate settling itself over the bait and moving up to position its mouth to take it, the massive wings rubbing the trace or line as it manoeuvres. Comes a brief pause, then the line will begin to run out in jerks. The rod is usually rested securely against the gunwale with the reel on light drag and with audible ratchet on. The hook is pulled in firmly – in the case of light tackle by

simply switching the lever to 'in-gear' and holding on until the rod curves over, then lifting it back into a fighting curve – and an attempt made to keep the fish moving around off the bottom. The light tackle makes this difficult, but not impossible; it means using the tackle very close to its limit. Smooth pumping is essential.

The belly pad should be worn all the time one is fishing for skate since there is no time to put it on before picking up the rod. The strain must be put on the fish immediately and maintained throughout.

Common skate are not eaten as a rule, although it is said the wings of fish under 50 lb (22.6 kg) are tolerable. Therefore, unless there is a very good reason, the boated fish should be returned to the sea, not killed. To bring the fish aboard two gaffs are usully used, each being inserted through the leading edge of opposing wings about 3 in back and 1 ft out (8 and 30 cm) from the nose. The two gaffers then haul the fish over the gunwale and into the boat. A trophy photograph should now be taken and the fish, still on the gaffs, put back over the side and the gaffs slid free. The small holes are but superficial wounds to a large fish like a skate. Weighing a fish on a boat is seldom very accurate.

Whenever possible, it pays not to allow the tackle to fish too far downtide of the boat: with light tackle especially it is best to try to keep right over the fish, and sometimes a skate will try to swim uptide when hooked, a very helpful move for the angler, who can try to exert only just sufficient pressure to make the fish strive to remain in that position, often fighting slight tidal flow too.

The mouth of the common skate has no sharp cutting teeth but is well equipped with massive crushing pads and muscles, so a strong forged hook, well sharpened as always, is necessary. Baits which commonly succeed include mackerel, herring, small whole coalfish (about 1 ft long – that's 31 cm), pollack of similar size, lumps of dogfish (lesser spotted) and pouting.

Skate fishing is worthwhile from mid-April to early November, with May, June and September providing the best of the sport as a rule.

Having mentioned shore-caught common skate, this aspect had best be dealt with briefly. It must be borne in mind that such fishing can usually only be successful where fairly deep water comes inshore in the form of broad channels; and it should also be remembered that most of the shore-caught skate have come from one place, the deep-water ocean pier at Fenit, Tralee Bay, County Kerry. Good specimens have also been taken from deep-water piers and projections in Scottish sea-lochs on the west coast, how-

This skate from Scapa Flow in Orkney was taken by the late Terry Brown (left) on 45 lb (20.4 kg) line. It weighed 147 lb (66.6 kg) and the fish had the advantage of an increasing tidal flow.

The svelte appearance of this fish belies his dangerous character. An Essex stingray is pictured before return to the sea.

ever, and anybody given to experimenting could – with perseverance and much patience – discover other places.

Obviously, the heaviest shore outfit in the list in chapter 2 would be used, with the running leger rig as described previously for shore tope. If possible, the 4 ft (1.2 m) of wire trace should be retained, even though it might be a little difficult to cast, since rubbing on the fish is liable to be over a long period, due to the light tackle being used. Casting is made easiest by using an anchor lead and hooking the hook on one of the wires before casting. Air resistance makes it fly free in mid-cast. The reel, Ambassadeur 9000, 9000C, or 7000, or Policansky Monitor 2, should be loaded with 30 lb (13.6 kg) class line.

Unless there is access down to the water level, when two long gaffs may be used, a special gaff made up from three 12/0 hooks brazed together at their backs and weighted with lead pipe (as for conger fishing from rocky shores) is useful. It is let down on a strong rope in the same way, of course; or else, the long, screw-connected sweep's brush handles in conjunction with a normal big gaff hook (as for shore porbeagle) may be brought into service.

The Policansky Monitor No. 2 multiplier, made by craftsmen in South Africa, is an ideal reel for battling big congers, common skate and other heavy fish from the shore. It can cast about 100 yd (91.4 m) and has a smooth lever-drag and strong spool machined from aluminium alloy.

When shore fishing for common skate, and with even a reasonable chance of connecting, it will pay to carry a belly pad, since the fight is bound to last a long time, and stomach and groin injuries could easily be sustained when imposing firm pressure on a skate over a long period. As in the boat, maintain the pressure as firmly as the tackle will stand. The fish is likely to move around the bottom, often stopping to try to hold the bottom. Try to prevent the fish from lying still by pumping, jerking a little perhaps, or bombarding the area with anything handy. It is not only a sulking salmon that can be woken up with a well aimed rock!

The stingray is the only member of the true ray family that warrants inclusion in a book on light tackle sportfishing, as opposed to fishing for the pot. The stingray is a fish of the summer months, moving into inshore waters to lie in the sun-warmed shallows – often only 18 in (45.7 cm) deep – over sand, sandy mud or gravel. Unlike the common skate and other common rays, such as the thornback, blond, undulate and painted varieties, the stingray has a very thick body and is very muscular, swimming fast when hooked and sometimes leaping clear of the water, too, when hooked. Its tail is slender and whip-like, equipped about one third back from the body with a sharp, serrated spine set dorsally. When frightened or otherwise stimulated it tries to bring the tail over and drive the spine into any nearby aggressor, and it often succeeds only in spearing itself. The spine is not only sharp but carries venom-producing tissues in a groove.

Mid-June is a good time to begin hunting the stingray, which certainly reaches weights in excess of 60 lb (27.2 kg) and is regularly caught in the 20–30 lb (9–13.6 kg) class. The fish seem to move to deep water in late summer, around mid-August. They appear to favour extensive estuaries and shallow water interspersed with banks of mud or gravel, especially when the area is protected from prevailing winds.

Although stingrays occur fairly widely in the southern North Sea, the favoured areas extend south from The Wash, the coast between Felixstowe and North Foreland being famous. Stingrays also occur on shallow sandy areas on the Sussex coast, especially along the shore between Hove and Selsey Bill, Lancing and Rustington being hot-spots. The Solent is also well worth visiting, although Solent fishing has dete-

riorated somewhat during the seventies, mainly due to industrial and domestic pollution plus some excessive commercial fishing. South Wales' Gower Peninsula also produces, as does Tralee Bay in Kerry.

Stingrays, like the other skates and rays, are bottom feeders: they avidly take baits of king ragworm, crab (soft, peeler or hermit), sometimes lugworm or herring strip.

Since this ray is such an active fighter, much lighter tackle may be used than for common skate. It can be fairly said that a 40 lb (18.1 kg) stingray fights about three times as hard as a common skate of at least double that weight. The fight, however, is more like that of a round fish, like the tope, and so it is possible to make the fish run and tire itself, even with, say, 10 lb (4.5 kg) test line.

Warm and settled weather with a calm sea are the optimum conditions for stingray fishing. From a boat it is wise to begin fishing, when possible, about half-way up the flood tide on the edges of shallow sandbanks leading to deep-water channels. As the tide approaches the hour before high water the boat should be quietly moved on to the sandbank or flat, where the fish may be expected in water little more than knee-deep, though often the depth in which fish will be taken may be 4–8 ft (1.2–2.4 m). As the ebb gets under weigh it helps to move the boat to the downtide edge of the shallows to ambush the fish as they move into the deeper channels, for often the best flats and banks for stingrays – and other sporting fish – dry out completely on many a low water period.

It is possible to fish with the 12 lb or 20 lb (5.4 kg or 9kg) class boat outfits. However, since both the shadow of the boat or noise can frighten or put off the feed fish that are in very shallow water, it is often a good idea to cast well away from the anchored boat, as little as 20 or as far as 50 yd (18.2 or 45.7 m).

A light boat rod of the two standards mentioned will permit the bait to be lobbed the shorter of the two distances, but for anything more ambitious a casting rod is called for such as the boatcaster (uptide rod) mentioned in chapter 2. It is also possible to use the bass rod. In either case, the reel may be an Ambassadeur 6000 series or 7000 model, or similar, and should be filled with 10–15 lb (4.5–6.8 kg) line, depending on the average size of the stingrays in the area.

The most useful tackle is a straight running leger, a link-swivel (about size 4) being slid up the line before another ordinary swivel of about the same size is tied to the end of the line (which is doubled first) with a tucked half blood knot. The hook trace should be about 4 ft (1.2 m) of nylon of about 30 lb (13.6 kg) test, to which a strong forged hook is tied.

Mark of an experienced stingray man. Hold the fish well away from the legs. This is an Essex specimen, the Essex and Thames Estuary areas being well populated by large stingrays.

This should be from size 3/0 for ragworm and small-ish baits, up to 5/0 for a big crab or any big bait. Stingrays do not have cutting teeth, only grinding, crushing pads, so wire traces are unnecessary while sharp hooks are, of course, needed as always.

When using king ragworm for stingrays use a big one whole, do not cut it in short lengths. Pass the hook into the worm's mouth and thread it well round the hook so that the worm's head ends up well above the hook eye.

The bite of a stingray can be sudden and savage, stripping yards of line from the reel. Sometimes, if the angler is paying attention, advance warning in the shape of little twitches will be seen or felt. The fish should be struck firmly when it has taken a yard or so of line, which in most cases means as quickly as one can pick up the rod, put the reel in gear and lift the tip back.

The first move of the ray is normally a fast run away from the boat, and it is essential that the drag on the reel has been previously adjusted to yield line safely below the strain the line will stand. Any extra pressure can be put on the fish by pressing a thumb on to the line or the edge of the spool. When the fish comes in close to the boat, apparently beaten, always be ready for it to dive suddenly under the boat. It must be countered by thrusting the tip of the rod far under the water, pushing the line down so that it cannot rub on the keel and be broken.

For stingrays up to 20 lb (9 kg) or so a big landing net, such as the Stag model, or a home-made one of rugged construction, is a good idea. For anything bigger use the gaff, clipping it just inside the leading edge of the wing to one side of the mouth.

It is useful to have a wet sack to throw over the ray once it is aboard to forestall its tail lashing; keep a foot on the tail while the hook is removed with strong, long-nosed pliers. If the fish has been netted, put it back by holding the net over the side and inverting it quickly. If a gaff is used, keep the fish on the gaff while unhooking, then put it back still on the gaff, which is disengaged with a quick push.

Shore fishing is very similar to the casting system from the boat. Expect the fish to be in range from about halfway up the flood tide as it comes over the sandy or muddy flats. The rod can be rested in a suitable monopod with the reel out of gear and on check, if this is possible in the tidal conditions prevailing. To hold bottom it may sometimes be necessary to use a breakaway lead, though it will usually be found that a straight bomb will hold position since most stingray shore grounds are out of the main run of the tide.

Although stingrays, big ones especially, will leap clear of the water, even when boat fishing, this occurs much more regularly when shore fishing, since the bait will frequently be picked up in little over a foot of water. The spectacle of a bat-like shape kiting out of the water on being struck is quite exciting.

A long-handled gaff is best for securing a ray from a flat beach, and keep a foot on the tail when unhooking the fish, as before. Anglers are not often spiked, but once is likely to be enough!

Finally, once in a while when stingray fishing a strange-looking 'sting' will come along. This specimen is the eagle ray, which has a tail spike but also has a small dorsal fin just in front of it. The stingray has of course no dorsal fin. The eagle ray also has a pronounced Concorde-like nose, distinctly separated from the actual body disc, and rising in a steep line to thicken out when joining the disc. The author once saw an eagle ray of about 30 lb (13.6 kg) taken on lugworm by an angler fishing for soles on a Kent beach in late summer. Everybody thought it was a stingray, and that's how it was reported in the newspapers.

An easy quick check is to look at the tips of the ray's wings: if they are round it is an ordinary stingray; if they are pointed (plus the other features mentioned) a comparatively rare eagle ray has been caught.

8 Cod

The cod is a fish sought in autumn and winter in the southern part of England, to which shores the shoals migrate, usually in late September/early October. In the North Sea, however, from Yorkshire to beyond Caithness and back down the western coast of Scotland as far as the Firth of Clyde, fish are present throughout most of the year.

That statement needs clarification, since it is an oversimplification of the picture, a rough generalisation.

In brief, from the Norfolk bulge down to Hampshire the inshore cod fishing is done during the October to January season, with the odd fish being taken before and after those days by as much as a month or so. The Essex/East Anglian coast gets a run of small cod in March. But some cod, usually big ones, are taken during the summer months as well, from boats fishing deep water, miles offshore in that area – and right down to the Atlantic coast of Cornwall and North Devon.

In Scotland spring and summer cod fishing from the shore can be good, especially in some of the west coast sea-lochs. Irish cod fishing is virtually all boat fishing on deep-water reefs and wrecks, though a few fish are taken by shore casting on steep to rocky shores.

Although the cod does not figure high in the 'best fighter' tables, it earned itself a great reputation in the sixties when modern tackle and long-casting techniques, pioneered largely in the south-east of England by an angler whose name became a much revered one for his huge successes, Leslie Moncrieff, produced one-man catches on the beach for a day of 100 lb (45.3 kg) or so. Since then, alas, cod fishing has declined alarmingly, especially in the areas where sport depends on the autumn and winter migration. The cause has been argued from many aspects. Some of the cause – pollution and weather pattern changes, for example – may have a certain effect, but the author has no doubt at all that callous short term exploitation by commercial trawlers, both in distant waters and along the beaches, has been responsible. The fishery scientists at Lowestoft have been stressing

Modern shore cod gear: matched Conolon blanks with Ambassadeur 7000s loaded with 15 lb (6.8 kg) test line – not a ring out of place!

that overfishing has severely reduced what was once considered to be an almost inexhaustible stock. However, it appears that neither the other European, British nor Irish governments have taken heed: our own link-up with the continent has had its dark side.

To be interesting to the shore angler, especially the sportfisher with his light tackle (much of it developed

in a very short while to take those great cod of the sixties) cod must be available in good numbers and in a variety of sizes. The run in late September/early October usually has a vanguard of 4–10 lb (1.8–4.5 kg) cod (cod weighing 2–6 lb (900 g–2.7 kg) are commonly called codling), and by mid-November there should be fair chances of catching 20-pounders (9.0 kg) or even 30-pounders (13.6 kg) from some beaches and piers.

Most of the good cod beaches (shingle/sand or just sand) lie along the coasts of south Yorkshire, Lincolnshire, Norfolk, Suffolk, Essex, Kent, Sussex and Hampshire and Dorset (Chesil Bank). In these areas there is good pier and harbour wall fishing, as well as inshore and offshore boat fishing.

In North Yorkshire the shore cod scene is different. There are sand beaches, often hemmed in by rocky cliffs and rock outcrops, but much cod fishing is done from the cliffs themselves, casting over beds of tough kelp to fish the bait right among the rocks. Yorkshire rock anglers once used 50 lb (22.6 kg) line and more for this fishing, with massive rods and special wide diameter 'Scarborough' reels, the single action spools being made either of walnut or a tough mixture of linen cloth and resin called Tufnel. Some still do, but a more modern and light tackle approach is now asserting itself there – while catching plenty of good fish.

When fishing from a shingle or sand beach the cod are usually found at a certain point from the fishing stance: on a shingle beach giving way to sand, that is usually a few yards beyond the junction of stone and sand and normally when the tide is sufficiently high to give a depth of water of 15–50 ft (4.5–15.2 m); on a flatter sandy beach it is often necessary to place the bait well beyond the breaking waves.

Thus, when cod fishing from beaches, either the steeply shelving shingle banks, like those at Orford Island in Suffolk, Dungeness in Kent or Chesil Bank in Dorset, or from sandy beaches like those in the Spurn Head area north to around Bridlington, in Yorkshire, for example, there are two criteria for consistently successful cod fishing. They are good fresh bait and the ability to cast it to where the cod may be at any point in the tidal situation: distances of 120–140 yd (109.7–128 m) or more with a lead weight of

Left: A typical winter scene at Dungeness, Kent's famous cod beach. Casts of well over 100 yd (91.4 m) are usually required to catch good fish, and such distances are best achieved with light reel lines and heavy leaders. Light lines also hold out better than thick lines.

4–6 oz (113–170 g). Not only that, either: cod beaches are crowded places and it is essential to be able to fish out beyond most of the other men on the beach, yet not tangle their gear when your own is wound in, either to be rebaited or when playing a fish.

The tackle to choose for shore fishing in the sporting context should be the 4–6 oz (113–170 g) surf rod, the reel to match, the range of multipliers preferably, or the suggested fixed-spool reel, loaded with nylon monofilament of 12–18 lb (5.4–8.2 kg) test – and loaded in either case to within about 1/16 in (1.5 mm) of the lip of the spool.

The business end is a simple nylon paternoster. There are two good ways of making it. Either tie a blood-loop into the casting leader about 18 in (45.7 cm) from the end, to which is looped the hook snood, or tie the blood-loop in the same position, leaving 2 ft (60 cm) of end, thread a size 8 barrel swivel on, then tie another blood-loop 6 in (15.5 cm) or less below it. Trim off the loops closely and you are left with the swivel running freely between two stop-knots. The hook snood is tied to the free eye of the swivel with the tucked half blood knot. This second system is very useful when pouting and whiting are numerous and prevents tangled snoods when constantly reeling in these 'nuisance' fish, since they spin on the way in and can ruin a blood-loop snood quickly.

The tackle is completed by a forged ringed or eyed hook, bronzed for preference, or a spade-end hook. Sizes 2/0 up to 5/0 will cope with small codling or a 30-pounder (13.6 kg). Bait clips can be good for long casts.

Avoid all wire booms, running or fixed, big swivels and clips. They are unnecessary, expensive, hamper casting and are just old hat. The only metal on the terminal tackle should be the hook, the tiny snood swivel (if that system is used) and a small link-swivel at the end of the gear to take the wire loop of the lead, a breakaway type.

Bait the hook as recommended in chapter 4. The number one bait for successful shore codding is lugworm, perhaps several big ones threaded up the snood. Razorfish is also excellent but more likely to be jerked off when casting for distance. Crab, too, is a fine bait but is very difficult to cast a long way; it is best for piers etc, where range is not so important. Mussels are useful and need to be tied on the hook in a big bunch with fine elastic thread. After a big onshore storm, many baits will be left on the high water mark. They will probably include whelks, hermit crabs, sea mice and other types of shellfish. All of them can be excellent.

It is necessary to realise that the reason for using

Some years cod begin to come onto the beaches in September. Here are typical 'matched pairs' of rods and reels set up together in monopods.

thin line is to be able to cast a long way, keep the tackle out there without the tide getting a grip on the line and dragging it shorewards in a bow, as well as that of having to exercise some skill in bringing the cod, if it is a big one, to the beach. Line of 12 lb test (5.4 kg) is not ridiculous, although some of the old guard who still use 25 lb (11.3 kg) test and upwards, plus massive rods and wired leads, think so.

Thin line is an advantage in many ways, as outlined in chapter 3.

With anglers lining the beach it may be a problem to find a gap: 15 yd (13 m) between two other anglers is the absolute minimum needed, and even then one should ask permission of the other bordering anglers. Most cod anglers use two rods, the very keenest having matched pairs, identical in all respects, with matching reels. With care, two outfits may be used, even on a crowded beach.

Watch the anglers on either side. They probably cast straight out, or slightly at an angle. If you can cast

further, then the following system is almost foolproof. Again, explain to neighbours first.

Walk uptide of your selected position, say about 20 yd (18.2 m), behind the other anglers, then make your long cast from a gap in the ranks, so that when you take your high-held rod back over the rods of your neighbours to your spot, the tackle comes to rest a little uptide of your fishing position. Do it with both rods if you fish two. Place the rods in monopods, preferably made from alloy angle, as shown, about a yard (1 m) apart and at an angle of about 20 degrees from the vertical pointing towards the sea.

Friction can occur between anglers on a crowded beach, and if it is possible for several friends to fish together in a line, this system of walking up to cast works well when adopted by all the anglers. Often anglers who cannot cast far will cast over the lines of those who can, dragging them in whenever a rebaiting is carried out. And naturally, if the long caster simply casts straight out from his position, by the time his tackle has sunk and the lead taken a grip of the seabed, it will be 20–30 yd (18.2–27.4 m) downtide of his pitch. When he reels in he is likely to hook up 50 yd (45.7 m) downtide the lines of his downtide neighbours. It is necessary to have patience, for unpleasantness never makes angling enjoyable. Watching to see if one's line is underneath or over the top of that of a neighbour can help to bring the gear in without affecting the neighbour's, by passing one's rod over or under the other line.

It is important to spill line when the lead hits the water on completion of the cast, else tide will drag it as it sinks. It is impossible, no matter what other anglers may say to you, to fish with a line straight from rod tip to lead. Everybody's line will form a downtide bow, the greatest bows being in the lines that are out furthest, of course.

Once the lead has taken a grip, wind the line in until the tip of the rod takes on a curve and the line is as taut as it can be short of springing the anchor wires on the breakaway lead. By the way, the wires can be adjusted to break at a wide range of strains by bending them to clip more firmly or more loosely into the recesses or collars, depending on the type used, or, in

Two cod at the same time – each weighing about 20 lb (9.0 kg) – prove quite a handful, but when using light tackle, one hook is enough.

Leaving rods to 'fish for themselves' like this can result in the loss of the whole outfit if a lively cod grabs the bait and drags the rod from its rest.

the case of elastic band types, on the size of or number of turns given to the elastic band.

Most cod bites will move the angle of pull on the lead and free it, so that the rod will spring back as line slackens downtide. At other times the rod tip will shudder, then be pulled over hard, nodding away as the fish swims off downtide. The rod is picked up and the line reeled taut before striking firmly as one walks back up the beach in the second case; in the event of a slack-line bite, grab the rod from the rest and run up the beach until the line goes taut and you feel resistance, then strike hard. Nylon stretches and absorbs attempts to move the lead and the hook and sink its point.

When the surf is rough and there is a strong undertow there is no room for a mistake with the gaff. Here the author brings out a 10-pounder (4.5 kg) for a companion. Many fish are lost by inexperienced 'helpers' grabbing the line between rod and fish and hauling.

Right: Anything you can do I can do . . . well, maybe not better, but how about this for the lady's first cod! Anne Lewington beat this 14-pounder (6.3 kg) on 15 lb (6.8 kg) line in a strong tide.

Hooked at long range, cod usually come towards the angler, swinging downtide, and seldom is there any real battle at first, although there are exceptions, and a cod of 15 lb (6.8 kg) or so will sometimes hare off with 20 yd (18.2 m) of line against the reel drag immediately the hook goes home. With the fish within 30 yd (27.4 m) or so from the beach it is likely to liven up, not liking the shallowing water and the noise of the breaking surf. Be ready to yield line if a run along the surf or out to sea comes suddenly. Such runs are seldom longer than about 10 yd (9 m). With levelwind multiplier reels the thumb of the rod hand can apply pressure to the line on the spool, the hand being positioned behind the reel; with open multipliers, the rod hand is in front of the reel to lay the line in close coils across the spool (which is immensely important to good, backlash-free casts) so the drag has to do all braking. It is necessary to adjust the brake (star-drag) to work when the fish is way out and when it is close in, although extra pressure can be imposed with the thumb of the reeling hand if a long run develops.

Cod of up to about 6 lb (2.7 kg) can be beached, as they are rolled up the shore by any incoming breakers, but anything bigger requires the angler to call for assistance with the gaff.

Never must any attempt be made to haul a decent size cod through a surf when a backtow (receding wave) is occurring: the pressure imposed on the line will break even 30 lb (13.6 kg) test if the fish is 10 lb (4.5 kg) or so; in fact, a fish of that size must not be held against a receding wave. Time an incoming wave to bring the fish in, when the line is rapidly recovered until a turn or two of the leader is round the spool. At this point the man with the gaff, who ought to be in thighboots, nips into the swash and plants the gaff just behind the fish's head and brings it ashore. The fish is immediately killed with a blow over the eyes with a pebble or a priest.

If a very large cod, 20 lb (9 kg) plus, runs off downtide in a rough sea – which is the best of all conditions for daylight codding – the angler with light gear must follow, passing his rod under or over the lines of other anglers to avoid tangles. It is an unwritten law among surf anglers on a crowded beach to make way for a man playing a big fish – anybody who doesn't can be sure of getting well cursed by all and sundry!

Good daylight fishing conditions usually come after an onshore blow when the sea is crumping on to the beach in slow 'walls' and is turbid with disturbed sand and mud. A hazard then is weed drifting into the line and dragging the lead out of the sand. There is no cure for this, except to keep bringing in the gear and recasting after clearing any heavy collections of weed. But if the weed is only present in the inshore breakers, as it often is, a move to the highest part of the back of the beach and keeping the rod tip almost vertical, will help keep the line out of trouble.

It is surprising just how rough the sea has to be to make fishing impossible, and with a thin line and skill such conditions can be effectively mastered and some terrific catches of cod made. In fact, very rough seas produce the memorable cod hauls, both in overall weight and in size of fish.

Quite apart from keeping line clear of the big waves crashing on to the beach, it is necessary to combat increased tidal run (strong winds and big tides usually coincide) and maybe debris in the water. An extension of the walking-up-and-casting technique is the way to achieve success, but it may be necessary to walk up 50 yd (45.7 m) to get the lead to hold, pushed into the seabed by the tidal stream instead of being swept away by it. The lead must come to rest uptide of the fishing position to permit the method to work – and this may have to be achieved with the lead only 70–80 yd (64–73 m) from the beach. Casting into an onshore wind is not easy!

Fishing at night is very popular with some cod anglers – in fact, some will not fish in daylight. Certainly, in anything less than rough seas and with clear water the cod tend to feed inshore best after dark. There is no great change necessary from daylight tactics, save that a few anglers who are able to use a multiplier in daylight find they have to use a fixed-spool reel at night. That is strange because an angler's headlamp enables the line leaving the multiplier to be seen just as well as in daylight; it also permits levelling line on the open reel spool when recovering line.

A paraffin or petrol pressure lantern is essential. It is placed behind the rod or rods and leaning backwards up the beach at an angle (a pile of sand or shingle can be put under the lantern's base) to shine up the rods to the tips, making the rings gleam and the rod tip(s) easy to see without straining the eyes. Anglers who habitually fish at night either paint about a foot (30 cm) of their rod tip white or they apply reflective tape to show up in the light glow. Avoid clip-on rod lights such as Beta; they do not work as well as expected and strain the eyes.

Cod fishing on a winter beach with a north-east gale blowing can be extremely painful. Some anglers use portable canvas-covered shelters or windbreaks, but they need to be moved up and down with the tide. Good clothing is the answer for comfort and mobility, and lying down in a shallow trench scooped from shingle will avoid excessive exposure to the elements.

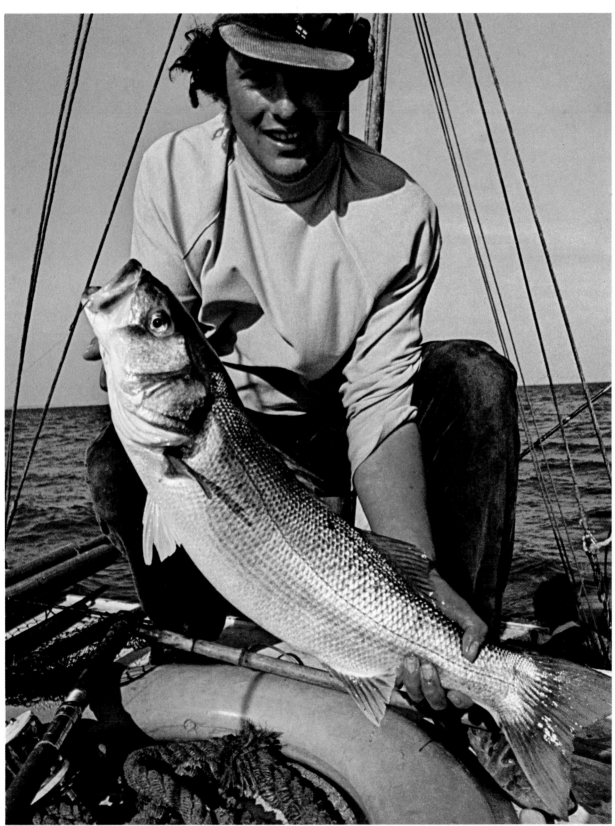

The coast of Essex, especially the Blackwater, Crouch and Thames estuaries, is famous for the many large bass taken, both inshore, and many miles out on the various banks. This fish held by John Rawle weighed 10½ lb (4.7 kg).

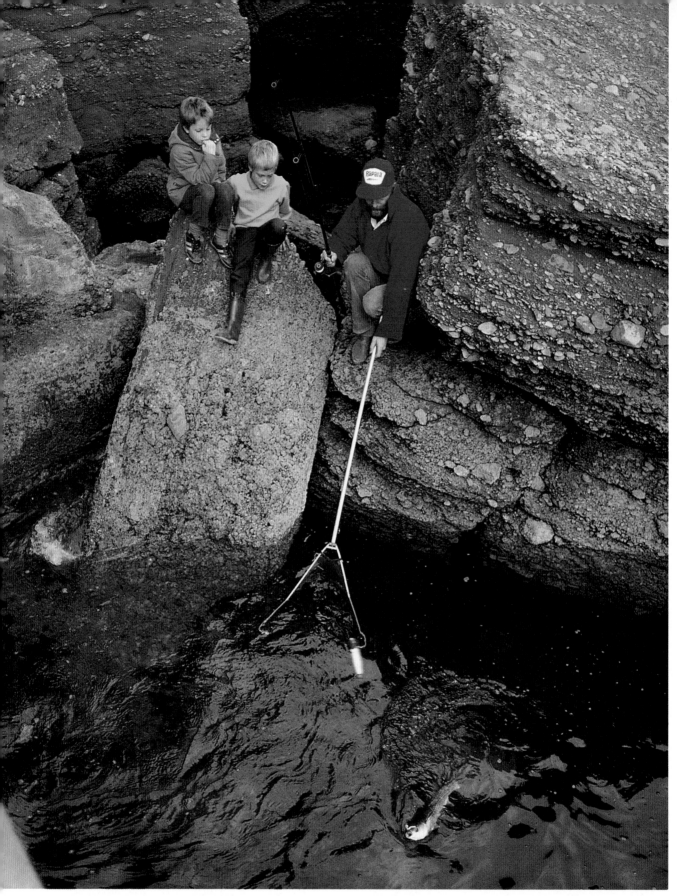

Two youngsters learn the ropes about float fishing for mullet at a rocky cove in the West Country. The angler is using a fixed-spool reel and a long flexible rod – an ideal combination in this context. The landing net is necessary to secure the fish since the light line would not be able to lift it. On a higher rock, a dropnet might be necessary.

Right: Two bass nestled among the cliff-top flowers near the Seven Sisters range of cliffs near Seaford in Sussex. The fish swim among the rocks at the base of the cliffs, searching for crabs and small fish. Besides being a skilled operator with his tackle, the bass angler seeking fish in this kind of habitat needs to keep a watchful eye on the flooding tide lest he be cut off.

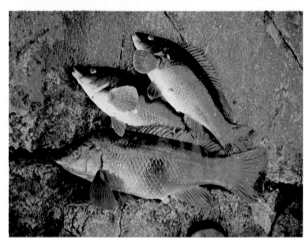

Ballan wrasse come in a wide variety of colour combinations and markings, and all these specimens were taken at the same place. The author shows a dark green specimen before returning it alive; there is a fish with a dark back and reddish mottled flanks; a 'patchwork' fish of chestnut and dull orange . . . and a varied trio.

Below: Kelp-draped rocks giving way to deep clear Atlantic water are typical ballan wrasse habitat. The fish vary greatly in colouration.

The black bream is not black, of course, but steely blue, silver and white. This fish is a female.

Below: The garfish is like a miniature swordfish and, like the swordfish and billfishes, often leaps out of the water when hooked. Because of their long slim jaw, many fish are lost as the hook cannot find a secure hold.

Piers are good vantage points from which to floatfish or spin for garfish. They are very good to eat, being rich and oily, but some people are put off by their green bones.

Right: A big mackerel is a handsome fish, and this one caught by angling photographer Mike Millman weighed 2¼ lb (1.02 kg) and took a squid strip. Most big mackerel are taken deep down on baits while after other species, such as black or red bream.

Fresh from the sea a big plaice is a very attractive fish with its brilliant orange spots on a smooth olive-brown background.

Fishing from piers, breakwaters, and rocky projections giving access to deep, clean-bottomed water is carried on in the same basic way as from the beach. Of course, a big rectangular dropnet is needed to bring up the fish once it has been played close to the base of the pier, but otherwise there is little need to say anything further. The fact that some anglers advise the use of rods 8–9 ft (2.4–2.7 m) in length for piers etc, holds no water; the long rod not only casts further, absorbs sudden strains quicker, but it also helps to push a fish out when it tries to gain sanctuary of rough piles, concrete supports and the like.

Boat fishing for cod can be done in two ways: bottom fishing with bait, as for shore situations, and lure fishing. Boat fishing with the bait legered can also be subdivided into fishing shallowish water where the tidal stream is not vicious, and fishing deep fast water well offshore. And the boat may be a 12 ft (3.6 m) dinghy used up to maybe 2 miles (3.2 km) from shore with two anglers aboard or a 40 ft (12.1 m) charter boat with eight or more anglers.

Lure fishing can be dealt with quite summarily. It is mostly done over deep water and over a wreck or reef where cod are known to gather. The lure can be a pirk, usually a chrome-plated, banana-shaped or elongated, faceted, diamond-shaped piece of metal, weighing from as little as 6 oz to as much as 2 lb (170 g to almost 1 kg), or a king-size version of mackerel feathers, usually white.

The lure is fished on a 12, 20 or 30 lb class boat rod (5.4, 9 or 13.6 kg), depending on the water depth and weight of lure, and allowed to tap the bottom before being lifted about 1 yd (1 m) and being jigged sharply up and down with short rod movements. Long lifts are both unnecessarily exhausting and less effective. A trace of three feather or plastic lures with the lead at the bottom of the trace is fished in the same way.

However, so far as the sportfisher and his light tackle is concerned, the use of more than one hook or lure is not advised, since shoaling fish can be hooked two or more at a time, which does not, as might be thought, add to the fight but simply allows one fish to pull against the other, thus causing tackle breakage. Also, sporting anglers eschew the pirk or jig because its use results in a high proportion of foulhooked cod, fish that may try to grab the lure but are instead hooked outside the mouth, in the eye, or many other parts of the body by the upward jerk of the rod.

Lure fishing is only really useful in clear water.

On the other hand, cod fishing with legered gear from a boat can be excellent sport. Using one of the conventional boat rods in the 12–30 lb (5.4–13.6 kg) range the bait, which may be a big bunch of lugworms, crab, whelks, sprats (single or a bunch),

half a fresh herring, a whole small squid, or a strip of a large squid or cuttlefish, is dropped overboard and allowed to touch bottom. It may be left with a suitable weight to hold it there, or lifted and bounced downtide to cover some 50 yd (45.7 m) behind the boat. Weights for such boat work may be simple cones with the loop at the apex. The trace is the same as that for stingray, as is the running lead on a link swivel.

Usually 12 lb (5.4 kg) or 20 lb (9 kg) class rods and lines will be adequate, but in very deep water well offshore where up to 2 lb (1 kg) of lead might have to be used to reach bottom, it may be necessary to increase the gear to 30 lb (13.6 kg) class. That condition is met in very few places.

Up to this point no mention has been made of the use of the wire line outfit for boat fishing. The reason is that, although wire is used for conger and ling fishing in very deep, fast-flowing water, it is not a good idea for a number of reasons.

For example, should a big fish break the wire line, or should a bad snag be encountered which makes a deliberate break-off necessary, not only is the second action dangerous, due to the cutting power of thin steel wire under great tension, but when it does break the slack wire off the reel will undoubtedly form a terrible tangle and will have to be cut from beyond the rod tip.

So, wire should ideally not be used on rough ground for big fish, but it does permit good fishing to continue at periods of strong tidal flow that make normal lines either unusable or distasteful, due to the great amount of lead that has to be used to keep the tackle down.

It is as well to keep a reel loaded with 30 lb (13.6 kg) stainless-steel single-strand wire in the boat kit, or a spare spool for a reel such as the 9000 series, or Penns and Mitchells with quick take-down systems – not for level-line reels. The spool should have been filled as described in chapter 2. Always keep the end of the wire taped tight round the spool in some way; an elastic band serves the same purpose. Failure to do this results in the line springing off to form a terrible coil which is not easily untangled.

Any terminal tackle has to be attached to the wire line on a separate length of nylon monofilament as this will permit a running leger set-up without creating angles in the wire, which can kink and break and work-harden and break. The nylon is also a useful buffer when a big fish is hooked as the wire is to all intents and purposes non-stretch.

Six to 10 ft (1.8–3 m) of nylon is about right, and the attachment can be made by forming a loop in the end of the wire line by first twisting for four turns, the

The Albright Knot
for joining wire to nylon monofilament

Having made a loop, by twisting the end of the wire, pass the nylon through and begin wrapping over the wire loop back towards the point where the nylon was inserted.

Keep the turns touching by holding them with finger and thumb.

As the turns build up the pressure begins to close the loop. After about a dozen turns pass end of nylon through wire loop in the opposite direction to that which it was passed originally.

Pull on both the main line and the tag ends to snug turns into position. Trim off the end leaving approximately ⅛ in (3 mm).

thumb and forefinger holding both strands of wire, then turning the tag-end at a right angle to the standing part of the wire and wrapping it around the standing part in close, touching turns (like whipping) 10 times. This loop is permanently left on the line, as well as the length of nylon, which may be attached using the Albright knot.

The running swivel or boom is put on to the nylon terminal piece, after which the trace is added in the normal way via a barrel or box swivel.

It is important when using wire always to keep in mind how potentially dangerous it is. Keep fingers clear of it when it is under any degree of tension and never try to free it from a snag using fingers, gloved hand or by wrapping it round a length of wood etc, as is usual with other lines. Always keep wire cutters handy for such jobs!

Also remember that roller rings at tip and butt, preferably all through, are necessary to fish wire successfully, else the wire will kink and snap or work-harden and snap.

So, wire is not often used in sportfishing but when it is needed, nothing else will do the job half as well.

The cod is the only species in this book for which wire line is fully recommended in special circumstances.

If there are only six friends sharing a big boat, then casting away from the boat with the boatcaster (uptide) rods and matching tackle will be useful for, say, half the party: the casting covers the seabed at the sides of the boat while the dropped-down conventional gear gets the cod that come up the tide from behind the boat or drop down in line with the bows.

Casting uptide and from the sides of a dinghy, especially in shallow water, is a deadly way of fishing and will, of course, permit the bottom to be held with lighter leads than otherwise, as is the case with beach fishing. Great care must be taken when casting from a crowded boat as serious injuries will result if the lead or hook hits a fellow angler as the power stroke is made.

When fishing downtide from the boat the bite is likely to be a sudden heavy drag, in which case a firm lift of the rod is all that is necessary to sink the hook; however, the casting system mostly results in a nod or two of the rod tip, followed by fast slackening of the line and further trembles as the lead is lifted from its anchorage and trundles round on the seabed. The fish is often only skin-hooked and it is necessary to wind rapidly until the weight of the fish is felt before striking firmly. Failure to follow this advice will result in many lost fish.

In strong currents a big cod can impose a terrific pull on the tackle by simply opening its mouth and increasing water resistance; whether it does this deliberately or whether it is due to exhaustion after battle is immaterial. What is important is that the light tackle angler recognises this fact and does not try to force the fish to the surface or haul it uptide to the boat 'just to have a look'. In the words of the proverb . . . 'softly, softly catchee monkey'.

There are times when vast shoals of whiting and pouting prove a nuisance to the cod fisher, either from the shore or boat. From a boat the answer is either to move, thus trying to avoid them, or to use a large dead one of their number mounted on a 6/0 hook and legered.

From the shore the problem is made worse. The favourite cod bait in this situation, the lugworm, is torn to pieces and pulled off the hook quickly by the hordes; and even if one wishes to kill one of them and cast it out for a big cod, the size, weight and shape of a dead whiting or pouting makes adequate distances remote. There is a way, though, to fish a big fish way out, and a live one at that!

The ordinary snood is used, but having knotted on the 5/0 hook, a tag-end of about six inches (15 cm) of nylon is left. To this is tied a size 1 hook which is positioned about two inches from the big hook. The little hook is baited with an inch or so (3 cm) of lug.

The rig for fishing a live whiting at long range. The large hook is a salmon-fly hook whipped with Terylene to the nylon snood, the turns afterwards being well varnished.

A beaten cod rolls belly up at the side of the boat. Note that the hook is only just inside the bottom lip. Any strong hauling might have ripped it free, but gentle yet firm handling made sure of some tasty fillets.

The long-distance cast is made and the line tightened up. Soon a whiting or pouting will rattle the rod tip: leave it well alone. After a minute or so your livebait has swallowed the lug and the little hook and is struggling to get free from the restricting lead. As its struggles cause vibrations and scale flashes a large cod will home in and grab it – the vast mouth engulfing it – and thus swallow the big hook which by now, as the fish is swallowed head-first, is lying alongside the whiting's gills.

The rod tip goes heeling over and the strike is made, the big hook getting the cod in the throat or mouth.... Very big fish are caught this way, but often this is a waiting game since there are many other live fishes out there apart from the one on the hook.

Some areas of coastline seldom get runs of cod proper, only codling of up to about 4 lb (1.8 kg). However, the use of the salmon spinning rod with 7 lb

(3.1 kg) line and 1 oz (28 g) of lead, where tidal conditions are gentle, will provide some shore sport. In a boat the baitcasting rod, light lead and 7 lb line will do likewise.

Finally, although the cod is certainly not among the top fighting species in British waters, it can sometimes be surprising. There was the time when, having taken half a dozen cod up to double figures from a Kent beach, the author was thinking of packing up, the tide being on the ebb and well down the beach. He was 20 yd (18.2 m) away from his rod and gutting his catch when a noise caused him to look up, just in time to see his rod pulled out of the rest and set off down the shingle at a rapid rate. He had to sprint and do a rugger tackle on the extreme end of the butt as it was disappearing into the waves. The cod that resulted from the ensuing five-minute fight weighed only 12 lb (5.3 kg) but was short and thick and extremely beautiful.

This indicates that if the rod is left to fish for itself it is essential that the drag is light and the check on, so that if a large fish does grab and rush off, the rod and reel will not be lost – it happens every season, many times.

9 Coalfish and pollack

These two members of the cod family share many similarities of body shape and fin conformation. The coalfish, *Pollachius virens*, is silvery-grey with a dark green, almost black back, the flanks being rounded and marked by a white straight lateral line. This fish grows to more than 30 lb (13.6 kg), but the bigger specimens over about 6 lb (2.7 kg) are found only in deep water over offshore wrecks and reefs. A good coalfish weighs 15 lb (6.8 kg) or so and the chance of catching heavyweights is best in winter when the hens are carrying big roes.

Small coalfish of about 1 lb (450 g) form huge shoals and roam inshore rocky waters for small fish. They are of little interest to sportfishers, except perhaps as bait for other species.

The coalfish swims on both sides of the Atlantic, but in American and Canadian waters, where it has been caught to over 40 lb (18.1 kg), it is called 'pollock', just to add to the general confusion on fish names.

The pollack, *Pollachius pollachius*, does not swim on

Artificial sand-eels are also good lures for big coalfish, too. This 26½-pounder (12.0 kg) was caught off the Cornish coast.

the American side of the Atlantic. It is a less rounded fish than the coalfish, softer all round, with a beautiful green back and olive and gold flanks. The pollack also swims in much shallower water than the coalfish; fish up to about 12 lb (5.4 kg) being caught from rocky shores where there is 15–40 ft (4.5–12.1 m) of water.

In sportfishing terms, the worthwhile coalfish can normally be caught only from a boat, usually in depths of over 20 fathoms (36.5 m) while the pollack, which reaches weights of 25 lb (11.3 kg) or more in deep water, does provide excellent shore and inshore boat fishing. Devon, Cornwall, the Isle of Man, Scotland and its islands and also Ireland's west coast are good coalfish areas. Iceland is superb in this respect.

Coalfish are superb. This one weighed 26 lb (11.7 kg) and was taken in the West Country by Tony Allan.

Coalfish

First, then, coalfish from a boat way offshore. Winter weather conditions sometimes make the distant wrecks and reefs unreachable and summer and autumn fishing is more reliable.

Ideally for sportfishing the big trawler-type boat that specialises in deep-water wreck and reef fishing should be chartered by only six like-minded anglers, although one or two such enthusiasts can sometimes persuade those fishing for bottom fish on a wreck to allow them places in the stern to fish with light gear. As has been stressed earlier, light tackle fishing from a crowded boat is the way to frayed tempers.

The boat will either mark the wreck or reef with a small buoy or buoys, called dans, then anchor uptide so that the baits may be fished down into the rough ground, or the skipper may make repeated slow drifts over the ground, slowing his drift with engine power.

For summer fishing the 12–20 lb outfits will be fine, and once the run of fish has been established one set may be discarded, ie for big fish keep the 20 lb outfit in action; for small fish under 10 lb (4.5 kg) keep the 12 lb outfit, or drop down to use the double-handed spinning rod and 7–8 lb (3.1–3.6 kg) line.

Some regular wreck anglers will scoff at such comments since they regularly use 40 lb (18.1 kg) line and get broken by fish. However, they mostly fish several baits or lures on snoods and when two or more large coalfish can pull against each other the heavy line or trace will not stand the strain.

Light tackle work means one bait or lure and one hook. The best way to fish is with a 10 in (25.4 cm) long stainless-steel wire boom, fixed by its lower eye to the wire loop of the lead with a split ring and attached to the main line via a link swivel tied to the end of the line. The free eye of the boom takes another link swivel, about size 4, to which is tied the hook trace, 15–20 ft (4.5–6 m) of nylon monofilament.

Coalfish do not bite through traces but they have hard mouths and fight with such speed and energy that they can quickly wear through thin, soft nylon. Choose a hard nylon for the trace. For 12 lb (5.4 kg) class or thereabouts the trace should be 25 lb (11.3 kg) test; for 20 lb (9 kg) class tackle the trace should be about 30 lb (13.6 kg) test. Even when using the spinning rod and 7–8 lb (3.1–3.6 kg) line, keep the trace at 20 lb (9 kg) test.

The hook, when bait fishing, can be about size 4/0 and should be strong and forged, the O'Shaughnessy pattern being very suitable. The bait should be cut in a long, slim strip, whether it be mackerel, squid or whatever; a whole big sand-eel is a very fine coalfish bait.

Coalfish tend to increase in size as the depth increases, the bigger specimens of 20 lb (9 kg) or so being taken in 40 fathoms (73 m) or more. So, by asking the skipper the depth on the echo-sounder as the mark is passed over, it is often possible to select the tackle outfit that will suit the size of fish.

The use of the wire boom in this instance serves a very useful purpose: it prevents the long trace tangling round the main line as the gear is let down over the side of the boat.

When the lead, which may need to be 6 oz–1 lb (170–453 g) taps bottom, the reel is put in gear – making sure the drag is properly set to the line test – and a slow, steady retrieve is begun. Often the fish will take soon after the bait begins to lift from the wreck or reef; at other times the fish will follow into midwater, then take with a bang that continues in a crash-dive of almost frightening speed and power. The fish must be given line, but not too much or it will make the wreck and cut the line. Frequently the bait is taken on the way down, as it nears the bottom, and in this instance the tackle must be tested to the utmost to prevent snagging.

Coalfish do not suffer as much from decompression as other fish do and will fight from the depths to the surface. A big strong net is a good way of bringing coalfish aboard and if this can be arranged the fish may be returned and will be able to get down to the depths again.

The famous Red Gill sand-eel is the best of the artificials, and it is fished on the same tackle as the moving bait, and in the same way. Also good is a pirk, especially on snaggy wrecks, and it helps to tip the big treble or single hook with a strip of fresh mackerel or squid.

Left: Not just sheer cliffs but an overhang – yet the angler got down to fish. This is Brandon Creek in Kerry where congers, pollack, ballan wrasse, mullet, mackerel, garfish and other species may be caught at one time.

Right: A big pollack is a handsome creature and a worthy opponent on light tackle.

A famous light tackle angler, Rita Barrett, shows a 22 lb (9.9 kg) wreck pollack taken on a 28 oz (794 g) pirk.

This is the famous Eddystone Light marking the reef of the same name, where pollack, ling, conger and bream are caught and where big bass once shoaled in their thousands – before the commercial fishermen reduced their numbers.

In winter, when the very heavy females are about, fishing a wreck is best done with either a pirk or just one Red Gill fished on a snood about 1 ft (30.4 cm) long and about 3 ft (91 cm) above the lead. Such gear will often be taken as the lure goes down and the short snood or single pirk tends to tangle less with the wreck than a long snood. If fish do repeatedly break 20 lb (9 kg) tackle, increase to 30 lb (13.6 kg) with 30 lb trace.

Reefs usually hold smaller coalfish than do the wrecks, and it is on the reefs that the long spinning rod and lighter line come into their own. A very subtle touch is necessary to hold the fighting fish just within the margin of strain the tackle will stand, and the longer rod is well able to cushion the sharp dives and directional changes of the fish.

Pollack

Much of the boat technique for coalfish also holds for deep-water pollack of the wrecks and reefs. However, there is seldom – if ever – any need to use tackle heavier than the 20 lb (9 kg) class outfit for pollack, and usually the 12 lb (5.4 kg) outfit or the long spinning rod with line around 8 lb (3.6 kg) test will be found suitable.

The long trace with the Red Gill is perhaps the most deadly of all methods for pollack from the boat, be it in very deep water or shallower water on a reef. However, the baits worked as for coalfish also do well.

Reef pollack run about 4–8 lb (1.8–3.6 kg) on average with the occasional double-figure specimen. On a newly found wreck the average can be more than 12 lb (5.4 kg).

Pollack usually take the moving natural or artificial bait more gently than a coalfish does. The lead touches, the reel is engaged and winding begins. Perhaps after a few turns a tap will be felt. Do nothing. Just wind on. There comes another light tap. Wind on. This can continue to mid-water or even to within a few feet of the boat, then the rod tip is felt to become heavy and a firm lift will set the hook.

Like the coalfish, the pollack is a crash-dive artist *par excellence*, and trying to slow and stop the fish before it reaches sanctuary is great fun and extremely testing to the tackle and 'hands'.

In some areas there are vast ranges of reefs quite close inshore – such as in Devon, Cornwall, Scotland and particularly west and south-west Ireland – where the water depth is about 30–40 ft (9.1–12.1 m) and dinghy fishing for pollack is fun, especially with the spinning outfit. With the small multiplier with 10 lb (4.5 kg) line or fixed-spool reel carrying line of about

7 lb (3.1 kg) test, casts are made from a slowly drifting or anchored boat. Use either a Red Gill with about 1½ oz (42.5 g) of lead in the form of a bomb on a nylon link about 4 in (10 cm) long and suspended from the top eye of the swivel, which joins reel line to 3 ft (91 cm) trace, or a 4 in (10 cm) goat hair fly on a 3/0 O'Shaughnessy hook. White and orange or white and blue hair is good, whipped tightly round the shank of the hook beside the eye with strong thread and varnished. An alternative lure is a heavyweight wobbling spoon, 1 oz (28 g) or so in weight, such as

Right: Obviously Scottish angler David Wilson thought the terrible climb he has just completed was worthwhile. A nice shore pollack is brought back to the hotel. They are very tasty when filleted and smoked.

This superb pollack weighed 25½ lb (11.5 kg) and took an artificial sand-eel fished in winter over a wreck off the Devonshire coast.

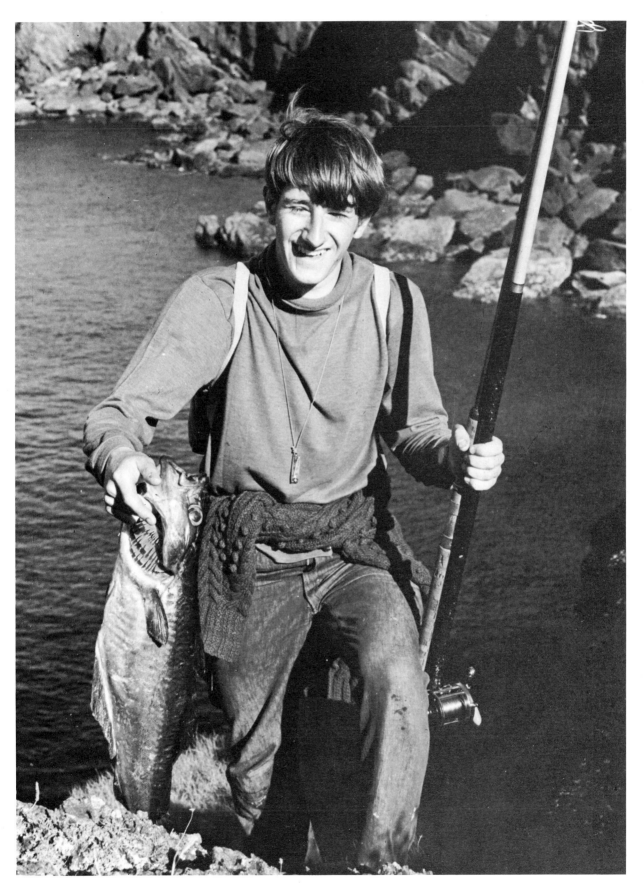

Koster, Toby, Condor and Ellips. No additional weight is used on the spoons.

The first cast must be counted down and the seconds memorised once the lead or lure taps the rock. Each cast must reach the same depth, the recovery being started just before the last number is reached, so that snagging is kept to a minimum. It is essential, however, to 'live dangerously', for a lure that swims too high over the kelp-covered rocks will often be left alone by pollack.

Even when chasing the spun lure the take of the pollack is initially gentle, the rod tip just becoming heavy, followed by the judder and crash-dive as the fish feels the hook and panics.

It is essential to keep the rod tip high when striving to prevent the pollack reaching sanctuary. It is amazing what elasticity there is in a long spinning rod.

Shore fishing for pollack may be the best of all pollack fishing situations so far as sportfishing is concerned. The atmosphere is different when one is perched, perhaps somewhat precariously, on a rocky ledge above the surging green and white-laced water as it sucks and gurgles below, the rocks' dark patches on a sandy ground, maybe, the weed waving like a massive mermaid's hair.

Spinning is the most used and most productive method and it is carried out like that done from the dinghy. However, it is easier to see the rocky outcrops, the deep gullies between them shown by darker water, and to make long searching casts, testing depths, maybe bringing the lure along a rock face deep under water and only a yard out. Besides the high perches one is usually forced to use facilitating seeing into the water, they also enable the angler to see much of the fight of the pollack, its golden flanks flashing deep down as it dives and struggles.

Usually one has only to beat the pollack's initial dive to land it, since the subsequent struggles are seldom so severe, though some fish fight harder than others.

It is best to fish rocks where pollack swim in the company of one other experienced angler at least, both to permit the landing of the fish by dropnet and for safety's sake: clambering down cliffs and over slippery rocks to reach the best pollack grounds is a calculated risk; alone it is asking for trouble. Always be watchful of the occasional bigger-than-usual wave for they can come from nowhere and sweep the unwary to death. Venture with extra care on to rocks that are wet with spray; try to remain at least 6 ft (1.8 m) above the water's highest surges.

Another excellent light-tackle method is float-fishing. The long spinning rod will serve well, used with fixed-spool reel and 7–8 lb (3.1–3.6 kg) test monofilament. The float should be a balsa-wood or modern plastic type, cigar-shaped with a central hole, lined with plastic tube in the case of the balsa type. A bead larger than the tube through the float is threaded on the line before the float, and a stop-knot of nylon or elastic, or a linen thread is tied on the line at the depth at which the bait is to be fished. It should drift about 5 ft (1.5 m) above the rocks.

The hook should be forged, about 1/0, and on a yard (91 cm) of nylon. The trace is joined to the main line by a number 8 swivel, above which a barrel, pierced ball, Hillman or other lead of about ½ oz (14 g) is fitted.

The bait should be a 4 × 1 in (10 × 2.5 cm) fillet of fresh mackerel, garfish, herring, squid, or king ragworm, perhaps even live prawn, although the latter seems a little wasteful when much more easily come by and easily kept baits are satisfactory. A live sandeel, of course, is the absolute ultimate pollack bait for float-fishing, and if they are available and can be kept alive (or freshly killed) on ice, they will be worth the work of collection and carriage. The good fresh mackerel strip, though, will seldom be ignored.

A final point about pollack fished from the shallower waters along the shore is that, even though they may not often reach double figures like the fish of the deeps offshore, it is possible to catch them and put them back unharmed, with a good chance of survival. Fish from deep water, however, suffer greatly from decompression and most come to the boat with their 'innards' protruding from their mouths, and they cannot swim back down if they are returned to the sea.

Seeing that reduces the pleasure of offshore pollack fishing: every gallant fighting fish a dead fish.

10 Halibut

A few years ago the halibut was given the big public relations treatment by tourist agencies in Scotland, the northern isles and in Iceland. Until about the past 18 years little was heard about halibut in angling circles. In fact, it appeared that very few had been caught at all on rod and line in British and European waters, the most publicised being an 84-pounder (38.1 kg) by Leslie Moncrieff, the famous English sea angler, who caught it in deep water on rough ground south of Valentia on Ireland's south-west coast. The Irish record halibut of 152 lb (68.9 kg) was also taken there.

Within the past few years, however, the PR work has produced good results. First Orkney, then Shetland, and finally Iceland hit the headlines by producing fine halibut for the adventurous few, who were prepared to break new ground and could afford the expense. And more recently, the rugged ground off Caithness has rewarded those who kept faith and fished consistently. Other Scottish grounds also hold this giant flatfish that bears the superb scientific name *Hippoglossus hippoglossus*.

Perhaps most halibut taken by anglers in the past few years or so have come from Iceland's Breidafjordur during late summer. This recently discovered fishery has not only produced more fish – including many 20–50 lb fish (9–22.6 kg) that are ideal for the light-tackle angler – but it has done so in depths of only 15–20 fathoms (27.4–36.5 m) as opposed to the more usual halibut haunts of twice that depth. Lots of modest halibut in shallow water not affected by savage tides – truly ideal for sportfishing!

However, Iceland is a long journey for a tilt at a halibut if you live in Southern England. . . .

Not one angler in a thousand who fishes British saltwater has caught a halibut, and most of those who have, have done so on heavy tackle – 80–100 lb (36.2–45.3 kg) line. A few pioneers have used 30 lb (13.6 kg) class outfits with success, but there is little evidence that captures on such gear have included the 100 lb plus (45.3 kg) specimens.

However, since the author is among those who have not actually boated a halibut – though he did

hook and lose one in Orkney – it is difficult to assess the true picture of the halibut as a fighter. But experienced longliners, who regularly catch fish over 100 lb (45.3 kg) or more, have said that if the fish is coaxed gently but firmly to the surface immediately on hooking, without jerking, it will hardly struggle, and a quick stroke with the gaff will secure it. They also add that the fish will begin to fight in the boat and it is so strong that serious damage can be done by a fish boated 'green'.

Many anglers agree with this generalisation, but if the fish does become alarmed at the upward move and dives, to try to stop it reaching bottom is to risk breakage of even heavy gear. Yet the experienced anglers also say that if the fish is allowed to make the dives to the bottom against safe drag pressure, it can be coaxed to the top again, perhaps to come to gaff then, or make more dives before doing so. Thus, it appears that the usual game of give and take and patience works on the halibut as it does on most fish. But it will not work with 30 lb (13.6 kg) gear in 40 fathoms (73 m) or more of fast-flowing water! Not when the vast flattie weighs well over 100 lb (45.3 kg).

The halibut is a fish-eater, and in the Icelandic fishery inshore is thought to feed largely on lumpsuckers and sea scorpions. Baits of herring, mackerel, coalfish, whiting, codling and squid will be taken.

Halibut reach enormous weights – a fish which weighed over 600 lb (272 kg) after being gutted was taken off Massachusetts, and specimens of over 500 lb (226 kg) have been caught by the longliners off Iceland. In spite of the fact that such monsters are beyond the scope of this book, since they are usually taken in extremely deep water where vicious tides also occur, it is well to remember that British anglers have taken fish of over 200 lb (90.7 kg) on lines testing 50 lb (22.6 kg) or under.

Only the 30 lb (13.6 kg) and 50 lb (22.6 kg) class outfits detailed in chapter 2 can be matched to the halibut in any sensible way and even then the reel must play a very important part. Top choice should be a lever-drag model though rugged star-drag reels like

Leslie Moncrieff (right) with the 84 lb (38.1 kg) halibut
which he caught off Valentia Island in Southern Ireland.
This fish, unlike so many others caught by anglers, fought
very vigorously.

Penn Senators 4/0 or 6/0 and similarly built reels by Daiwa, like the SL600H, or Shakespeare's Sigma series are suitable. The exception to this advice can occur when, in places like the Breidafjordur, there are lots of small halibut in shallow and comparatively slow-moving water, in which case a 20 lb (9 kg) class outfit might be used.

Terminal tackle is usually made up with fishing on the drift in mind since halibut, like many predatory fish, have a penchant for a moving bait. A small Clements boom, or a big link-swivel is first run up the line and a swivel big enough to stop the weight-carrying link-swivel or boom from running down the trace is tied to the end. A trace of 80–100 lb (36.2–45.3 kg) test commercial monofilament, 4–6 ft (1.2–1.8 m) long, is connected to the free eye of the stop swivel, and another strong barrel swivel tied to the end. This swivel is linked to about 10 in (25.4 cm) of cabled trace wire by crimping, and on to its free end is slid a silver spoon with a split ring through the hole in the narrow end. A bead and about 2 in (5 cm) of brass or hard plastic tubing keeps the spoon away from the eye of a strong forged 6/0 hook, an O'Shaughnessy or Seamaster for preference.

The spoon flashes as the tackle drags along on or bumping the seabed and is an additional attraction to the fish. The late Reg Quest, who was a kingpin of the British Conger Club, brought back this spoon idea from Iceland following an exploratory trip for *Angling* magazine, reporting that it did better than traces without a spoon and was at its best with the angler working the tackle to keep bait and flasher lifting and dropping as the drift proceeded. Ivor Kilbourn, another keen British angler, gave Reg the tip-off.

To quote Reg: 'I would have no hesitation in using the same tackle on a future visit (50 lb IGFA) but the 30 lb (13.6 kg) tackle, although adequate over the inshore areas where the depths were not great and the tides very small, might be overstrained on a really big fish when the sheer dead weight might have to be pumped up to the surface, for although such tackle could handle the running fish, the accumulated weight might be too heavy to lift.'

The author's only comment here is that since other free-swimming species of the size reached by halibut are beaten on 30 lb (13.6 kg) gear, there is reason to expect some success with the giant flatties, although the deep, strong water is the main opponent of that success, not the halibut itself, since coaxing will persuade almost any fish to come to the surface, provided it is a live fish and not a dead or dying one. . . .

Peter Peck of ABU, the tackle company, is a confirmed light tackle angler. He is illustrated holding an Icelandic halibut.

The flasher spoon can be seen just outside this 105½ lb
(47.8 kg) halibut's mouth as it is gaffed aboard an Icelandic
boat.

11 Bass

The bass is one of Britain's most beautiful saltwater fish. Green or blue backed, silvery or brassy flanks, a stark white belly and large, strong fins, the head bony and ending in a vast mouth; it is a real anglers' fish. It reaches an ultimate size of over 20 lb (9 kg), but many anglers go to the grave not having caught a double-figure specimen. A good bass weighs 8 lb (3.6 kg) and fish of 2–3 lb (1–1.3 kg) are called school-bass because they tend to form big schools or shoals.

Bass are slow growing and long-lived: fish of 10 lb (4.5 kg) may be 15 years old in southern England, more than that in western Ireland. Bass over about 4 lb (1.8 kg) or so are nearly all hens, though some cock fish of 7 lb (3.1 kg) or so have been taken, mainly in south-eastern England. Any 10-pounder (4.5 kg) can be relied on to be a hen

In spite of all this, it was common until about 20

Estuaries provide excellent bass habitat. This fine fish was caught in south west England.

years ago to find most anglers using big, stiff rods, heavy leads, and lines of at least 20 lb (9 kg) test for bass fishing from the shore. In fact, some still use that outmoded gear. But since the bass attracts such angling pressure, it – like the cod – has been responsible for much of the trend towards lighter, more sporting tackle.

Bass, though greatly reduced in numbers by commercial exploitation, offer great opportunities for varied angling techniques. They will pick up a legered bait in the wild combers of a clear-water Atlantic surf beach, like those in south-west Ireland, west Wales and the West Country of England, coming into a foot of water to do so; they will swim among rocky, weed-draped gullies searching for

One cannot fish bass in the surf with tackle much lighter than this. John Darling shows a thick fish taken on a carp rod, tiny ABU 2100 reel and 10 lb (4.5 kg) line.

crabs, prawns and small fish, where legering or spinning or float-fishing may work; they move into estuaries and swim far up tidal rivers, where spinning, legering and float-fishing will catch them, and in rivermouths with extensive banks or rock outcrops; they will also come to the skilful fly fisher, as they will when the whitebait or sand-eel shoals are herded in the waves of steep shingle beaches during calm settled weather in late summer and autumn, or when the bass shoal up in thousands over offshore reefs. And on the reefs spinning, trolling, driftlining may all be expected to work on their day.

Bass can be sensitive and difficult to catch, but at times they can become almost suicidal, being caught in multiple hook-ups on mackerel feathers fished from boats. They will sometimes fight extremely hard, especially in clear water, but at other times they can be extremely sluggish opponents, hardly resisting rod pressure, indeed sometimes swimming into the angler and almost beaching themselves.

Bass fishing takes the angler to superb scenery, and since the best of this is the wild surf-pounded strands of south-west Ireland with the Kerry mountains as a backdrop, it is surfcasting on these storm beaches that will be dealt with first.

A rod of 10½–11½ ft (3.2–3.5 m) and to cast 2–3 oz (56–85 g) using 10–15 lb (4.5–6.8 kg) lines, is the one to choose, with the small multiplier or, alternatively, the fixed-spool reel. With surf bass averaging 4 lb (1.8 kg) or thereabouts, 10–15 lb test might at first appear to be stronger than necessary, but the gear has to be cast 100 yd (91.4 m) at times, and it has perhaps to cope with heavy rafts of weed and the abrasion of sand.

Top bait on surf beaches is lugworm, with clam, razorfish and sand-eel close followers. In autumn squid will catch the larger fish at the cost to the angler of obtaining fewer bites from modest fish.

The terminal tackle is simple: a single-hook fixed nylon paternoster made up in exactly the same way as for cod from the beach, except that the hook should be from 1/0–4/0, depending on the bait size used, and made of fine wire: Mustad's numbers 79510 and 79515 are favoured by most bass addicts.

Some anglers make up running paternosters for surf bass, but experience has proved them to be unnecessary: such well-known bass anglers as Ireland's Des Brennan and Kevin Linnane, Clive Gammon, John Darling, among others, use the fixed paternoster. It does not tangle, gives immediate signal of a bite, and, used with a breakaway lead and a very sharp hook, can result in many fish just skin-hooking themselves as they turn away with the bait, whereas a running line can give a fish warning by *slowly* increasing tension, at which the bait can be ejected in a flash. The fixed line brings the fish up *sharply*.

Casts of 40–100 odd yd (36.5–91.4 m) are the usual range, and chest waders are best when it is found necessary to wade well out into a rough surf to cast beyond the worst turbulence. In fact they are best at all times for true surfcasting since one can stand out in the troughs waist-deep when awaiting a bite; this shortens the line to the lead and bait, which means a faster strike and less line stretch. Failing chest waders, which are very expensive, thighboots will do, but wear oilskin or PVC over-trousers over them and put strong elastic bands over the lot at ankle level to prevent waves seeping up. Bib-type trousers with shoulder straps are best.

Since most of the bass will, I hope, be unhooked

Winter bass fishing in the white water of Derrynane Strand in Kerry. In the off season for tourists, the country is peaceful and the scenery breathtaking. Besides good bass, excellent flounders may be caught, too.

and returned to the sea alive immediately, it is best to carry all the gear you need on you, because the need for a new hook, lead, swivel or bait often entails a walk of more than 300 yd (274 m) over wet sand to the dry base or the car in the dunes; and further if you've walked *along* the beach, too! Breast pockets on a waterproof parka or anorak will keep following low water, there is no hard and fast rule of thumb on timing. Bass roam surf beaches and can turn up at any time during the tide, and sometimes the best fishing will come after high water and right down the ebb. The high water period – lasting about an hour – is usually a slack period for bites, but even then there are exceptions. For daylight fishing plenty of surf rolling in from about 200 yd (182.8 m) out is desirable, conditions which can follow a local onshore blow or a vast storm way out in the Atlantic. At night surf is still needed, but bass will come very close inshore after dark when there is little in the way of white water. Dull days can be better than sunny days, but again radiant sunshine, blue sky and a roaring surf have produced superb fishing.

One hears advice about 'casting to the third breaker where the bass lie' – as if the fish were glued to the sea-bed at that point. It helps to cast about 50 yd (45.7 m) for a start in a moderate surf and extend casts seaward from there until fish are contacted. Failing that, try shorter casts: bass will often take in the swash of the last comber as it runs up and down the clean sand, the water calf-deep. Good spots to try are where freshwater streams cross the beach, or where there are gullies or banks of sand – made visible by the pattern of the breaking waves seen from a distance, preferably above on the mountainside.

On these surf beaches there is very rarely any trouble from lateral tidal currents, the breakers running in straight up the line from the position of the lead. In such cases, for maximum comfort and sensitivity, it may be found best to cradle the rod along the forearm, butt under the arm, the tip pointing down, either straight at the lead or, as the author prefers, at an angle of about 60 degrees from the lead pointing slightly out to sea and along the line of the surf.

This latter stance gives quick response to a rapid pull or pluck or a rapidly occurring slack line, the body and arm simply swinging away from the direction of the lead and bait. The rod must be held always when surf fishing for bass, else many fish will be missed. Sometimes even the most comfortable stance will impose strain on arm or back, in which case try a suitable alternative for a few minutes, such as back to the sea and the rod 'at the slope' over the shoulder. A strike can be quickly made from that position, too, and it is particularly useful when holding the rod tip high to keep the line clear of drifting weed inshore, which can be a big problem after a prolonged onshore gale.

Bass bites in the surf vary from slack lines, a few fast taps followed by a firm pull, a mind-bending

Fishing from a rocky ledge at the base of a sheer cliff in Sussex, Ian Gillespie caught this 6½ lb (2.9 kg) bass on peeler crab legered in the boulders. The rod is made from a freshwater carp rod blank.

things fairly dry; if it's too warm to wear any form of jacket, then both the bait and the end-tackle spares may be carried in a small canvas or plastic bag round the neck.

Although most surf beaches fish well on the flooding tide, particularly during the first two hours lunge, the savagery of which can take the rod from the hand of the unwary, or a gentle sucking sensation. All must be struck, all must be recognised. To be able to do this consistently takes time and persistence.

Bass in the surf usually make short, jagging runs immediately on being hooked. Then they either race inshore, the angler running back to help the reel take up the slack line, or they kite along the crests of the rollers. The occasional fish, not always a monster, will rush out to sea, the clutch on the reel whining, for maybe 30 yd (27.4 m) or so. In the swash of the final wave the shoots up the beach and rushes back like a torrential river, a bass can rush around and put a lot of strain on the line. Keep the rod tip up and the drag light, thumb or finger pressure on the spool to provide sensitive control of any lunges.

A damp piece of towel or similar, kept in a pocket or the little bag, is useful for handling fish while

unhooking without leaving the water. The fish is held in the cloth under the arm and cradled along the forearm while the hook is disengaged. One has only to stoop and let the fish slide from the cloth into the water. For those who don't know, beware of the sharp spines on the dorsal fins of the bass, also the razor-sharp anterior edges of its gills. Very bad gashes can be sustained from these.

When wading out to cast – and when returning to the shallower swash – always watch out for the incoming combers. Time the cast between them: to be hit by a big wave in mid-cast can roll even a heavy man over and up the beach. It is seldom very dangerous, but it can be very uncomfortable and embarrassing!

The slimmer the line used, the less lead it is necessary to use, and the more the bass will be able to fight without the encumbrance of a lead 'necklace'. The 10 lb (4.5 kg) test line is usually ample, but when casting further than 40 yd (36.5 m) the line will break from the sudden shock, even with 2 oz (56.6 g) leads. A leader of 15 lb (6.8 kg) will prevent this happening. If breakaway leads are used it will not be necessary, 99 times out of 100, to use a lead of more than 3 oz (85 g) in any surf beach conditions, and most fishing will be comfortable with 2 oz (56.6 g).

John Darling again, a very successful bass angler and a light tackle fanatic. Here the scene is Sussex rocks at the base of high chalk cliffs, where casting crab baits into the gullies produces exciting tussles with bass like this brace.

Bass in the surf of Kerry and west Cork can be caught all the year round due to the relative consistency of the water temperature. April and May are usually very good months, late September to the end of November excellent, especially for big fish. In the depths of winter bass of 3–6 lb (1.3–2.7 kg) can provide some hectic sport, and although it is likely to be wet and windy, Irish west coast weather is seldom bitterly cold. The winter surfs can be quite magnificent, the power of the waves never to be forgotten.

Bottom fishing for bass in other places, like the steep-to shingle beaches of the southern Irish, Welsh and west, east and south-east of England coastlines can be covered by the same casting outfit in general. The difference lies in the behaviour of the bass and the depth and character of the water.

There will usually be lateral tidal currents with which to contend, and the bass tend not to be so numerous as on surf beaches, where one good angler can catch 20 fish on a good tide. The bass can average 6 lb (2.7 kg) or so, however, and bigger baits of crab, squid or cuttle, half a mackerel (side fillet) or herring, a sand-eel, small pouting or rockling,

Spinning and bottom fishing around old towers in the Thames estuary produces plenty of action with shoaling bass.

bunch of slipper limpets, king ragworm and so on will tend to work.

Bass will work very close in on such beaches with their often turbid water and little wave action, and a running paternoster allows the fish to get the big bait into its mouth and move off without feeling untoward resistance, provided a slack line is fished, thus permitting the angler to set the hook – as big as 5/0 at times – even when awaiting bites over long periods with the rod in a monopod and the reel out of gear but with the audible ratchet on.

Such beaches usually fish best when there is some turbulence after an onshore blow, although at night calm seas can produce fish. In England, and most of Wales, the surf beaches of the extreme west apart, the bass season begins in late April or mid-May and ends about the end of October, only occasional fish being taken in winter. There are some exceptions, warm water outfalls for instance; but even at some atomic power stations the fish have mostly quit by mid-November.

Estuary bass fishing is conducted in a very similar way to that of steep-to beaches, but estuaries vary widely in character and some are confined by man-made structures, deep and fast flowing on flood and ebb; others are wide and natural, with sandbanks, gullies, rocky outcrops *ad infinitum*. On both these steep, deep water beaches – 10 ft (3 m) or more – and

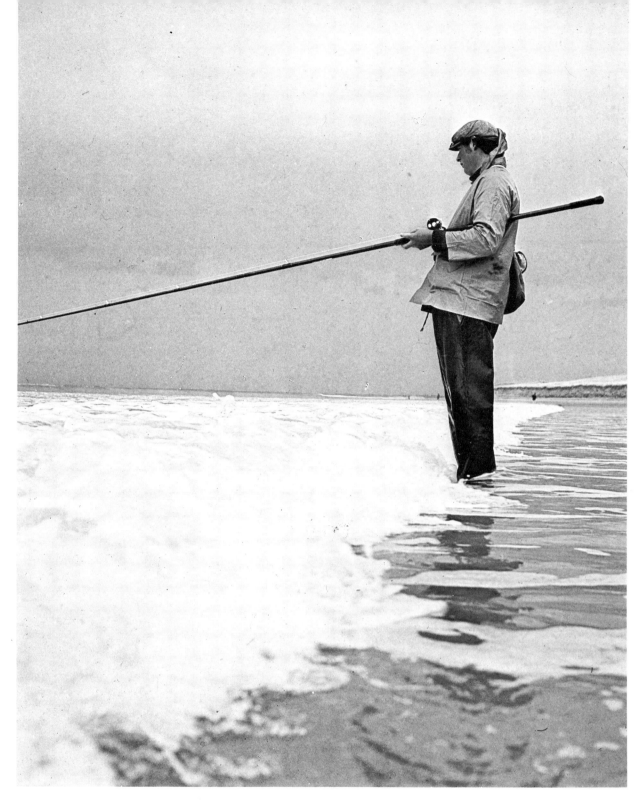

in most estuaries the flood tide fishes best, from just after low water for two hours, then there follows a lull until the last two hours. On some estuaries, though, the ebb fishes best, and some beaches can produce at such times. It pays to know that the estuary of any river fed by acid water draining from moorland can be extremely unpleasant to bass in times of flash floods: the fish will usually move away to pure saltwater until the floodwater is dispersed, and this can even occur when small streams crossing Irish surf beaches run vinegar-hued with peat drainage.

White water rolls around the angler's legs as he points his rod down the line, out to the spot where his lug-baited hook lies in wait for the bass in the surf: Inch strand in County Kerry.

Estuaries sometimes provide very short periods of activity, perhaps only for three hours at the top of the tide, due to very fast currents in their constricted channels on flood and ebb. Also, estuary bass have to be understood, because they move in and out of the rivermouth and up the main channel along very

185

closely defined routes. Never be put off by shallow water when bass fishing, either on open beaches, in estuaries or among rocky foreshores. Depth matters little to the bass; the fish is a wanderer and goes where the food is. The author knows two river-mouths where bass are taken on the ebb in 2 ft (60 cm) of swift water over gravel, whereas a bait placed a short distance away goes unnoticed.

With light lines estuary bass sometimes need careful playing when they get into the full flow of the river's ebb-tide current. Often concrete groynes, wooden breakwaters etc. are good vantage points, both on estuaries and open beaches, but a dropnet is needed to secure the beaten fish.

In many estuaries, especially the more natural ones, and those in which bass run several miles upstream on the flood, the surfcasting rod is unnecessary and the double-handed spinning rod with as light a lead as possible and 6–8 lb (2.7–3.6 kg) line makes a great combination. A good bass, even a six-pounder (2.7 kg) will go well on this outfit.

When wading in rivermouths with sandbanks and channels, always fish with a friend and keep an eye on the incoming tide. It is easy to become engrossed in the fishing and be cut off by the flooding tide.

Various piers and breakwaters at seaside resorts can provide good fishing for bass, by legering any of the deep-water beach baits mentioned, by float-fishing with live prawns, bunters in bunches (they are small, brackish-water shrimps), soft or peeler crab, king ragworm, bunches of white or red ragworms, small live fish, such as pouting, blennies, butterfish, preferably live or else freshly deep-frozen sand-eels, or slim strips cut from mackerel, herring or squid. The tackle is rigged as for float-fishing for pollack from the shore and the bait fished from mid-water to just clear of the bottom.

Bass, like most predators, like to hang in the shadow cast by a pier, bridge or groyne, to dash out at food that comes by. Float-fished baits should be held near such places and even encouraged by the use of currents and wave action to drift under the pier structure. Bass hooked thus need to be held firmly and 10 lb (4.5 kg) line may be necessary, whereas without obstructions – with smooth concrete walls going down into the sea – 6 lb (2.7 kg) line on the double-handed spinning rod will provide some exciting battles.

Fish strips, live small mackerel called joeys, live pouting and so on may be driftlined from the ends of piers and breakwaters where there is sufficient tidal current to take the bait away. Just the baited hook is needed for much of the time, although a small amount of lead may be necessary to get the bait down in stronger flows. A live fish may be guided to swim where the angler wants it to go by judicious gentle twitches in the opposite direction. A single 3/0–5/0 hook nicked through the back of the pouting or mackerel just behind the front dorsal fin works well. When the bass takes, a strong pull is felt, at which line must be allowed to run off in free spool – or the pick-up arm must be open with a fixed-spool reel – for several seconds. The bass will usually go for about 10 yd (9 m) and slow down, then move away in jerks. That is the time to pull the hook into the fish's jaw. But make sure the line is taut first.

Spinning can be good active sport from some piers and seaward projections, provided the water is fairly clear – visibility from above should be for a distance of at least 8 ft (2.4 m) down into the water. Spinning in murky water seldom works for salt-water fish.

The Red Gill sand-eels, the soleskin lure about 3 in long (7.6 cm) with a small mackerel spinner at its head, Toby, Condor, Koster and Ellips heavy-weight wobbling spoons, even a silver Devon minnow about 2 in (5 cm) long with a willow-leaf shaped piece of chamois leather about the same length on one hook of the tail treble, will work at times. Carry a selection. Make casts far out where tide-races form, along weed-covered walls; fish deep and fish shallow, fast and slow. Usually the artificial sand-eel recovered at a modest pace around midwater will find the fish. The wobbling spoons in 1 oz (28 g) or heavier will usually cast far enough and fish deeply enough without additional lead.

For the rubber sand-eel and soleskin lure, a bomb-shaped lead suspended from the top eye of a size 8 swivel, which links a 4 ft (1.2 m) trace of matching nylon to the main line by a few inches of nylon, will serve as sinker, anti-kink device and it will cast much farther than the more usual Wye or spiral spinning leads used.

In a boat, a dinghy close to the shore or a bigger boat way out over reefs or wreckage, shoaling bass may be tackled with trolled Red Gills or spoons, strips of mackerel and squid, or by casting and spinning such lures and baits from an anchored position. When tackling bass from a boat it is usual first to find the shoal by looking for birds working, especially terns. The bass may be feeding on sand-eels, whitebait or shoals of mackerel, even whiting and pouting that are tumbled around in the turbulence of the water flowing at speed over the obstruction. Then it is essential not to motor into the shoal but to keep to the edges, casting along the shoal's edge. A lure right in among the shoal may be ignored; a lone lure wriggling or twinkling along the edge in open water stands a better chance of being taken.

Spinning for bass is usually best in the period from late June to mid-October when there are shoals of either mackerel or of sand-eels, whitebait and sprats.

When fishing from a small boat which forms a stable platform or from steep-to beaches, rocks or wide-open estuaries, this period also produces excellent sport with the fly rod, a technique which has been developed to a high art in saltwater in warmer parts of the world but is yet in its infancy in Britain and Europe. The prerequisite is visible activity near the surface by bass, not necessarily a vast shoal but reasonable numbers of fish showing. Again, as in spinning, clear water is essential to success, as is a quiet approach with the engine turned off and casting along the fringes of the shoal, not into its middle. Dawn and dusk are favourite periods.

The reservoir fly rod and reel suggested in chapter 2 are the backbone of the outfit, and since casts of at least 25 yd (22.8 m) should be easily attainable, even into a stiff breeze at times, with well over 30 yd (27.4 m) when necessary, the obvious choice of fly line is either a weight-forward saltwater or bug taper, or a shooting head backed up with monofilament or braided monofilament shooting line. And since the bass may be near the surface or several feet below it, both a floating and a fast-sinking line should be carried – one on a spare spool for the reel.

If braided monofilament shooting line is chosen, it is very easily and smoothly joined to the back end of your shooting head (also called a shooting taper) by insertion and glueing. Braided monofilament nylon lines are hollow and one of 25 to 30 lb (11.3–13.6 kg) test will be most suitable.

First pass a darning needle into the open end of the braided line for about 1½ inches (3.8 cm) and hold a flame to it until the needle gets hot, but not red. Watch the braided nylon closely and you will see it begin to crinkle, then the frayed ends will begin to disappear, a melted blob of nylon appearing at the end. Remove the flame and let the needle cool.

Pull out the needle and you will find that the hollow in the line will remain open, with the end of the line welded. Lay the line on a wooden block and, with a very sharp scalpel or razor blade, cut cleanly through the blob at a right angle, removing just a fraction, so that the open end of the line is exposed. Push the end of the shooting head (or it may be the tapered back-end of a weight-forward

A little dinghy can be ideal when sea conditions are right, for bass fishing just offshore, trolling or spinning, especially at dawn and dusk.

flyline whose running line has been worn out – a good way to use up such worn weight-forward lines, this) into the braided monofilament for about 1½ inches (3.8 cm). Then, with the joined lines on an old piece of cardboard, apply a tiny drop of cyanoacrylate adhesive (Superglue) at the point where the flyline ends inside the braided line. Leave for about five minutes to set.

This will hold the joint so that you can apply a tight whipping round the braid's end, just as when whipping a rod, and finishing with the end of the fine nylon whipping thread being pulled under the turns with a separate loop of thin monofilament nylon – about 3 lb (1.3 kg) is about right. Trim the end of the tag close.

Coat the whipping with liquid vinyl (Vycoat), to resist abrasion. The whipping will anchor the braid to the soft flyline coating, and the more the line joint is pulled apart, the harder the braid beds into the line.

You can join a tapered leader to the tip of the flyline using the same method, passing the flyline halfway into about 2 inches (5 cm) of braided monofilament and the leader into the other end, so they meet. Apply the adhesive as before, and whip over the braid where it ends on the flyline.

An alternative method of joining shooting head to monofilament nylon shooting line – and the leader to the flyline tip – is with a nail knot modification. For those who do not know how to do this, the diagram explains all.

Since long lengths of fly line and shooting line are going to be draped all over the place in a boat, or underfoot on the beach or rocks, as a shoal of feeding bass are followed and cast to, a line basket worn low on the left hip (for a right-handed caster) is an essential item of equipment. It helps not only shoot

Instructions for attaching monofilament to fly line.
1. Make a hole through the end of the fly line with a pin or needle, passing this out on the side of the line. While the pin is still in the hole, heat its head with a match flame to redness, then let it cool before removing the pin. Pass the end of the monofilament in at the end of the fly line and out at the side.
2. Wind the monofilament three·times round the end of the fly line and lay the end of the monofilament parallel to where it leaves the hole in the side of the fly line.
3. By winding the turns of monofilament backwards over the end, and carefully pulling on the ends and adjusting the turns, snug down the resulting knot. With a good pull applied between the end of the monofilament and the part

emerging from the end of the fly line, squeeze the turns of the knot down into the fly line dressing.

Remove some of the dressing from the end of the fly line so as to expose the braided fly line core. In doing this, be careful not to cut or nick the monofilament. Fray out the end of the braided core and apply varnish.
4. Whip over the frayed core with fly tying silk or, preferably, very fine nylon thread, building up to a taper shaped by successive layers of turns, to form a smooth transition between the diameters of the monofilament and the fly line respectively. Thoroughly cover this binding and the turns of the knot with Vycote.
(Reproduced from *Angling Magazine*, by kind permission of Richard Walker)

line for long casts, but prevents damage to the line by treading on it or the line tangling with weeds when wading.

Leaders need only be 6–8 ft (1.8–2.4 m) long and of level nylon – about 7–9 lb (3.1–4 kg) test. The strength is not important with regard to the fight or weight of the fish, only to the stiffness of the nylon which must be sufficient to turn over a comparatively big, heavy fly.

Flies should be dressed on strong hooks, such as the Yorkshire Stronghold or similar, even on O'Shaughnessy bends when fishing deep from a boat. It is important that the fly takes a streamlined and mobile aspect in the water and that it should have some white hair and silver tinsel in its make-up. The author dresses a fly which he calls the Bass Blond, modelled on the Blond series of flies invented and popularised by the great American sportfisher, the late Joe Brooks. The author added colours suggested by the English writer John Bickerdyke, who fished fly for bass in the middle 1800s.

The Bass Blond is dressed with white tying nylon and has a carrot-shaped body of white Orlon baby wool ribbed with wide silver Lurex. An underwing of pale blue bucktail is put on halfway between eye and beginning of bend, the body being then continued forward and fattened. The wing is built up of, from top to bottom, white, red and yellow bucktail and the head is built up big and thickly covered with white varnish before black eyes are painted on.

The fly is made on hooks 1–2/0 and besides being attractive to bass satisfies the fly dresser's whim for artistry. Much plainer bucktails and streamers, white or black, especially with deer-hair Muddler heads, have also been effective.

The fly is cast ahead of or near visible signs of bass chasing fry, from open beach or rocks, and is then fished back in smooth pulls, not at a fast pace, but so that it darts and stops, like a little fish. When fishing across an estuary with a flow coming from the side, the line may be allowed to swing round with the current, as in wet fly trouting or seatrouting, before being brought back with smooth pulls. If the fly furrows the surface this will often trigger a smashing take.

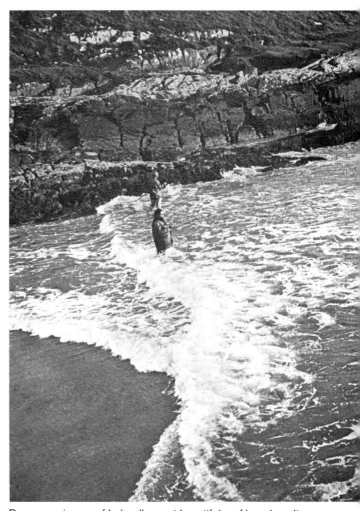

Derrynane is one of Ireland's most beautiful surf beaches. It provides superb surfcasting for bass – and big flounders – and fishing from the rocks at high water at the mouth of this little river.

There is much to be learned in saltwater fly fishing in the waters of the United Kingdom and neighbouring countries. Because it is a difficult technique to master in the sea and not so numerically rewarding with fish, progress will be fairly slow due to so few anglers having the mental attitude to persist in the face of many failures. Success, when it comes, however, is extremely sweet.

12 Grey mullets: thick-lipped and thin-lipped

The mullet family, of which the two above named species are members, inhabits nearly all the warm and temperate coastal waters of the world. They favour brackish water and during the angling season – in British waters from May to October in general, although in some western harbours mullet are taken in winter as well – are seen in great shoals. They move up and down with the tides in estuaries, penetrating tidal creeks, lagoons and drains, and wandering in harbours to mop up the dross and offal of human habitation.

This thick-lipped grey mullet was taken on float-fished bread in Christchurch Harbour, Hampshire. Note how the hook is near the edge of the mouth.

The thick-lipped grey mullet, which is the more plentiful and more widely distributed of the two, runs the rivers only to the limit of the tide, but the thin-lipped grey mullet presses on into pure freshwater where it may spend the whole summer sojourning with coarse fish.

Chelon labrosus is the scientific name for the thick-lipped mullet; *Liza ramada* is the thin-lipped mullet. Thick-lipped mullet reach weights of 10 lb (4.5 kg) and more, the thin-lipped probably weighing almost as much, but because fewer are caught by anglers, and some not recognised for what they are anyway, positive records are scanty. A third species of grey mullet, the golden grey mullet, inhabits our coastal waters. It attains weights of about 3 lb (1.3 kg) but is less numerous.

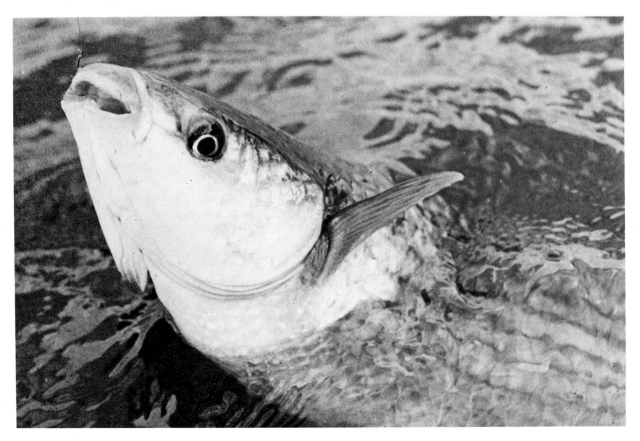

Both thick- and thin-lipped mullet are superb fighters. They can make long fast runs, they bore doggedly for the bottom, and just when the angler is reaching for the net they will make another run, and maybe circle under the rod for up to 5 more minutes. Many anglers hold the view that, size for size, mullet are the hardest fighters of all British saltwater fish.

Grey mullet are a very successful family of fish because they can tolerate living conditions that kill other fish, both sea- and freshwater fish, such as pollution and low oxygen content and a diet that most other fish do not touch. These two species of grey mullet eat a basic diet of diatoms, plant detritus and algae which they skim with their lower scoop-shaped lips from mudbanks, boat hulls and harbour walls. In freshwater and water only slightly brackish, the fish have been found to contain a small proportion of midge larvae (bloodworms).

However, in areas where human waste gets into the water, such as harbours with plenty of boats, fishing ports, seaside resort piers with cafés and marinas, the mullet, more so the thick-lipped species, happily waxes fat on a diet of pulpy bread, plate scrapings of meat, fat and vegetable matter, fish guts and filleted carcases and many other unpleasant items that are washed in from sewage outfalls and drains. In Ireland mullet swarm round pipes carrying creamery waste to the sea or tidal inlets.

In muddy harbours and in tidal reaches of muddy-bottomed rivers and creeks, the mullet do sometimes happen across free-swimming tiny harbour ragworms, usually 1½–2½ in (3.8–6.3 cm) long which live in millions of tiny burrows in the bottom and banks. Periodically the ragworms emerge to migrate.

Although similar tactics may be used for both species when they are either in the sea or in harbours, estuaries and creeks, a separate system must be adopted for catching thin-lipped mullet once they have entered freshwater or are moving up and down a river between freshwater and the brackish water lower down.

In this situation the thin-lipped mullet will accept only one bait for 95 per cent of the time and that is harbour ragworm. Once in a while a coarse fisher will catch one on a maggot, or even a piece of bread flake, but anybody who wishes to catch thin-lipped mullet up the rivers with any regularity should use harbour ragworm. Details of obtaining these are given in chapter 4, but always keep an eye open for Water Authority men or harbour staff when digging. They seem to think anglers damage the banks by digging ragworm, although how they

A fine specimen thin-lipped grey mullet so typical of the shoals that run up the eastern Rother in Sussex, one of the most famous rivers for this species. On light tackle these fish are dynamite.

justify such thinking when they use draglines and dredgers in the same places leaves most anglers wondering – and they dig regardless. In truth, it is best to fill in any holes made, just to keep the peace!

The tackle for upriver thin-lipped mullet consists of the Avon-type rod and line of 3–4 lb (1.3–1.8 kg) test, which on wide rivers or other upriver waters can be on a fixed-spool reel and in narrow rivers, up to 15 yd (14 m) in width, a centre-pin, for sheer

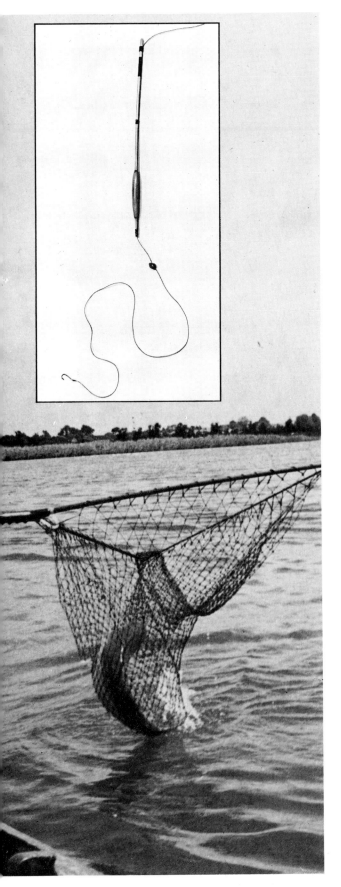

pleasure and control of the fish from the direct drive.

Nearly all the fishing will be with a float, with many rubber rings to prevent slippage, and best of all is a long slim one, either a peacock tail quill, gull quill or hard balsa-wood. The length needs to be about a foot (30.4 cm) and when it is supporting a swan shot, or equivalent load, about 2 in (5 cm) at least should remain above the surface of the water. Even though the ragworms to be used as bait, singly or as many as three at once, are tiny, the hook must not be too small. Long experience by anglers of thin-lipped mullet has shown that size 8 is most useful, sizes 10 and 6 being carried for special circumstances.

The shot is usually fixed about 6 in (15.5 cm) above the hook, first slipping on a sliver of balloon rubber so that the squeezed shot does not damage the line and is prevented from slipping to the hook when hard, fast strikes are made.

Warm and settled weather in June is a good time to begin looking for thin-lipped mullet. Travel light with either a small haversack, landing net and lightweight waterproof or fly-fisher's waistcoat. Always carry polarising glasses, both for searching for shoals of fish and for freedom from dazzle when float watching.

Unless the local mullet anglers can, or will, tell where the shoals of thin-lips are to be found, one must do the work oneself. On many occasions mullet can be spotted by watching for swirls and Vees on the surface as the shoals move up or down the river. The swirls are usually large, an oily upwelling of water from a sudden movement by a powerful body deep down. Mullet men call them *whelms*. Once the direction of the shoal, which may be half-a-dozen fish or several hundreds, has been pinpointed, head it off and cast the tackle with two ragworms, head-hooked, in front of it, the fishing depth initially at about 1½ ft (45 cm), regardless of the depth of water.

Feeding mullet will usually indicate interest quickly, the float suddenly disappearing in a flash,

The author nets a good harbour mullet for his son, who has caught fair numbers of these so-called difficult fish on light tackle, proving the point that even boys can succeed when properly guided.
Inset: A typical float rig used by the author for bread or ragworm fishing for mullet in harbours, creeks and tidal rivers. The float is cane and elder-pith and held firmly by several long lengths of cycle valve rubber. The shot is pinched on over a piece of balloon rubber, again to keep it in position when rapid striking is necessary.

or dithering over several seconds before shooting down; often the tip of the float will tip one way, then the other, before going down. It is essential that any strike is delayed until the whole of the 2 in (5 cm) of float above water has disappeared, since mullet will pull the float halfway without having the hook in a sinkable spot.

However, once the float has gone the strike must be made like lightning. It takes lots of practice to be able to connect with thin-lipped mullet bites regularly, and unless plenty of bites are being obtained, it is a problem to get keyed up to the right pitch anyway! The float tackle, being set so shallow, will be whipped from the water at great speed when a bite is missed and can do some damage to anybody standing on the bank beside or behind the angler. One spectator had a porcupine quill float embedded in his forehead by one mullet angler who was getting on the ball!

If the initial depth setting gets no attention from the fish, but they are obviously still in the area, try 2 ft (60 cm) and then down from there. Rarely are thin-lips found to take red ragworm at much more than 3 ft (91 cm), or more than half the total depth of the water, as a rule.

If the fish are not visible on the surface, one has to fish up the river, trying every 10 yd (9 m) or so, until a bite (or bites) is forthcoming. It is obviously a far quicker operation if a number of mullet enthusiasts do this together, leap-frogging to cover the water quickly. Once mullet bites or fish are forthcoming, it is recognised practice that the anglers cast their floats into the taking area, even a foot or so from each other. The effect of a number of baits being close together is that more scent is given off and the fish home-in – a form of mutual groundbaiting.

To make a big catch of thin-lips in freshwater, or in places where there is little salinity, it is essential that the fish are feeding, or are prepared to feed once stimulated, and that they will either remain in a small length of river, dyke or similar or can be tempted to do so. Many shoals of mullet in a river system may be uncatchable because they are not feeding when the bait is cast to them or will not begin to do so when a number of baits are put in. Another method that will sometimes work and hold a shoal together involves throwing in an evil smelling mixture of mud in which ragworms have been kept and where some of them have died, plus a

One of the most highly respected mullet-men in the United Kingdom, Gerry Green, showing a fine fish from the Sussex Cuckmere.

little soaked bread mixed in with the mud. This does not work, however, if the river flow is such that the odour is carried away. The best conditions for thin-lips are no current or a slight current and a wind against it to keep surface water in a state of near balance.

One's first mullet, if it is much over 1½ lb (680 g), will be a revelation. It is likely to streak away with the reel clutch whining, swirl savagely on the surface and run up and down the channel, all at great speed and with such power that a fish many pounds heavier is suspected. When you think it safe to reach for the net, the fish will begin boring round and round under the rod tip, in spite of maximum pressure. A 4 lb (1.8 kg) thin-lipped mullet may take 10 minutes to bring to net on the kind of gear mentioned, sometimes even longer. The occasional fish of 5 lb (2.26 kg) upwards will be contacted that will whip 50 yd (45.7 m) of line from the reel with one run, and then keep pulling.

To strike both quickly yet avoid the impact breaking the tackle is tricky: a low, sidewise strike can help, trying to cushion the line near the float in the surface of the water. Unless there is a troublesome surface drift or wind that will drag the float out of position, always keep the line well greased and floating. This helps make striking fast. If a sunken line is the sole way of being able to fish, the chances of connecting with fast bites are narrowed a lot.

On occasions the thin-lip will relent and one gets a slow sinking of the float, in a sidewise direction. Such bites are fairly easy to hit, but are rare. Occasionally winding in *slowly* produces better bites.

Thick-lipped grey mullet are another matter. In tidal reaches of rivers, in creeks, in harbours, lagoons, from breakwaters and piers, they may be fished with almost the same tackle, except that when fishing in water 25 ft (7.6 m) deep or more a sliding float will be needed – one with a central plastic tube through a cigar-shaped balsa-wood body has proved as good as any and better than most – with a tiny rubber or linen thread stop on the line. Avon trotting floats are useful at other times. Also, it is as well to increase line test to 5 lb (2.26 kg) in deep water, especially in places where mullet can run and foul the tackle, such as boat moorings, bridge and pier supports and the like. Striking firmly enough to hook fish in deep water, and at long range, can break 3 lb (1.3 kg) line surprisingly easy. The amount of lead on the line may need to be increased to two to three swan shots for proper tackle control, too.

Depending on whether the saltwater location is a

busy resort marina or port, a pier with a café, or a tiny cove in Cornwall, Devon or Ireland where a few inshore boats land fish and throw the offal into the sea, the bait may be fresh bread-flake, red ragworms, small cubes of skinned mackerel flesh, or tiny strips of skin and flesh cut from mackerel, herring or garfish. Cubes of flesh can be about ¼ in (6 mm) square or as big as ½ in (12 mm) square; strips of fish may be about ¼ in by about 1½ in (6 mm by 38 mm).

Thick-lipped mullet will also take small pieces of shellfish, especially mussels and cockles, and in places where these shellfish are landed and cleaned, the shells and some of the contents being returned to the sea or creek, mullet come in and are caught quite readily on these baits.

Where creamery waste is discharged to sea or estuary, as in a number of well-known places in Ireland famous for mullet fishing, cream cheese makes a good bait. A wisp or two of sheep's wool or 'cotton-wool' is whipped to the hook just below the eye to give the soft cheese something to which to cling, else both water action and mullet can take it off, the latter sometimes without getting hooked in the mouth.

Des Brennan, the Irish mullet addict, reported in *Mullet* (Osprey Anglers series) that he had caught mullet feeding wildly on creamery waste on a hook adorned only by cotton-wool, or anything else white!

Imagine a day for thick-lipped mullet from a pier or wall where the fish take bread. It is usual to fish at times and in places where tidal flow is minimal, so that the tackle fishes in a small area where mullet congregate or can be gathered together: at slack tide, or before and after it when there is little ebb or flow, and then usually around the high water period rather than the low; or in places away from the main tidal stream, such as occur where pierheads have T-shaped sections, or where harbour walls that project out to sea have strengthening abutments, or inner harbours where the water is smooth and slow-moving.

Often, when the weather is sunny and the water calm and clear, a look along the projections, especially with the help of polarising spectacles, will reveal mullet swimming slowly to and fro. The first thing to do is find a fishable spot where the fish are, or to which they may be lured. Then lower down an onion bag or something with similar size holes, containing several stale loaves which have been well soaked and mashed up. The bag or bags must just touch the water surface, so that any rise and fall washes out bits of bread; failing that, give the bag a shake on its cord occasionally. Don't forget to raise and lower the bag with the rise and fall of the tide!

Soon, however, mullet should begin to shoal around the bag as the water turns milky with the mashed bread breaking up. Simply lower the float tackle gently down beside the bag and let it waft around. Fish are likely to be taking any bits from the bag as they sink slowly, and so the bait should also sink slowly. This means that the shot should be at least 2 ft (61 cm) from the hook, when fishing less than 3 ft (91 cm) deep, although any attempt to fish the slowly sinking bait with the float much more than 4 ft (1.2 m) above the bait will result in fish taking the bread without registering very much on the float.

Avoid as much as possible making surface disturbance. Watch the bait as it sinks slowly; it is possible to see the fish move up to take the bread before the float shows anything. It is best, however, to await the float going down before striking quickly but gently.

If the fish will not take the slowly sinking bread in the first 3–4 ft (91 cm–1.2 m), then increase the fishing depth by a foot at a time. Once the fishing depth exceeds the length of the rod it is necessary to use the sliding float. It is seldom necessary to fish the bread deeper than half the depth of the water.

Usually a pinch of flake ½ in (12 mm) square on a size 6–8 hook will be about right, but if many bites are missed, or bites are finicky, try smaller pieces on a size 10 hook.

If float-fished bread fails and the mullet below your stance persistently swirl on the surface or swim with their backs out of the water round the bread bag, it is well worth trying floating bread crust, just as when freshwater fishing for carp, chub and so on. Only the hook is used and baited with a piece of crust ½–¾ in (12–19 mm) square; unless it is necessary to cast the crust any distance, in which case a bubble-float with some water in it for weight, or a short piece of balsa, with a swan shot pinched on either side of it, is threaded on the line to remain about 4 ft (1.2 m) from the bait.

When a mullet cruises slowly up to the bait, swims round it, backs off, returns and then sucks it in, do wait a second for the fish to turn down before pulling in the hook.

Usually one finds that on seaside piers, as well as in tidal reaches of rivers, thick-lips will accept both bread and float-fished red ragworms, perhaps taking both baits on the same day in the same general area. However, with ragworms on the hook and from the comparatively deep water off piers, harbour arms or bridges, it usually pays to fish the bait deeper than one would bread: for example, in water

Just to prove those earlier pictures were not of the odd lucky fish . . . father and son with thick-lipped mullet from Christchurch Harbour. On 3–4 lb (1.3–1.8 kg) lines these fish will make runs of up to 50 yd (45.7 m).

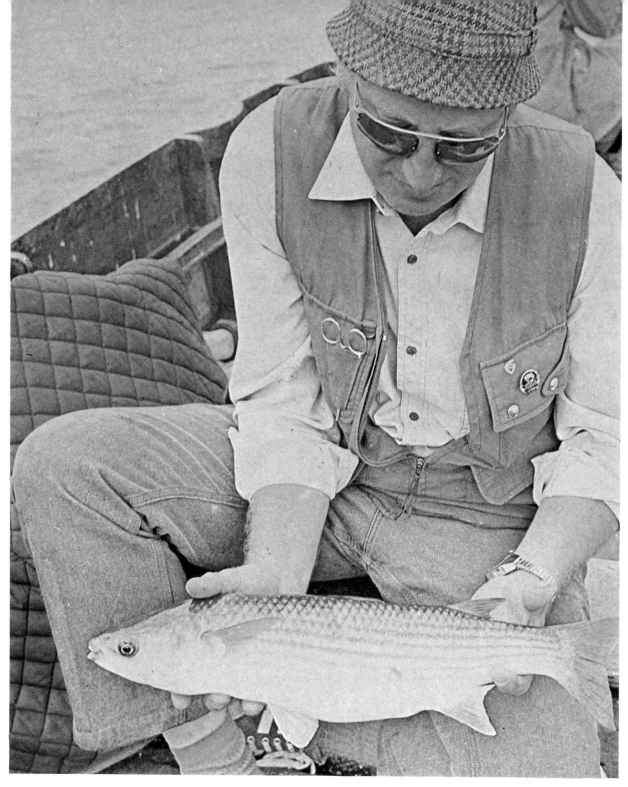

A mullet of over 4 lb (1.8 kg) taken float-fishing bread in 2 ft (60 cm) of water in an estuary. On this day a number of good fish were caught on 3 lb (1.3 kg) test line and roach tackle.

15 ft (4.5 m) deep the best results with ragworm would be likely with the bait 8–12 ft (2.4–3.6 m) below the float. That does not apply in the river, where tactics as for thin-lips in freshwater apply.

There is one advantage in fishing bunches of red ragworms from piers etc. It is that mullet often take them in a more leisurely way than they do bread,

which gives a better rate of hook-ups to strikes.

This rate can be improved upon in fishing harbours where the thick-lips feed on fish offal. Mullet seem to eat fish flesh and guts – often rotting fish flesh, too – more deliberately than they do most foods, perhaps because it has to be dealt with in a tougher manner than pulpy bread or soft worms, which are sucked in. Mullet can often be seen feeding on fish carcases littering the bottom among moored trawlers, standing on their heads or driving themselves into the pile with vigorous tail-wags. It was in such a situation that the author saw the two biggest thick-lipped mullet he had ever seen. It was in the harbour at Dingle, Co. Kerry, and the fish were at the end of the fish pier, the bigger, at a conservative estimate, 12 lb (5.4 kg), and the smaller one about 9 lb (4 kg).

Float-fishing with fish strips or cubes or pieces of gut at various depths, from near the surface to just off the bottom, will work when the fish are prepared to co-operate. When fishing very close to weed-covered walls or rocks, or among moored boats, it sometimes pays to paternoster a fish-bait rather than fish the float, using two hooks on nylon snoods about 4 in (10 cm) long, the first about 18 in (45.7 cm) above the small pear-shaped lead, the other about a foot (30.4 cm) above the first. This technique is good when the water is rough and in cold weather, when the mullet tend to go deep.

Simply lower the gear down and touch bottom, then lift it about a foot (30.4 cm). Hold the line just ahead of the reel, and feel for the bites; they are normally very gentle, sucking bites and the rod should be lifted sharply at any signal that perceptibly lasts a little longer than the norm.

If bites are not forthcoming at a foot above the bottom, raise the baits another foot or so, until midwater is reached. Then begin again near the bottom. For fishing close to walls or among moored boats, the short spinning rod may be found more useful than the Avon rod used for most mullet fishing.

Mention of the spinning rod brings us to the final technique in this chapter and one which for sheer light-tackle enjoyment may well be the best of all. However, it works only in a few selected locations, and there appears to be no common ground on which to base the decision of the fish to react or not. The method is spinning.

The trout spinning rod, fixed-spool reel with 3–4 lb (1.3–1.8 kg) test line and a tiny bar-spoon is required, together with some red ragworms or even red worms from a farmer's dung-hill. The method usually works only for thick-lips in estuarine waters, and especially those in which there is a walking-pace current, and where the mullet are seen swirling, *whelming* and actually jumping clear of the water.

The French do quite a lot of this type of fishing and perfected a small bar-spoon backed up with a single hook for the worm instead of the usual treble hook. The spoon is aptly termed the Muge, and is about ¾ in (19 mm) long. Other good spoons include Mepps, Veltic, Droppen, and any other similar bar-spoons up to ¾ in (19 mm) in spoon length may be used. Silver seems a little better than gold. The trebles may be left on or changed to single

hooks, about size 8 or 6, which should sit approximately an inch (2.5 cm) behind the spoon.

The cast is made across the area in which the mullet are seen and the lure wound back as near to the surface as is possible; the rod tip is kept high to keep the spinner an inch (2.5 cm) or so under the water.

When first done successfully, this technique is a revelation to the angler who has erstwhile taken mullet – that shy, gentle-mouthed grey ghost – float-fishing or on floating bread: the fish chase the spoon and take it with a thump as hard as any other European saltwater predator.

At times when the mullet are a little choosy the ragworm on the hook is essential (or an ordinary red worm from a dung-hill, as mentioned above, will do instead). At other times the bar-spoon alone will be taken; maybe the day will begin with the need for the baited hook, then develop to the stage where the unbaited spinner is taken.

Whatever method the mullet falls to the fish will fight hard – always. Much has been said about the fish's soft mouth and how hooks tear out easily if the fish is held too hard. While it is true that the prehensile part of the mouth, the front lip and its connecting membrane, will tear easily if the hook penetrates there, it is also true that most mullet are hooked further back in the mouth, and that part of the fish is as tough as that of any other fish.

Mullet have to be played firmly, and in tight spaces – like around moored boats or snaggy pier stanchions – may have to be held hard. The Avon rod will take a lot of the shocks in such cases, and the trout spinning rod will also help a lot, unless one of the tip-action types is chosen. An easy action, though not a sloppy one, is best.

Use the rectangular dropnet from high vantage points, a round-framed landing net 2 ft (60 cm) in diameter with a deep bag net from places that can be reached with a 6 ft (1.8 m) handle.

A coarse fisher once hooked a mullet by accident while trotting bread flake for roach in the lower reaches of a tidal river. His remark as the fish tore off 40 yd (36.4 m) of line is unprintable. His commentary as the fish rushed up and down the stream for nearly ten minutes included 'bloody great bass' . . . 'foul-hooked a seatrout' . . . 'must be a stray carp'. And when finally he slid the net under a mullet of about 3 lb (1.3 kg) the comment is again unprintable.

Mullet do that to people. The angler fished for nothing else and in no other river for the next 15 years or so, after which he had to stop fishing anyway!

13 Ballan wrasse

Unless one is exceptionally fit, 50 is the usual age beyond which the best of ballan wrasse fishing from the shore must remain unattainable. Indeed, the climbs necessary to be able to fish most of the really good wrasse spots deter many young and agile anglers the first time they are taken to view the locations.

This is not a criticism of those anglers who just will not go down to wrasse spots: the author knows many a brave man (with military medals for gallantry, even) who just cannot face precipitous rock faces and cliffs. It is not fear but the honest recognition that such climbing is beyond one's capabilities and that one would be a risk to other members of the party.

And wrasse fishing from precarious, wave-washed ledges at the base of sheer cliffs, such as there are in Devon, Cornwall, parts of west Wales, Scotland and the south, south-west and western coasts of Ireland, must be carried out in properly planned groups, preferably three or more anglers travelling together. Never, ever should an angler go down a cliff on to wave-washed wrasse rocks alone; even with one companion the climbing and carrying and the landing of fish is arduous work. A slip, either down the rocks or cliff, or, worse perhaps, into the water could result in broken bones, or very likely be fatal; with two anglers there is somebody to give first aid, rescue or go for help. But many locations demand the use of ropes and anchoring stakes at cliff tops, plus food, tackle and other supplies to be lowered or passed down and up in stages from ledge to ledge. It is then that three to six anglers can make the trip safer, more successful and more enjoyable.

Ballan wrasse are among the most colourful salt-water species in these islands. They can vary in the same locality from a rich orange-brown, through red-brown, to a chestnut hue and a lovely dark green, sometimes with blue overtones. Some are delicately spotted with lighter markings, others may have blotches of irregular size, or vertical stripes, and perhaps the most beautiful of all is the fish with chestnut back, reddish sides marked with light spots

and blue sheens, the belly being bright orange and the fins edged with bright green, the rest being either orange or yellow.

The fish tend to shoal in sizes, and in the very best places, such as some rugged holes in Cornwall and west and south-west Ireland, nearly all the wrasse taken will be 3–4 lb (1.3–1.8 kg) with several over 5 lb (2.26 kg). The author has fished in Ireland when fish over 5 lb were fairly common and several over 6 lb (2.7 kg) were caught. No doubt the species reaches 10 lb (4.5 kg).

Ballan wrasse like warm Atlantic water and the normal fishing season lasts from mid-May to mid-October. Rocks of a hard nature, such as various forms of granite and volcanic material, are the usual composition of good ballan wrasse ground, which is an advantage, since this rock is usually safe for hand and foot holds, whereas softer rocks can appear firm but are in fact treacherous as they crumble when weight is put on them. Also, the hard rocks do not form discoloured water as do some softer rocks which are eroded by wave action.

Although wrasse may be caught in calm water conditions, there is little doubt that the fish's feeding activity is increased when rough water crashes into the base of the cliffs and surges among the jagged, weed-covered rocks. Obviously such a pounding dislodges crustaceans from their holds and batters and confuses small fish, sand-eels and crabs. The wrasse make hay at such times.

Ballans eat lots of tiny mussels, where they exist in large colonies, and these and small limpets are bitten from the rocks by the fish's ivory-white front teeth – massive in comparison to the size of the fish, and very powerful too. Anybody who gets a finger bitten by a big ballan will not be ignorant of this fact. Ballans also eat whole small hardback crabs, prawns, barnacles and marine worms, both lug and rag.

As far as bait goes the fish will accept lugworm as well as any other, usually, and since lug is fairly easily obtained it is an obvious choice. But small hardback shore and hermit crabs are also fairly easy

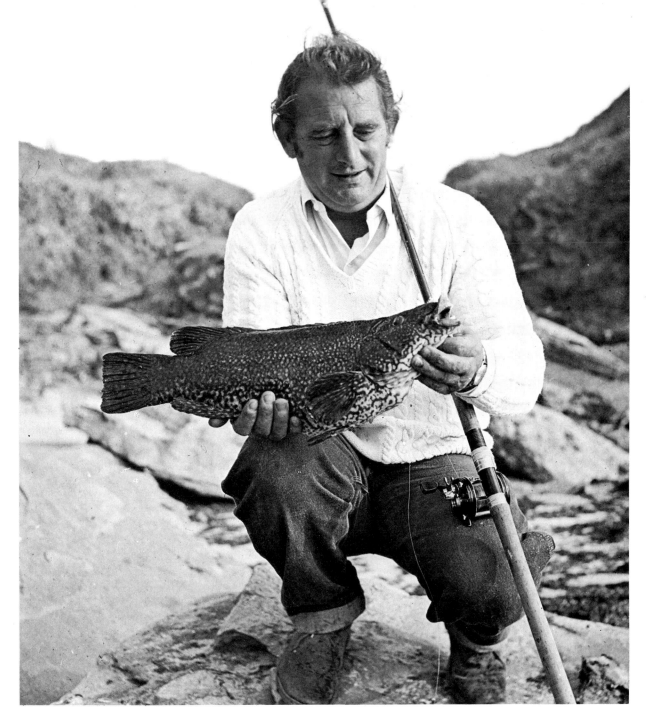

A ballan wrasse weighing well over 6 lb (2.7 kg), caught in Ireland by Cornishman Stan Hoskin. The fish was killed in this instance and found to contain hundreds of tiny mussels. Wrasse lose their colours somewhat after death.

to find. Mussel flesh is excellent and slipper and ordinary limpet flesh works, too, though less well than lug.

It is obvious that in some areas especially, the larger ballan wrasse feed heavily on sand-eels when they are shoaling thickly. The author has caught large numbers of big ballans on Red Gill rubber eels when fishing with friends in south-west Ireland, and the fish somehow managed to engulf the whole eel so that the hook was well back in the mouth! The artificials had to be fished at high risk, just bumping over the odd big rock. Other anglers simultaneously using spoons did not catch any wrasse, only pollack and mackerel.

Before dealing further with the actual business of catching wrasse on lightish tackle it is necessary to say something about the requirements of a party

going down a cliff or over treacherous rocks. Although some advice has been given in the chapter dealing with fishing for shore pollack, the extent of climbing and risk when attaining some ballan wrasse spots is quite a lot higher.

In some places the access to low rock ledges may be quite easy, simply a series of ledges leading down to just above sea level. In such cases the only thing to watch is that footwear is suitable, both for getting a good grip on the rock and for a degree of ankle support. Fellboots or climbing boots are naturally excellent, but some can be very expensive. Leather, strong rubber or synthetics may all be used as uppers, but the soles had best be good thick rubber, well moulded with gripping tread. Metal studs are effective on wet and weedy rock, provided the studs are constantly renewed so as to be really sharp; blunted, worn studs can be very dangerous.

The author has worn felt-soled and rubber-soled training shoes on rough volcanic rock, but when the rock is wet they do not serve well and a slip can mean a broken ankle or a bad sprain. Also, rock surfaces are very rough, knife-edged and the foot arch does need good support, else a day's wrasse fishing can be agony.

If the access means descending any sheer faces, especially when drops of 30 ft (9 m) straight down have to be negotiated, with the total cliff height perhaps 150 ft (45.7 m) or more, a rope of climbing quality nylon and of adequate length to cover the total drop must be used to avoid unnecessary danger. If there is no firm tree or rock at the cliff top to which the rope can be firmly anchored then carry several lengths of angle iron or aluminium-alloy angle, the faces of which should be at least 1½ in (4 cm) across and the length about 2 ft (61 cm). One end is sharpened to a point and the other is drilled through the apex of the triangle (that is, the hole passing through two sides) to which is fixed a strong steel welded ring, or a rigging clip (used for sailing) to which the rope is tied.

Test all ropes and fittings regularly for top security.

When climbing, especially the first drop which is often soft topsoil with rock in it, never put any weight, by hand or foot, on any projecting stone or rock that has not been given a good strong pull to establish if it really is part of solid rock or just a lump of rock embedded in the soil. The author once fell 20 ft (6 m) down a face to a ledge, where he was caught by a companion who had gone down first; had he continued over an overhang to crash 60 ft (18 m) on to fanglike rocks in the water below, death or terrible injuries would have been inevitable.

Once on the lower rocks and ledges from which fishing is to be done, ensure a comfortable stance, well above the reach of the occasional big wave, and keep all the tackle together well back on dry rock platforms. Tie the bags on if necessary on a windy day. Keep the bait in a bag round your neck and spare nylon, weights and hooks in pockets. The dropnet should be tied to a rock at the distance it will easily reach the water and there should be a net

Left: A rope being used to reach a ballan wrasse spot safely.

Right: The dentition of a ballan wrasse. These teeth can rip shellfish from their anchorages on the rocks and crush limpets, barnacles, mussels, crabs – and an angler's finger if he's not careful!

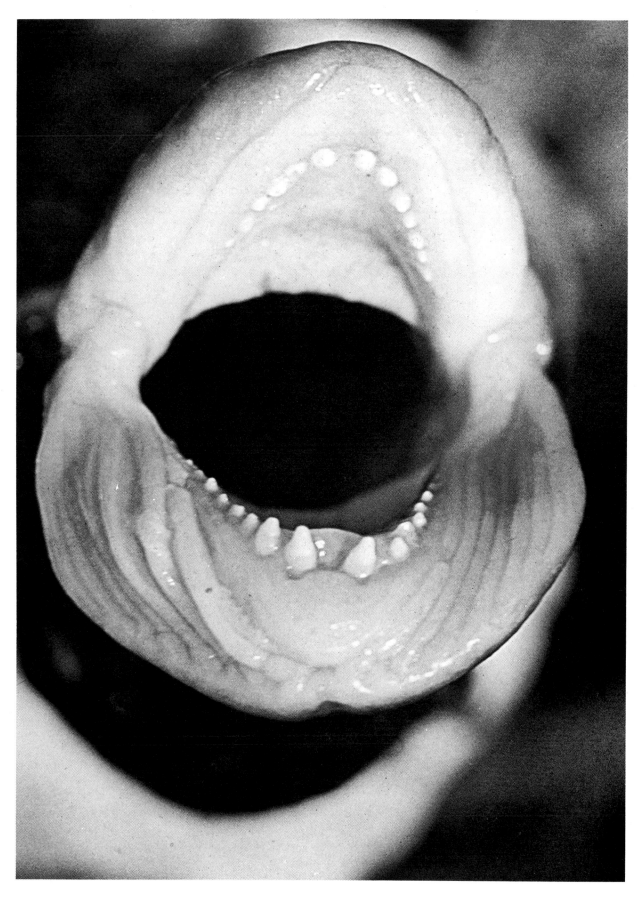

between every two to four anglers, who usually fish together in small areas. Each angler needs long-nosed pliers or stout artery forceps in his pocket with which to remove hooks from the rubbery mouths of the wrasse.

All the above is aimed at avoiding unnecessary clambering about on the rocks. Advice is often given, not to venture at all on to wet rocks; it is sound advice but anglers ignore it when they have travelled long distances for a wrasse session and it is raining, or spray has wet the rocks. The author and his friends do fish on wet rocks, but it is imperative to be twice as careful when moving about as when the rock is dry and footholds safe.

And now to the fishing.

Apart from spinning with Red Gills, which is done in exactly the same way as for pollack, except that the lure is fished even more at risk, touching rock, and with the double-handed spinning rod, multiplier or fixed-spool reel loaded with 8–10 lb

(3.6–4.5 kg) test line, there are two basic techniques for ballans: paternoster and float-fishing, and the float-fishing may be with a form of paternoster rig or more conventional float gear.

Because these fish live in jumbled rocks and deep in tiny crevices and caves, all weedy, in the ground right below your feet or a yard or so out, tackle must be simple, cheap and easily made up, because losses may be high.

For the paternoster system use either the bass surf-casting rod with 12 lb (5.4 kg) line or the double-handed spinning rod with 10 lb (4.5 kg) line, depending on the average size of fish and the ruggedness of the underwater terrain. The line tests might seem excessive to anybody who has yet to tangle with ballan wrasse, but the idea is to yield as little line as is possible to the fish, else it will get into a hole or crevice and either hang on until you pull for a break or cut the line on the sharp rock.

Tie a blood-loop about 18 in (45.7 cm) above the end of the line. This takes a snood about a foot (30 cm) long, made of the same line as the reel line, and with a strong size 1–1/0 eyed hook. Yorkshire Stronghold hooks have proved excellent, as have several long-shanked strong trout lure hooks with forged bends.

This close-up photograph of the head of a large Irish wrasse clearly shows the beautiful markings that have earned the species the title of Britain's most colourful sea fish.

To the very end of the line now tie either a small split ring or plain brass ring, or form a small loop. This takes a length of about 4 lb (1.8 kg) nylon, to which is tied the weight, consisting of any object that weighs between 1–2 oz (28.3–56.6 g), such as old bolts and nuts or strips of lead or whatever. The length of the weak link to the weight should be about 3 ft (91 cm).

Examine the water below. If it has areas flecked with foam, where great rocks and caverns and cracks are revealed as each rise falls away, lob the tackle to the edge of the foam. Immediately the weight touches bottom, stop the reel, keep the line just taut without moving the weight if possible, and hold the line in front of the reel. If the ballans are around and feeding, a bite will usually come within a minute or so: a sharp pluck or two, then a strong pull. Strike and begin lifting the fish simultaneously in one smooth movement.

The first dive of a ballan wrasse of 3 lb (1.3 kg) or so will astound newcomers to the sport: the fact that the fish are hooked right at their own front doors, as it were, makes it easier for them to get 'home', of course; but even so, it is a fact that such a calibre of fish can easily break 10 lb (4.5 kg) test line with the shock. Some fish, like some pollack, will give up after that first dive, but others will fight on, diving several times. Bringing a big ballan to net in the surges of Atlantic water that can rise and fall 10 ft (3 m) on fair days is quite an art. The net and the fish have to rise and fall at the same time, and this takes some tricky arranging.

If you do hook one of the really big old fish there is no way, even with 15 lb (6.8 kg) line, that the first dive will be severely curtailed. Line must be given, grudgingly, but if the fish is determined to get deep into the kelp and rocks it is better to risk it becoming inextricable or wearing through or cutting the line on rock than to break off in mid-dive. There is a small chance that the fish may be fooled into leaving its holt by slackening off tension for a few minutes.

The weight will often be lost – one every two casts is average – and it is an unfortunate fact, too, that a fair number of hooks are also sacrificed by wrasse hunters: the hook is bound to snag as often as the weight. However, the fact is that the bigger wrasse invariably seem to be winkled from deep fissures running way back into the rock, or kelp-draped caverns that have been gouged out of the lower ledges by the gnawing waves.

Some anglers delight in making big bags of wrasse and eschew the light tackle to do so. The bass rod is used and the line increased to 15–18 lb (6.8–

A husky wrasse for the late Ian Gillespie, taken on float-paternoster on the Dingle Peninsula, County Kerry.

8.1 kg), the fish being skilfully lifted on to the fishing platform instead of being netted. The weak link to the weight is retained. And even with those strong lines the bigger specimens can actually impose such an impact strain on the line on a dive that breakages occur fairly often!

When a wrasse is landed it is a good idea to have a damp towel available in which to hold the fish cradled under and along one's arm while the hook is removed with pliers or forceps: wrasse have exceptionally tough mouths and are slippery customers as well. When putting them back try to drop them head-first, and do it when a swell comes up the rock, to minimise the drop of the fish. If the fish is just thrown back from a height and hits the water with its flank, the impact can daze it sufficiently for it to be incapable of diving, the result being a battering against the rocks. Some fish may drift on the surface for several minutes before suddenly recovering and swimming down.

The float-paternoster method is basically the same hook and weight set-up, with the addition of a sliding 'float' above the ring or loop connecting main line with weak link. In fact, the thing that keeps the tackle upright in the water and to an extent allows it to drift around, the weight bumping against the rock, is a lump of cork, a proper cork stopper from a big wide-topped jar, or a piece of

A ballan wrasse has lots of fin area to help it force the issue in a rough-and-tumble battle.

white expanded polystyrene. To stop the sliding 'float' running down on to the hook snood some form of stop must be used if a loop and not a ring connects main line and weak link. A swan shot or a bead will do. A swivel would do the job, too, but is more expensive to lose.

The cork or polystyrene must just support the weight used, and polystyrene about 2 in (5 cm) square is about right. A number 8 swivel may be attached to the float by lashing with nylon, cord or wire; or by softening the wire of eyed or ringed hooks (sizes 1/0–2/0 are recommended) and then pushing the barbed end into the cork or plastic foam. The swivel can be fitted into the opened eye or ring, after which it is closed again with pliers.

The usual stop on the line is made and the tackle does to an extent help to avoid snagging, since the weight is supported and has less tendency to drop down into cracks in the rock. It also can be allowed to drift around with currents or wind action. Strike when the float goes under.

Finally, it really is amazing where big wrasse will make their homes. The author has several times in Ireland winkled them from cracks in rocky ledges several yards back from the seaward edge of the ledge on which he stood and only 18 in (45.7 cm) wide at the top! The paternoster was lowered carefully down the crack until it touched bottom, the water depth apparently being about 15 ft (4.5 m), and almost immediately the rod thumped down and some exciting battles ensued; it is peculiar playing a strong fish down a crack – a bit like fishing in a street drain! There are obviously wide caves at the bottoms of such cracks.

Of course, the fish has to be lifted up the crack unless it can be guided along to the seaward opening.

14 Black bream and red bream

Round about late April – the exact time of year depending on the warmth, or coolness of the water – vast shoals of black bream turn up in the eastern part of the English Channel. They spawn between mid-May and July, mostly on the rough ground interspersed with sandy patches known as the Kingmere Reef off Littlehampton.

In fact, this little harbour on the estuary of the River Arun is the mecca of black bream angling and many anglers, both regular sea anglers and coarse fishermen filling in the gap due to their close season, converge there between May and mid-June.

Black bream obviously winter in deep water, though it is also believed that some fish migrate to the Channel from the Mediterranean. Having turned up in spring off the Sussex coast, the fish later spread out, and by June can be caught just south of the Thames estuary and along the coasts of Hampshire, Dorset, the West Country and Wales, but very rarely in the North Sea. However, Sussex is by far the best fishery. Black bream occur only occasionally in Ireland.

Typical of the sea breams, the black bream has a small mouth, small teeth and deep body with plenty of fin area. The spined dorsal fin is beautifully constructed and can be retracted into a channel along the fish's back, to reduce drag and increase swimming speed. It fights extremely hard and since it averages about 1½ lb (680 g) and is caught to 4 lb (1.8 kg) or so most seasons, it is an ideal light tackle species.

A good 95 per cent of black bream fishing is done from boats since it occurs 1–6 miles (1.6–9.6 km) offshore as a rule. However, some are taken from the shore, especially in the Selsey area of Sussex and Devon and Cornwall, and occasional specimens turn up from South Coast piers. Shore captures are usually made in late summer, even in autumn in

Black bream are caught from the shore in summer and early autumn. This is a Selsey (Sussex) specimen caught by John Cooper.

the West Country. The bass casting rod, 10 lb (4.5 kg) line and a single-hook nylon paternoster is right for shore bream.

Black bream, as one might expect, are not black! They are usually a steely blue on the back, shading to purple, with flanks of silvery grey or pink-hued with streaks of metallic gold-brown below the lateral line. Some have vertical bars of dark grey or blue, and mostly these turn out to be the cock fish.

They are active feeders and are found in shallow water – most good Sussex fishing takes place in 4–6 fathoms (7.3–11 m) over chalk rubble inshore or over the reef further out. The tackle for shallow water bream can vary, depending on preference, but line of 3–5 lb (1.3–2.6 kg) is always adequate and

fishes nicely with leads varying in weight from about 1–2½ oz (28–71 g). The rod can be a crank-handled baitcaster of 6–7½ ft (1.8–2.28 m) and of the type designed for very light weights, or the trout spinning rod or the double-handed spinning rod, although the latter overguns bream of average size.

The reel for the baitcaster is obviously the small multiplier; the same can be used on the spinning rods, although the centrepin reel will provide better sport and more direct contact with tackle and fish. Some anglers use fixed-spool reels for black bream when fishing from a boat, but since no casting is done the reel has tackle control disadvantages due to its construction.

There are two basic black bream techniques: a paternoster let down and fished sink and draw for 100 yd (91.4 m) or so downtide of the anchored boat

Black bream.

and, for the slack water period (when the fish go off the feed and require a moving bait to attract them), float tackle is used.

First the paternoster. The author's type is of variable setting and has proved very successful, as well as tangle-free. First push up the line a ¼ in (6 mm) length of nylon tube – ballpoint pen ink-tube is all right – then a number 10 swivel, followed by another piece of tube. A tiny piece of matchstick is pushed from the sides opposite the link swivel into the bits of tube, thus jamming them in position on the line with the swivel between. The lead goes on a number 8–10 link-swivel on the end of the reel line and the hook trace to the free eye of the swivel that is between the jammed tubes.

The usual distance to set the swivel from the lead is about 6 ft (1.8 m), but if this does not catch fish well, it may be reduced to a yard (1 m) or raised to 10 ft (3 m). The hook trace, of the same nylon as the reel line, is never less than 6 ft (1.8 m) and often as long as 15 ft (4.5 m). This will be wafted enticingly in the tide, lifting and falling as the angler fishes the bait down the tidal stream.

Premium positions in the boat are at the stern, but the other anglers will still catch fish, and there should be a change-over of positions every two hours to give everybody aboard a fair turn. The bait – on a sharp number 1–2 hook – can be lugworm, or slim strips of squid, cuttlefish or fresh mackerel. A workable size is ⅜ in (1 cm) wide by 4 in (10 cm) long and the hook should be nicked through once very close to one end. That way the bait flutters attractively in the water but has no tendency to spin and cause line kinks.

The gear is dropped overboard and once the lead taps bottom, it is lifted about a yard and line spilled off the reel as it drops down again. After a few seconds repeat the lift and drop, but never lift too high and never spill more than a yard or so of line, else the tide will billow the line downtide and lift the

Useful leads for black bream, plaice and flounder fishing as well as spinning and float-fishing: a fold-over, pierced bullet, swivelled bomb, pears and Hillman leads for clipping on to swivel eyes.

In places black bream may be caught from the shore. Plump specimens like this Channel Islands fish provide superb sport on light tackle.

lead, the whole gear becoming deadened, and bites cannot be felt.

Done properly, the technique results in the bait fluttering up and down and dropping downtide from the boat, covering plenty of ground and behaving in a manner very attractive to black bream. It is essential to be able to feel the lead tap bottom occasionally. Then, even 100 yd (91.4 m) back of the boat the bites will be distinguishable.

Bites usually take the form of a light pluck or two followed by a sensation of the tip becoming heavy. Never strike a black bream bite in the accepted sense of the word. You must do the same as suggested for pollack: lift the rod and take a turn or two on the reel; the fish seems to make a firm grab, feel the hook go home and turn to dive. Just hold firmly and the hook will penetrate.

The fish will dive, pull, make runs of up to 20 yd (18.2 m) if it weighs 3 lb (1.3 kg) or so and is hooked well back of the boat with a good tide running, and even when it has been pumped and battled to the boat it will still have the energy to scuttle deep in a wavering motion that never fails to impress. Holding bream too hard will result in line (trace) breakages; they really can pull and impose sudden shocks on the gear with end-swapping direction changes.

Good boatmen will have a bucket of squid, cuttle or mackerel with them and chop it up into small pieces to feed over the side. This stream of groundbait will keep a shoal feeding behind the boat or make it feed more readily if things are slow. When the tide is running hard, however, the bait is washed away too fast to do any good for the boat, but it might help another boat anchored 200 yd (182.8 m) downtide!

A big net, not too deep, and bag-shaped rather than deep and pointed, is best for bream, and the mesh need be no more than ½ in (1.27 cm). The fish should be netted from the stern of the boat and the angler must back up the boat to get the fish on his long trace in reach. The best of the Littlehampton skippers like each angler to retain only six fish to take home and put the rest back – a very sensible conservation measure because the fish have been reduced drastically in recent years, and there have been disgusting scenes with unwanted dead fish drifting in scores down the Arun estuary from the charter-boat moorings.

The bream usually stop feeding properly at slack water and it is then that the odd fish can be lured into taking by using float tackle. The ideal rod for this is the Avon rod used for the mullet: in fact, the sliding float set-up for mullet in deep water adequately serves for bream.

Try to get the bait to swim about 4 ft (1.2 m) above the seabed and use any wind or slight tidal flow to get the float away from the boat.

Bites are signalled by a couple of preliminary bobs, then the float dives sharply; some fish will take it under without any preliminaries.

Bonus fish when black bream fishing include garfish and mackerel, of which more later, whereas pouting and lesser-spotted dogfish are regarded as a nuisance.

Red bream are similar in general outline to black bream. They are a beautiful red or orange hue, dark on the back, shading to a silvery pink belly. Like the black bream, the red bream is a great fighter, but the bigger fish are found in much deeper rocky water

offshore, or around wrecks, which means heavier tackle is usually necessary.

Red bream are far more widely distributed than black bream, inhabiting the western end of the English Channel, the neighbouring Atlantic and the south, south-west and western coasts of Ireland. Only rocky, reefy areas or wrecks on sand or mud are home to adult red bream, although little fish of under 8 oz (226.7 g), called chad, are taken from shallow water – under 20 ft (6 m). The worthwhile specimens of 2–5 lb (900 g–2.26 kg) usually come from depths of at least 15–20 fathoms, which is 90–

A red bream weighing 5¼ lb (2.38 kg), showing the large eye characteristic of deep-water species, and the spiny dorsal fin.

120 ft (27.4–36.4 m) and although the species has been caught to nearly 10 lb (4.5 kg) in the western Channel, these larger-than-average bream nearly all come from more than 200 ft (60.96 m).

However, red bream can fight all the way to the boat because they suffer little from the decrease in pressure. This makes up for the slightly heavier tackle needed in deep water.

The baitcaster or the double-handed spinning rod will do fine, with 250 yd (228.5 m) of about 8 lb (3.6 kg) test line on the small multiplier or centrepin reel. A blood-loop is tied in the line about a yard (1 m) from the end, to which is attached a snood of

the same nylon about a foot (30.4 cm) long ending in a 1/0 or 2/0 hook. A lead of 3 oz (85 g) will take the tackle down to the depths quickly enough, most times.

Deep water red bream fishing is rarely made a deliberate session, for the expense involved in getting out to distant wrecks and reefs has to be borne in mind. Therefore breaming is usually indulged in for perhaps an hour during slack water and when the big fish-baits meant for conger, ling and so on are being torn off in minutes by hordes of red bream.

Baits of lug or king ragworm, small sand-eels, slivers of mackerel, squid or cuttlefish are all acceptable and the strip baits may be larger than that used for black bream – say about ¾ in (2 cm) wide and 5 in (13 cm) long.

The red bream's big eye marks it as a fish of deep water, where light gathering qualities in the eye are of great importance.

Slim strip of squid hooked for black or red bream. It will also catch plaice when moved along the seabed.

A system that works well is to let down the tackle until it taps bottom, leave it there a second or two, then lift the rod tip slowly, and reel in a yard or so of line, also slowly. Often a fish will attack with sharp jerks. Reel in, and at the same time lift the rod tip back quickly, for a red bream is adept in ejecting the bait or stripping it from the hook without getting 'spiked'. If the lift brings no response, drop the bait and lead down again and repeat the exercise.

The red bream fights in a way that is very similar to the black, but it tends to lift in the water more than the black, often giving the angler the feeling that the fish has broken the line or shed the hook. When this slack line is followed by a shuddering power-dive the impact on the rod and line is very considerable and it pays to have the clutch set very finely on the multiplier.

Like the black bream, the red has a spiny dorsal fin and should be handled with care, the damp towel coming in useful again. Red bream are good to eat but, once more, conservation should be borne in mind: six fish per angler should be plenty to take home. Red bream appear to be capable of regaining great depths, from which they are often brought, after being put back in the water, though some drift away on the surface out of sight of the boat, so some perhaps do expire.

The season for red bream usually lasts from mid-June to mid-October.

In the West Country, where most of the good catches of red bream are made, black bream are often caught in great depths of water on the offshore wrecks, alongside the red bream. The fish are no bigger than those taken in the Sussex shallows earlier in the summer, and are probably fish that have moved away from Sussex having spawned.

In the deeps the same tackle as for red bream is justified, of course, with the resulting loss of the fish's full fighting potential. The author would never deliberately fish for black bream in the deeps since, if the fish cannot be caught on the ultra-light gear mentioned, then it really isn't worth fishing for at all. As an aside, the black bream just appears to have the edge, so far as fight is concerned, over the red, comparing both fish on the same gear from the deeps.

In the Sussex shallows the black bream is one of the top-rated fighters; but if the red bream could be caught in the same area and on the same tackle, maybe . . .

15 Mackerel and garfish

Very few anglers appreciate how well both these species can fight on light tackle because very few anglers bother to seek them with light tackle, only regarding them, mackerel especially, as baits for bigger fish.

Certainly they reach no great size in British and neighbouring waters: mackerel rarely exceed 2 lb (900 g) and garfish rarely 1½ lb (680 g), although mackerel over 6 lb (2.7 kg) and garfish over 3 lb (1.3 kg) have been recorded.

The season for these two species, which may fairly be dealt with together (since fishing for one will as likely as not yield some of the other, and they are widely distributed round most of the coastline of Britain and Ireland) lasts from late May to late September in general.

Both may be taken from the shore, especially from any projections giving access to deep water, such as piers, harbour arms, breakwaters and rocky promontories, during late June to early autumn, and in boats offshore about a month earlier; in some circumstances, there are 'jumbo' mackerel runs deep down, in the autumn months.

From late June until mid-September, when the

weather has been settled and calm and warm for a week or more, mackerel and garfish shoals move inshore, often right on to the beaches, herding small fry. At such times the newspapers report fish leaping on to dry land and holidaymakers harvesting mackerel with buckets.

At such times the trout spinning rod, fixed-spool reel and 3–4 lb (1.3–1.8 kg) line with a slim, heavyweight wobbling silver spoon, such as a Condor, Toby, Koster, Krill and similar designs, will prove a killer. Cast to the edge of the milling shoal and recover quickly. No trace is necessary: tie the line to the nose swivel of the lure; the Condor needs splitring and swivel to be attached since this lure is sold without.

Keep testing the knot on the swivel since constant casting of these heavyweight lures of around ¾ oz

(21 g) can weaken such delicate lines; in fact, if constant long casts of 40 yd (36.5 m) are necessary to reach the shoals, tie on a leader of 6–7 lb test (2.7–3.1 kg) monofil to absorb casting shocks and help hauling fish ashore. It should be long enough to take three to four turns round the reel with the bait hanging about 2 ft (60 cm) below the rod tip.

From piers, similar projections or an anchored boat, especially a dinghy in calm inshore water, there is great sport with both mackerel and garfish with either the trout spinning outfit or, better still, the Avon rod, centrepin or fixed-spool reel and 3 lb (1.3 kg) line. A sliding float similar to that used for mullet and which will support either 1, 2 or 3 swanshot will usually be found about right. The hook, a fine-wire eyed number 1, is baited with a thin sliver of mackerel or herring, cut across the flank, or squid, cuttlefish or tiny sand-eels.

Blind-fishing where mackerel are supposed to be is all right, but the sport is best when the conditions are fairly calm and the fish are seen boiling on the surface. Garfish often leap clear of the water as they chase fry and they also do this when they play

The garfish is a mini-marlin and if it grew any bigger – even by a few pounds – it would rate one of the top three places in the United Kingdom sport-fishing honours.

around flotsam in the water – such as a plank, raft of weed or an old container. From a boat the delicate tackle justifies the use of a landing net; trout size is sufficient, or roach size, if coarse fishing is also done! From piers etc. use the dropnet.

The bait is nicked through one end and then the float is allowed to drift away with the tide or wind. Starting depth can be about 4 ft (1.2 m) if the fish are seen on the surface, but if no bites are forthcoming increase the depth by a yard (91 cm) at a time until fish are found, or the boat is moved to a new location, or you change position on the pier.

It pays to reel the bait back quite slowly, when a fish will often grab it.

Although mackerel pull hard and swim fast, they lack any 'plan of campaign' and instead of long runs, simply indulge in their characteristic jagging fight, driving down and dashing round in circles. However, on the light tackle this can be good fun. Garfish, on the other hand, are spectacular fighters, and are often more out of the water than in it, greyhounding across the surface and tail-walking just as their bigger brethren, the big game billfishes do. A fair number of garfish will come unhooked due to the difficulty of finding a hook-hold in the hard bill.

In the autmn, when the whiting are moving inshore, very big mackerel, called 'jumbos' by anglers, swim among them, both species obviously feeding on the migrating shoals of small fish of that season's breeding. Quite often the first indication of these big mackerel – 2 lb or more, maybe up to nearly 4 lb (900 g–1.8 kg) – is when one is taken on lugworm or herring strip being fished for the whiting, just off the bottom. For a real slogging battle, the trout-spinning rod is brought into use and employed with 3–5 lb (1.3–2.26 kg) line and a single hook on a yard (1 m) trace fished about 2 ft (60 cm) above the minimum size of lead that will take the gear down and keep contact with the seabed. Often an ounce (28 g) will do; sometimes 2 oz (56.6 g) is necessary. In strong tides fishing this way will not be possible for very long, only near the slack periods.

Strangely, these 'jumbo' mackerel will often prefer lugworm to fish strip, even though their very presence is to feed on small fish.

Finally, when the sea is calm and the whitebait are showering from the water as the mackerel and/or garfish attack, as occurs on many a summer dawn or evening period, the fly rod used with a sinking line, from shore or small boat, can produce wonderful fishing, the garfish being especially acrobatic on this gear. The 'fly' need be nothing more elaborate than a reservoir trout-fisher's White Lure on a number 6 long-shank hook or on a tandem system, both hooks facing down. The easy way to make such a fly is to wrap the shank of the hook with broad silver tinsel – or thread on a suitable length of Mylar silver tube, tied back and front for security – and add a wing of white goat hair or deer tail hair.

Garfish seldom grow longer than 3 ft (91 cm) and are very slim, but the author once thought he had the 'mother and father' of them all when fly fishing for bonefish on the flats off North Andros, Bahamas. The bonefish fly was taken with a great pull and a vast 'garfish', apparently 4 ft (1.2 m) long leapt high out of the water, went back in and proceeded to scream away with line, leaping every 2 yd (1.8 m) or so. In fact, the fish turned out to be a houndfish, or that's what it apparently was. It's a billed species very similar to the gar, except that it grows to about 8 lb (3.6 kg).

It's a pity garfish and the common mackerel do not grow to about 10 lb (4.5 kg). If they did they certainly wouldn't be considered only as baitfish, nor hauled up six at a time on feathers!

16 Flounders and plaice

These two species of flatfish are widely distributed in the British Isles and if they are found in areas where the tidal conditions permit light tackle to be used, both can produce good fishing.

Both species are happiest over ground that consists of a mixture of sand, mud and fine gravel, but the flounder has a penchant for brackish water, especially in its youth, and (up to palm-of-hand size) spends a fair amount of time in pure freshwater. The plaice, however, likes the real salt, but also inshore and offshore grounds and banks where loose, coarse sand harbours sand-eels; or grounds where low ridges of rock abutting sand provide rich feeding on small mussels; as well as sand that is the home of razorfish, lugworms, cockles, various other bivalves and the ledges of soft rock or peat that contain the boring piddocks.

Both flounders and plaice also have a yen towards moving baits, and for that reason many of the techniques used to catch them hinge on the fact that a visual attraction can lead to final engulfing of the baited hook.

A flounder and a codling. Also some good flounder baits: the bivalve that is often washed ashore after gales and known to anglers as 'butterfish'.

Many areas that were once great plaice grounds, where good bags could be caught from the shore, now no longer exist. Trawlers and trammel nets have not only ravaged the stocks, but have used chains and heavy weights on the trawls to tear up the very grounds that harboured the fish: mussel-beds, cockle-beds etc.

Even the so-called protected areas – which include the nurseries of valuable food fish – have been plundered, perhaps because the British Government's fishery protection organisation has proved to be less than adequate.

Two examples come to mind. Foreign and British trawlers have for years plundered the Skerries bank off Dartmouth in Devon, an area where trawling has been expressly forbidden, yet the boats get away with it repeatedly in broad daylight! Thus for years Britain has been seen as the lion with no teeth. The

Common Market agreement has without doubt signed the death warrant of many flatfish-producing grounds. Another example, of which there is ample knowledge, is the Rye Bay area of Sussex where the greedy trawlers from Hastings were not content to have a decent yearly return but felt obliged to get 'the lot' before visiting trawlers got it. The result was annihilation of the mussel-beds which attracted the plaice in the first instance: trammel nets were set and trawlers went up and down between them, dragging tons of ironmongery that broke up the mussel-beds, tore up the sand and stones, and sent the plaice into the waiting nets.

But the plaice have never re-colonised the area. All this, and more, has gone on under the eyes of the local fisheries inspectors. Almost every tide, Hastings trawlers make that last sweep and end up landing tons of undersized fish which are left to rot on the beach in full view of anybody who cares to look! Just over the back of the beach trippers can buy plaice, dabs and other illegally landed *undersize* fish from men who can sell them at bargain prices. Even photographic evidence and dates and times pub-

A fine brace of flounders caught in Devon's tidal River Exe. On a light spinning rod and fixed-spool reel, fish like this can fight very hard.

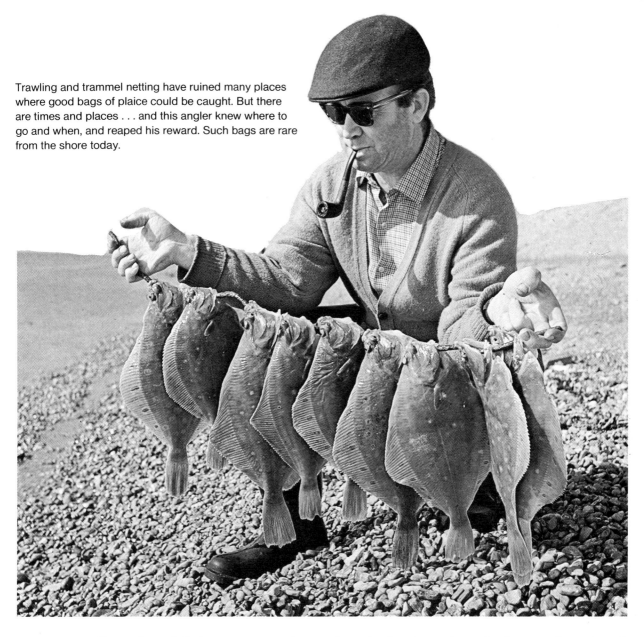

Trawling and trammel netting have ruined many places where good bags of plaice could be caught. But there are times and places . . . and this angler knew where to go and when, and reaped his reward. Such bags are rare from the shore today.

lished of the offences have failed to get any reaction from the authorities.

So what follows concerning plaice and flounder fishing in a sporting manner is advice on the fishing as it has been, still is in a few places, and could be were it not for government complacency.

First, the plaice. It's a well-known food-fish and a favourite in the fish-and-chip shops. In actual fact its popularity with the public stems from a mixture of good public relations in the fish trade and ignorance of other good and more tasty flatfish. Widely distributed, as has been said, the plaice is a sucker for sandbanks and sandy ground among rock round most of Britain and Ireland.

Any disturbance of the sand makes it curious and it will move to investigate. So, anglers have devised methods of disturbing the seabed to get the fish's interest, and these include drifting with special rigs from boats, and moving baits by reel and rod action

from the few shore places that have not been ruined by commercial fishing.

From the shore, depending on the depth, strength of tidal current etc., be it from pier, rocky promontory, shingle or sand beach, the bass surfcasting rod, or the double-handed spinning rod may be used, with 2–3 oz (56.6–85 g) lead (or lighter) and 6–10 lb (2.7–4.5 kg) line. A trace of 4 ft (1.2 m) minimum is best, ending in a number 2–1/0 hook baited with the bait that locally does best: this can be lugworm, razorfish, mussel, soft or peeler crab sections, cockles, butterfish (shellfish), ragworms of big and small varieties, piddocks, or sand-eels, to name some.

The lead, fixed via a small link-swivel running on the reel line, is augmented by a barrel or spiral lead of about 1 oz (28.3 g) set about a foot (30 cm) ahead of the hook, or with a small fluttering bar-spoon, set at the same distance from the hook, give or take an inch or so. Many books advise a big

219

spoon, 2½–3½ in (65–90 mm) long, but a spoon 1–2 in (25–50 mm) will do just as well. Its job is to create flash and sand/mud disturbance, and the smaller spoon helps casting to greater range when necessary.

Having cast the tackle to the required area, the lead is allowed to touch bottom, when a few turns are made on the reel, at the same time swinging the rod smoothly away from the sea and low – almost parallel with the beach. A pause of a few seconds is made, followed by another few turns on the reel and a sweep of the rod. The take, when it comes, occurs most commonly as the reel begins to move the tackle along the seabed after a pause. A plaice really wallops a bait fished in this way and fish of 2 lb (900 g) or so can really put a bend in the rod, fluttering and pulling with a surprising strength. Even the bass rod can take a thumping from a good plaice, 3 lb (1.3 kg) or so.

In some areas the only plaice left by the inshore trawlers are those that inhabit narrow drifts of sand between rocky ledges and outcrops, and in such places the only method for the angler is to note the positions of the sandy patches and channels at low water, then cast accurately the lightest running paternoster – made up as for bass but even lighter in test. Such places often produce best results during evening flood tides, the chance being at peak following a moderate onshore wind.

There are still a few places, notably in Ireland and western Scotland, where shallow bays still host good stocks of plaice that the commercial fishermen have not found. If rocks or a pier give way to reasonably deep water – 6 ft (1.8 m) or so – float-fishing in a way that permits use of the Avon rod, 4–5 lb (1.8–2.26 kg) line and a light barrel lead just dragging the bait over the bottom can be very killing.

Basically the same methods work for flounders from the shore, except that they are much more plentiful than plaice and found in quiet creeks, estuaries, and harbours, the species being happy over mud or sand, even fine gravel.

Of course, both species are taken on normal heavy casting tackle from open beaches, specially after gales when razorfish and other shellfish and worms are being washed up by the waves. But as a pure sportfishing exercise, there is little in it. The bait or baits are simply legered and bites awaited, as in cod fishing.

The very best plaice and flounder fishing is from boats, especially in the case of plaice on offshore banks (often not much more than two miles (3.2 km) out, perhaps) where the depth is only 3–5 fathoms (5.4–9.1 m). For flounders the same areas can be fished, though estuaries and creeks are usually more accessible, and, maybe, more rewarding.

The boat is drifted over the ground, the baits being dragged behind, with either spoons, barrel or spiral leads, a few coloured plastic beads stopped from running right on to the hook eye by a swan shot, or a metal button threaded on the trace and stopped in the same way – all 6 in–1 ft (15.5–30.4 cm) from the hook.

For plaice the baitcaster and small multiplier is a good choice, although the longer spinning rod is also suitable. In shallow, calm estuarine water, the trout spinning rod and 3–4 lb (1.3–1.8 kg) line on centrepin or fixed-spool reel will let even 1 lb (453 g) flounders give a reasonable account of themselves and allow bigger fish to put up real battles.

Both plaice and flounders can dive in a most spectacular manner when suitably light tackle is used and a landing net is necessary to avoid losses by last minute struggles.

Plaice will accept avidly a strip of squid dragged behind a fluttering spoon or other sand-stirrer, whereas flounders rarely do. It really pays when seeking both these flatfish to make enquiries in the area to be fished in order to establish the best local bait. Both fish have localised tastes and plaice in one area may be on lugworm, while in others it will only accept razorfish or mussel. Flounders, likewise, may be locally fond of rag or lug, usually the former, but more likely take razorfish, cockles, butterfish or pieces of peeler crab, among others.

Some anglers have pointed out the importance of ensuring that the baited hook trailing behind a flasher spoon, barrel lead or other form of attractor, does not spin, but the author has had perfectly good results without fitting any swivels at all between the back of the hookless bar-spoon and the bait. Each angler must rig his tackle in a way that suits him and gives him confidence, however, and if you think swivels will help, use them. A good light hookless bar-spoon for bait fishing is made by Mepps; another good one for the job is the Normark Vibro – an oldie with a good reputation.

Naturally, when boat fishing there is no need to drift all the time. The boat may be anchored and casts made over the ground with spoon, lead or beads attractor and bait, or with float tackle run down the tide. The boat may be moved if nothing happens within about an hour.

Plaice are usually in poor condition in April and May when they return to inshore waters after spawning offshore, but they soon put on weight and by the early summer have become fat. The migration for spawning usually runs from around Jan-

Believe it or not, this is a flounder, not a plaice. It was taken from a Kent beach on razorfish and weighed about 4½ lb (2 kg). On a baitcaster from a boat such a fish would be a real handful!

In addition to spinners, spoons and leads ahead of the baited hook for flounders and plaice, coloured beads also prove very successful. The bait should be moved along the seabed with such a rig.

uary to March, inshore fishing not usually being very rewarding at that time.

Flounders also migrate offshore to spawn, usually from late February to May, but through most of the summer and up to January are catchable well up estuaries, in creeks or in the sea proper. A favourite sport in parts of Wales and in many parts of the south coast of England from East Anglia to Devon, is fishing tidal creeks and rivers with freshwater tackle, legering as if for chub or roach, the lead being an Arlesey bomb of maybe ½–1½ oz (14–42 g) stopped about 18 in (45.7 cm) from a size 6–8 freshwater hook. The bait is usually small ragworms, red or white, lugworm or (in areas of brackish or nearly fresh water) garden lobworms or red worms from a farmer's manure heap.

The rod is placed in a rest or rests, just as in freshwater legering, and bites signalled by the pulls on the rod tip, striking being timed to coincide with a long pull on the tip that holds it round.

On the conventional boat and beachcasting tackle used by most sea anglers, both plaice and flounders are of little account, sportwise. But by treating them almost as freshwater fish, and dropping down the tackle to that level, they compare very favourably with such freshwater species as tench, perch, carp and fast-water roach, size for size.

And few anglers denigrate them.

17 How modern 'high-tech' rod blanks are made

When I first seriously took up sea fishing, after several brief – if moderately successful – interludes using freshwater gear, my first surfcasting rod was a 12-foot (3.65 m) Burma cane, in two pieces, which could cast up to five ounces (141.7 g). It was a seasoned, raw length of natural jungle plant, complete with nodes, where the leaves had been, joined by reinforced brass ferrules and with the handle covered with a whipcord whipping, well varnished, which was the modern trend in those days.

The first boat rod I built to go with it, as it were, was a solid glass-fibre job, with a separate cork-covered handle, rather on the lines of modern boat rods. With it, I used a Nottingham reel, six inches (15.24 cm) in diameter and made from solid walnut, with a brass-lined drum (to avoid distortion of the wood when saturated) and a star back, which was a reinforcing element of the cage side of the reel. I could have bought an American Penn or Pflueger multiplier, but most advisers warned me off them. 'You'll get overruns and lots of trouble', they said.

In those days, over 30 years ago, there were plenty of fish to catch and that old Burma cane bent to the pull of many double-figure cod, and even tope and smoothhounds from the beaches. In the boat, big tope, turbot, conger and many other species punished the old blue solid-glass rod, but it never cried wolf.

Like most anglers, I welcomed tubular-glass surfcasting rods when they began to trickle into the country, mainly from America, and few of us would have guessed that much lighter and stronger and more flexible rods would ever supersede those early tubular-glass models.

Today's so-called 'high-tech' rods are also of tubular construction, and they all have a small (or larger) amount of glass-fibre in their make-up. But the heart of these modern rods is graphite – also known as carbon fibre. The material itself is produced by exposing a man-made fibre, polyacrylonitrile, to increasing temperatures and decreasing amounts of oxygen, the final process involving temperatures of up to 3000 degrees C without any oxygen present.

Graphite has great rigidity, yet can flex, which is why modern rods made from it are very thin, when compared to glass and wooden rods of the past, very light and have a very quick recovery from being bent. In short, they can project a lead weight at tremendous speed to very great distances.

The early types of graphite rods had varying amounts of glass-fibre integrated in their construction, to help the stiff carbon fibres resist fracture – a kind of buffer, if you like. As the boffins became more *au fait* with various modern fibre-construction techniques, a number of other materials were integrated with graphite fibres in rods, including Kevlar and boron.

But enough of technicalities, which most of us do not understand. It is enough to know that our modern tubular graphite, or graphite mixture rods are constructed from woven fibres, in the form of very thin cloth, with most of the graphite fibres running the whole length of the rod blank (known as unidirectional construction) with the bolstering glass fibres mainly circumferential, though other modern fibres are built in, in many ways, most of them closely guarded trade secrets.

The companies which make such rod blanks have their own techniques, which involve varying mixes of graphite, glass and other fibres, but all of them use rolls of material, impregnated with resins, or phenolic, epoxy or polyester. The material is cut into an elongated triangular shape, wrapped tightly around a precisely tapered metal mandrel, usually of chromium-plated stainless steel, and then cured in a kiln, after which the mandrel is withdrawn and the hollow blank is left.

Down in New Romney, an ancient town once connected with smuggling, in Kent, some of the most advanced casting-rod blanks available today are made in a small factory unit about the size of a family home. Due to the precision work involved, production is limited to about 4000 blanks each year, but when you know that the man behind the Zziplex rod company is former top-flight tournament surfcaster, Terry Carroll, you can appreciate why he aims for the ultimate in blank construction.

The quality of the pre-impregnated rolls of graphite fibre, known as 'pre-preg' in the trade, is, he says, higher than that used in the aerospace industry. He uses only unidirectional-fibre graphite, which means that the fine fibres, when rolled around the forming mandrel, run along the axis of the rod, giving it its rigidity. But it is not possible to use 100 per cent graphite fibres, and so the graphite is backed by finely woven fibre-glass cloth, to hold the fibres in place and add circumferential strength. In some rods, such as those used for bass fishing, woven graphite and Kevlar fibres are the basis of blank construction, to reduce weight further. Butts of tournament rods also contain Kevlar.

'The carbon-fibre (graphite) pre-preg we use costs five times as much as the usual standard pre-preg used,' says Carroll, who launched his business 10 years ago on a site at Shorncliffe, near Folkestone. Only four people make the rod blanks, and production is usually between two and three batches per day – from the raw cloth to the finished blanks, ready to go out to the tackle trade. 'We only make up-market rods,' Carrol explained, because of the labour-intensive work involved. Neil Mackellow, who holds the British casting record with a distance of 281 yd (256.9 m), works with Carroll, and the rod with which the record was cast – naturally made by the company – hangs on the wall in the factory entrance.

The company uses 40 different mandrels to make its rods, all produced by an American company in California, and made from hard-chromed stainless steel. They have widely varying tapers, the tips incredibly thin, and over them the various graphite and graphite/Kevlar pre-pregs vary in wraps from 4 to 12. It is essential that the mandrels are stored and treated with great care, for they are very expensive and must remain perfectly straight. If they are slightly bent, the blanks they produce will be bent.

The day's production begins with the cloth being cut to the required elongated triangle, using a sharp Stanley knife and straight edge on a special cutting table. Each pre-preg triangle is cut separately, so that the resultant, carefully calculated shape is precise. Cutting several shapes simultaneously can result in minute slippage. The next stage involves applying a tacking agent to the mandrel, first warming the mandrel to get the bond needed, then applying the leading edge of the pre-preg triangle to the mandrel, after first removing the protective backing from the pre-preg. A hot-iron gadget is used to seal the pre-preg's edge to the mandrel.

The pre-preg-covered mandrel is then placed on the high-pressure rolling press, which is highly adjustable, and rolled under great pressure, to compress the pre-preg on the mandrel. Two passes, each at different angles, are required, so that the same pressure is maintained, specially at the fast-tapering tip of the mandrel, to ensure uniform wraps without slippage and crinkling of the pre-preg.

Next, the rolled mandrel is wrapped on a special machine and under an average pressure of 80 lb per square inch (5.62 kg/cm²), with a special transparent tape. This further compresses the pre-preg, avoiding any air spaces.

When a batch of mandrels has been similarly treated, they are then suspended, butts up, in a vertical kiln where hot air is blasted through. This process can take from one to three hours, depending on the resin system used, but average examples are 150° C for 70 minutes or 140° C for 80 minutes. The heat first causes the resin to flow, enveloping all the fibres on the pre-preg to create a constant combination, after which the resin cures, hardening to form the rigid tubular rod blank.

After removal from the kiln, the still-hot mandrels, each of which has a bolt threaded into its butt end, are drawn from the blanks on a special device which applies great leverage, and the blanks are left to cool briefly. Then the spiral ridges formed by the compressing tape, which contracts in the kiln to create the final pressure on the pre-preg, are ground off using a finely adjusted belt-sander, after which the smooth surface of the blank is sprayed with a tough lacquer and placed in a temperature-controlled drying rack to harden. The result is a very smooth, high-gloss finish, ready for the angler or rod-maker to whip on the rings and fit a handle and reel fitting to the butt end.

The Zziplex butts to go with the blanks are made in the same way, and all the firm's blanks are made to fit into the butt sections, without the need for spigot joints, by careful grinding. The butt sections have built-in reinforcing wraps at the upper (open) end to strengthen them to prevent cracking under stress.

Carroll pays tribute to the British weaving industry for producing the finely woven pre-pregs that go into his rods. It is, he says, in this field that great improvements have been made. Thus, the amounts of the various materials – graphite, glass and Kevlar – can be varied along the blank, to produce the required stiffness in the butt and lower sections of the rod blanks, with flexibility at the tip, plus the required resistance to fracture.

Very few of the Zziplex factory's production ever

break in fishing. And when they do come back – maybe only half-a-dozen a year – it is nearly always due to abuse by the angler. The worst thing a man can do is to abrade the outer fibres of the blank, breaking them them so that there is a weak spot formed. Even then, the effect is usually a split, with the other fibres keeping the blank together. Carroll advises that rods should never be leaned against rocks or concrete, or anything else which can wear through the lacquer and outer fibres.

Some of the Zziplex blank and butt combinations cost well over £100, after which they have to be built into rods, which can add up to a rod worth about £140 or more, depending on the quality of the rings and handle fittings. The fact that Zziplex blanks are in constant demand bears witness to the high esteem in which they are held by competent casters.

The protective backing is peeled from the pre-preg after the correct triangular shape for the particular rod blank being made has been cut out with a Stanley knife.

Terry Carroll next applies the tacking agent to the warmed mandrel. The slender tip of the mandrel flexes in his fingers, illustrating its delicacy.

Now Carroll sticks the leading edge of the tacky pre-preg to the tacky surface of the mandrel, making sure both pre-preg and mandrel are perfectly aligned. A heated iron, rather like a soldering iron, is applied to the pre-preg where it abuts the mandrel, to help adhesion.

Left: The mandrel and pre-preg are carried carefully to the powerful rolling table and placed in position. Hydraulic power applies a pre-set amount of pressure as the rolling is done.

Left, centre: The second pass through the roller is done at an angle, so that the steeply tapered tip area is compressed at the correct point, to avoid slippage and blank distortion.

Left, below: The mandrel is now tightly wrapped with the pre-preg and ready for the next stage.

Below: This involves tightly wrapping the pre-preg covered mandrel with overlapping spirals of cellophane tape on a specially made machine on which the pressure applied is widely variable, but constant once set.

Left: Now the blank, to all intents and purposes fully enveloped in an internal and external mould, is suspended by the butt end of the mandrel, which sticks out of the butt end of the blank, in a vertical kiln. This first makes the resin in the pre-preg flow, then cures it to produce a tough, rigid but flexible rod blank.

Above: After removal from the kiln, the still-hot blank – the reason for the thick gloves being worn – is levered off its forming mandrel. The mandrels in the Zziplex range are visible on the rigid storage table.

Left: Suitably masked to avoid inhalation of particles, Neil Mackellow removes the cellophane tape, and the ridges it leaves, from the surface of the blank.

Below: Mackellow applies the hard gloss finish to the surface of the blank, after which he puts it in . . .

227

... a heated drying unit to harden.

Part of a day's blank production await packaging and delivery to tackle trade customers. Carroll flexes the tip of one of them, to illustrate the lower stiffness allied to tip flexibility.

Left: Neil Mackellow shows the Zziplex blank with which he set the British record.

18 The International Game Fish Association and British anglers

The IGFA, based in Florida, is an international organisation which sets out to encourage light tackle fishing and lists authenticated captures of what the association considers to be 'game' fish.

When the original edition of this book was published, only seven of the 50 or so British species of saltwater fish were accepted by the IGFA, but now any of the British species may be entered, provided their capture is made on tackle within the IGFA's line-class system, and that the tackle and method also conform to the rules.

IGFA was responsible for setting up line classes and prescribing certain lengths and designs of rods, reels, lines and hook arrangements as acceptable in the sporting capture of game fish of the oceans. As such, it has done a very good job, to the extent that even in the United Kingdom and its environs, it is possible to buy off-the-peg rods that are built to

IGFA specifications, opening up world records to those who may catch a big fish on such a rod.

In spite of the fact that IGFA has inspired great deeds of light tackle skill, which to many is much better than the sort of thick-eared angling mentality one finds too often in Britain, there are obvious loopholes that make a mockery of IGFA's *raison d'être*. Some of the alleged light tackle captures are obviously impossible if something a bit odd is not done: like chasing a fish with the boat to drive it into shallow water where it can be vanquished without being able to sound; dropping a bait into the mouth of a fish that has been chummed to within a yard or so of the boat, then gaffing it immediately the hook is pulled home without ever bending a rod in battle. . . . Long traces can be grabbed very quickly when necessary.

Fishing to International Game Fish Association rules

The 'angling rules', so called, of the IGFA cover some 19 points, but the basis of the system – as has already been illustrated in these pages – is one of light and balanced tackle used 'in accordance with sporting ethics and customs'.

Most of the rules apply to boat fishing tackle and methods in the line classes which run as follows: 6, 12, 20, 30, 50, 80, 130 lb (2.7, 5.4, 9.0, 13.6, 22.6, 36.2 and 58.9 kg). Lines must test, when wet, up to and including these weights. In addition to the records for these classes, the IGFA lists an all-tackle section for the heaviest fish of each listed species taken on any tackle class (only certain selected fish are eligible for IGFA world records).

When applying for a world line-class record, not only must the angler have been using tackle acceptable by IGFA but he must also have followed the procedure set by the organisation. For example, for 50 lb (22.6 kg) class and below, a 50 ft (15 m) sample of the actual line used, plus 2 ft (61 cm) of leader or trace must accompany the application. For classes above 50 lb, the 2 ft of trace must go in, but the length of line is increased to 80 ft (24 m) and if a double line was used (as in shark fishing, for example) the double line is included in the length.

It is interesting to note that if a fish is taken on two lines of different tests knotted or spliced together, the catch will be classified under the heavier of those two lines, samples of both having been submitted for testing.

The amount of double line and leader allowed is also controlled: on all weights up to and including 50 lb class 15 ft (4.5 m) of leader and 15 ft of double line may be used. For heavier tackle the double line must not exceed 30 ft (9 m), neither must the leader.

Rods must also measure up. The tip, measured from a point directly beneath the centre of the reel, must be a minimum of 50 in (127 cm) long. The butt, measured from the same place on the reel, must be no more than 27 in (68.5 cm) long. These figures do not apply to surfcasting rods 'used in surfcasting' and are intended to outlaw freak rods, obviously to preserve the sporting aspect and to protect anglers in combat with big fish.

Reels, too, must be 'in accordance with sporting ethics and customs'. Mechanical reels of any kind, including power-assisted reels, are banned. Strangely, so are reels with double handles! There seems no logic in such a rule. For example, our British centrepin mullet reel has two handles and is fitted out with light line: yet were our mullet to be listed by IGFA as a sporting species, captures on a centrepin reel would not be accepted.

Fighting chairs used for big fish must have no mechanical device which helps the angler fight his fish; and the only butt gimbal permitted (to take the extreme butt of the rod) is one which swivels in a vertical plane only. That is to prevent an unscrupulous angler just jamming his rod in a fixed gimbal and letting that take the strain!

Were one to catch a cod using the wire line technique mentioned, that fish could not be entered as wire lines, including lines with metal cores, are prohibited.

When using natural bait, no more than two single hooks may be attached to the trace, and then only if they are both attached to or imbedded in the bait. The eyes of the hooks must be no less than a hook's length apart, and no more than 18 in (45.7 cm) apart. On artificial lures, the eyes of the two hooks

must be at least a hook's length but no more than 18 in apart; the trailing hook may not extend behind the lure for more than a hook's length. No swinging or dangling hook is permitted. This is to prevent foul-hooking of fish, of course.

Treble or double hooks on plugs are permitted, but they must be limited to a maximum of two hooks – meaning two doubles, two trebles or two singles are eligible. When casting a lure from a boat the boat must not be under any form of propulsion. And any record claim made for fish caught by plug fishing or lure fishing must be accompanied by a photograph of the plug or lure.

Two-hook bottom rigs are permitted so long as the top hook is far enough away from the bottom hook so as not to hook into a fish taken on the bottom hook – or vice versa. Again, a photograph or sketch of the tackle must accompany record claims.

The use of floats, other than a small balloon, bladder or cork, is prohibited. This is to prevent large buoyant devices being used to tire fish which would have to tow such heavy floats under the surface and through the water. Floats are solely for the purpose of drifting the bait while suspended in the water; the release balloon mentioned in the shark chapter certainly fulfils those demands.

A gaff up to 8 ft (2.4 m) long may be used to secure a fish on a boat, and it may be attached to a maximum of 30 ft (9 m) of rope. Longer gaffs may be used for bridge or pier fishing. The angler must hook, play and bring the fish to the net or gaff unaided. If anybody else touches the tackle during the period after hook-up any record claim is outlawed.

The rod must not be rested on the gunwale while fighting a fish, but a harness attached to the reel and a belly-pad are permitted. An angler is not allowed to change rod or reel, or to splice, or in any way add to the line during the period a fish is being played.

The following acts and situations also disqualify a fish: Failure to comply with the rules or tackle specifications. A broken rod, including a broken butt. Any person touching the tackle during play, except that one person is permitted to hold the trace when a fish is being boated. Shooting, harpooning or lancing any fish. Any fish mutilated, either by sharks during play, or by propellers that remove or penetrate its flesh. Old scars or marks caused by line or trace during the fight are not considered to be disqualifying injuries. Chumming (rubby-dubby) with flesh, blood, skin or guts of any mammal; chum must be consistent in size with that of the bait being used. Beaching or driving fish into shallow water, after hooking it from a boat, so as to deprive the fish of its normal ability to swim.

In addition to all the above, record applications have to be made on special forms and a great deal of information and verification is required. For example, photographs that clearly show the physical features of the fish, plus the tackle used, have to be submitted. The angler must be photographed with the fish; also the scales on which it is weighed. For shark records detailed photographs of the head, especially dentition, are required.

All claims from outside the United States of America must be received by IGFA within 60 days of the fish's capture. Entries of fish caught elsewhere must be received within three months of capture.

To replace a record for a fish weighing 100 lb (45 kg) or more, the new record must exceed the existing record by 1 lb (450 g); a fish weighing less than 1 lb more will be considered to tie with the record. For records weighing less than 100 lb (45 kg) similar conditions apply, except that the stipulated weight difference is half a pound (226 g).

Finally, no officer of the IGFA may hold a world record for a line class.

The address of IGFA is 3000 E. Las Olas Boulevard, Fort Lauderdale, Florida 33316, USA.

The British Record (rod-caught) Fish List

The British Record (rod-caught) Fish Committee maintains lists of freshwater and saltwater species caught by fair angling with rod and line in British waters, including the Channel Islands. It is based at 11 Cowgate, Peterborough, Cambridgeshire, PE1 1LZ (telephone (0733) 54084).

There are strict rules concerning record fish claims, and in the first instance, an angler believing he has caught a possible record fish should telephone the committee's headquarters, when he will be given directions about how properly to make a claim. Usually, a committee-appointed person will need to inspect the fish, to verify its species and other details.

Both boat-caught and shore-caught lists are kept, and for the species included in this book the latest list to hand at the time of going to press included the following records:

Bass: shore – 19 lb 0 oz (8 kg 618 g), David Bourne, Dover Breakwater, Kent, 1988; boat – 19 lb 9 oz 2 dm (8 kg 876 g), P. McEwan, off Reculver, Herne Bay, Kent, 1987.

Black bream: shore – 4 lb 14 oz 12 dm (2 kg 232 g), D. P. Bohan, Alderney, Channel Islands, 1984;

boat – 6 lb 14 oz 4 dm (3 kg 125 g), J. A. Garlick, wreck off Devon coast, 1977.

Red bream: shore – 4 lb 7 oz (2 kg 12 g), A. Salmon, Alderney Lighthouse, Channel Islands, 1979; boat – 9 lb 8 oz 12 dm (4 kg 330 g), B. H. Reynolds, off Mevagissey, Cornwall, 1974.

Coalfish: shore – 20 lb 6 oz (9 kg 242 g), D. Cook, Flycellers, Newquay, Cornwall, 1982; boat – 37 lb 5 oz (16 kg 923 g), D. Brown, wreck south of Eddystone Reef, Devon, 1986.

Cod: shore – 44 lb 8 oz (20 kg 183 g), B. Jones, Tom's Point, Barry, Glamorgan, Wales, 1966; boat – 53 lb (24 kg 39 g), G. Martin, Start Point, Devon, 1972.

Common skate: shore – 133 lb 8 oz (60 kg 554 g), S. Morrison, Lochaline Pier, Sound of Mull, Scotland, 1988; boat – 227 lb (102 kg 965 g), R. Banks, off Tobermory, Inner Hebrides, Scotland, 1986.

Conger: shore – 67 lb 1 oz (30 kg 417 g), A. W. Lander, Natural Arch Rock End, Torquay, Devon, 1967; boat – 109 lb 6 oz (49 kg 609 g), R. W. Potter, South East of Eddystone Reef, Devon, 1976.

Flounder: shore – 5 lb 3 oz 10 dm (2 kg 370 g), M. R. Burgess, River Teign, Devon, 1987; boat – 5 lb 11 oz 8 dm (2 kg 593 g), A. G. L. Cobbledick, Fowey, Cornwall, 1956.

Garfish: shore – 2 lb 15 oz 9 dm (1 kg 347 g), M. Wills, The Lizard, Coverack, Cornwall, 1979; boat – 3 lb 2 dm (1 kg 363 g), J. Nardini, Penzance, Cornwall, 1981.

Halibut: shore – qualifying weight set at 10 lb; boat – 234 lb (106 kg 136 g), C. Booth, Dunnet Head, off Scrabster, Scotland, 1979.

Mackerel: shore – 5 lb 11 oz 14 dm (2 kg 603 g), M. A. Kemp, Berry Head Quarry, Brixham, Devon, 1982; boat – 6 lb 2 oz 7 dm (2 kg 790 g), W. J. Chapple, 1½ miles off Penberth Cove, Cornwall, 1984.

Mullet (thick-lipped grey): shore – 14 lb 2 oz 12 dm (6 kg 427 g), R. S. Gifford, The Leys, Aberthaw, Glamorgan, Wales, 1979; boat – 10 lb 1 oz (4 kg 564 g), P. C. Libby, Portland, Dorset, 1952.

Mullet (thin-lipped grey): shore – 6 lb 4 oz (2 kg 835 g), H. E. Mepham, River Rother, Kent, 1981; boat – 3 lb 7 oz (1 kg 599 g), D. Davenport, Christchurch Estuary, Dorset, 1983.

Pollack: shore – 18 lb 4 oz (8 kg 277 g), C. R. A. Lowe, Abbotsbury Beach, Dorset, 1986; boat – 29 lb 4 oz (13 kg 267 g), W. S. Mayes, Dungeness, Kent, 1987.

Stingray: shore – 53 lb 8 oz (24 kg 265 g), D. L. Harris, St Osyth Beach, Essex, 1987; boat – 61 lb 8 oz (27 kg 894 g), V. W. Roberts, Cardigan Bay, Gwynedd, Wales, 1979.

Blue shark: shore – qualifying weight 40 lb (18 kg

143 g); boat – 218 lb (98 kg 883 g), N. Sutcliffe, Looe, Cornwall, 1959.

Porbeagle shark: shore – qualifying weight 40 lb (18 kg 143 g); boat – 465 lb (210 kg 920 g), J. Potier, off Padstow, Cornwall, 1976.

Mako shark: shore – qualifying weight 40 lb (18 kg 143 g); boat – 500 lb (226 kg 796 g), Joyce Yallop, off Eddystone Light, Devon, 1971.

Thresher shark: shore – qualifying weight 40 lb (18 kg 143 g); boat – 323 lb (146 kg 504 g), S. Mills, 6 miles south of Nab Tower, Portsmouth, 1982.

Starry (spotted) smoothhound: shore – 23 lb 2 oz (10 kg 488 g), D. Carpenter, beach, Bradwell-on-Sea, Essex, 1972; boat – 28 lb (12 kg 700 g), R. Grady, Maplin Sands, Thames Estuary, 1980.

Smoothhound: shore – 17 lb 8 oz (7 kg 937 g), G. A. Hazell, Sowley Sedge, Hampshire, 1988; boat – 28 lb (12 kg 700 g), A. T. Chilvers, Heasham, Norfolk, 1969.

Tope: shore – 58 lb 2 oz (26 kg 363 g), R. J. White, Baggy Point, North Devon, 1982; boat – 79 lb 12 oz (36 kg 172 g), P. J. Richards, Bradwell-on-Sea, Essex, 1986.

Ballan wrasse: shore – 8 lb 6 oz 6 dm (3 kg 808 g), R. W. Le Page, Bordeaux Beach, Guernsey, Channel Islands, 1976; boat – 9 lb 6 oz (4 kg 252 g), M. Goodacre, Eddystone Gully, Devon, 1981.

Glossary

A

ABU-Garcia A manufacturer of tackle. Famous for its reels and lures.

Aluminium oxide A very hard material used as the bearing surfaces of rod rings, as a lining inside a metal ring.

Anodise A method by which aluminium and its alloys are colour-coated to prevent corrosion and used as a form of decoration.

Araldite An epoxy-resin adhesive first developed for gluing aircraft frames together. This two-part adhesive is much used in rod making.

Avon-type rod Basically a freshwater rod with a flexible middle and top section, capable of subduing big barbel or tench and good for mullet, bass, etc.

B

Backing Line used behind the main line as a reserve for playing fish, or for building up the line level to aid casting.

Backlash Line over-running during a cast with a multiplier or centrepin reel and winding itself in tangles the wrong way round the spool or drum. A surfcaster's nightmare!

Bag-net A landing net that ends in a U-shape at the base when suspended from the frame.

Bait clip A hook-shaped device, of wire or moulded plastic, fitted to the trace below the hook snood, to hold the baited hook in line with the main part of the trace, to streamline the bait or baits during the casting stresses. Also known as a relay clip.

Bait pump A cycle pump-like device becoming popular for extracting lugworms from their burrows in suitably soft sand/mud shores.

Balsa A soft, buoyant wood used in float making.

Bar-spoon A spinning lure on which a spoon- or willow leaf-shaped blade revolves round a wire bar when pivoted from its front end.

Berkley American fishing tackle makers of Spirit Lake, Iowa. They make excellent swivels, rods and nylon lines.

Beta-light A light, the power source of which is based on atomic reaction between tritium gas in a glass tube lined with a phosphorescent coating.

Bickerdyke, John 19th Century angling writer who was best known for his love of pike fishing, but who also enjoyed sea fishing.

Big-game fish Usually such species as marlin, broadbill swordfish or bluefin tuna, but in British waters including the sharks.

Blank A glass-fibre or carbon-fibre tapered rod, hollow or solid, from which a fishing rod is constructed; or a day's fishing during which no fish are caught.

Boatcaster A rod made for casting and legering from an anchored boat.

Bonefish A streamlined, fast-swimming sportfish found in shallow tropical and sub-tropical oceans.

Boom A rigid bar from which a hook link or trace is fished so as to help avoid tangling with the main line. Also, an attachment for a lead which runs on the line as in tope or skate fishing.

Boron One of the 'space-age' man-made high-tensile filaments used in rod construction. The material is produced by a process of attracting borax-contained particles to be deposited on ultra-fine tungsten filaments.

Braided monofilament nylon Nylon filaments braided to form a hollow line, mainly used in flyfishing as the shooting line behind a shooting-taper or shooting-head flyline, because it slides through the rod rings smoothly, is less prone to tangle and can be joined to the flyline without knots.

Break-off Line breakage while casting or when fighting fish.

Breakaway lead A bomb-shaped lead, for casting from shore or boat, on which the anchor wires are pivoted. They lock in the active position but break away under increased tension, to trail freely, thus enabling the tackle to be reeled in without the wire constantly catching bottom. This lead design permits very light reel lines to be used.

Broken Word used to describe losing a fish by line breakage: 'I was broken by a big cod.'

Bronzed hook A steel hook protected by a bronze

coloured lacquer.

Brooks, Joe A famous American all-round angler who pioneered saltwater flyfishing among other aspects of the sport.

Butt Thicker end of the rod near the handle; the lower joint of a rod. Also used in flyfishing: the thickest part of the leader where it joins the flyline.

C

Caged drum reel A centrepin reel – for trotting or flyfishing usually – on which the drum is enclosed within a two-sided frame with crossbars.

Carbon-fibre A modern material, very stiff for its weight and used in making expensive rods. It is produced, in simple terms, by burning special textile man-made fibres in the absence of oxygen.

Cast Excreta of a worm (lugworm) deposited on the surface of sand and mud shores below high water mark; also the action of projecting tackle to reach the fish.

Centre-pin reel A reel of the old type on which the drum or spool revolves on a spindle (or pin) fitted to the backplate. The bearing surface is minimal, which permits the drum to rotate extremely freely, paying-off line when letting float tackle move down-current, as in mullet fishing.

Charter-boat An angling craft which may be hired by the day or for longer periods. It can be obtained with a skipper – and sometimes a mate – to position anglers over fish and assist in boating them.

Check The audible ratchet mechanism on a reel that clicks as line is drawn off the spool or drum. Used to signal bites, at times, and to judge rate at which line is being drawn off.

Chumming American term for rubby-dubby – the minced and cut fish used to attract fish to an angling boat. In Britain used to describe cut chunks of fish rather than minced fish and oil.

Clutch Braking mechanism on a reel, also called a drag.

Collet A device rather like the chuck of a drill that holds the drilling tool; it holds the tip of a baitcasting rod in the cranked handle, usually, by screwing up against a tapered tube.

Collyer, Dave Well known English freshwater angler and flydresser.

Corrosion Destruction by chemical action, especially by the action of acids, rust, etc. upon metals; in saltwater angling usually caused by salt deposits on reels and other metalwork on tackle.

Crank (or cranked) handle Short handle on a baitcasting rod which retains a reel, usually a small multiplier or closed-face spinning reel, at a low centre of gravity and lying in a U-shaped clip.

Crimp Describes the act of crushing a metal ferrule on to a wire-to-hook joint or wire loop with a special pair of pliers.

Cure The process by which modern rod blanks of glass-fibre, graphite (carbon-fibre) and other composite structures are hardened around the forming mandrel in a heated kiln. The bonding agent, or resin, becomes hard but resilient.

Custom-built rod A rod that is made by a craftsman to the special order and specification of a customer.

D

Dacron American term for a man-made textile used in fishing lines. In Britain, the same material is known as Terylene. Dupont are the American makers, ICI the British makers.

Dingle Peninsula in south-west Ireland famous for its saltwater angling, particularly bass in the surf, pollack and wrasse from the rocks.

Doubled line Used in the capture of large fish, such as sharks and tropical water game fish. The end of the line is doubled for 15 ft (4.5 m) or so, both to resist abrasion weakening the line and provide a means of pulling the fish to the side of the boat by handling the doubled line.

Drag See clutch.

Drum Cylinder holding the line, usually on a centre-pin reel. On multipliers and fixed-spool reels the term used is spool.

Dressing Describes style and materials such as feathers, hairs and tinsel used in the manufacture of flies.

Driftlining The method of fishing with weightless or lightly weighted tackle, allowed to drift with the tidal currents.

Dropper Term most used in fly fishing to describe a fly (or hook) on a short piece of nylon fixed above the terminal fly (hook) and usually projecting at a right angle from the line or leader.

Duralumin An alloy composed of aluminium, copper, manganese and magnesium, originally used in aircraft frame construction, due to its combination of lightness and strength. Much used in the fishing tackle industry for stiff rod butts and for reels.

E

Estuarine Description of any fish, habitat, etc. in the vicinity of tidal mouth of large river.

F

Feathering Term to describe catching fish, such as mackerel or pollack, on traces bearing a number of feather-decorated hooks. Also a method of slowing down the rate of line leaving the spool of a fixed-spool reel by letting a fingertip just touch the coils as they come over the front lip.

Ferrules Joints in fishing rods, made from metal or from glass-fibre, graphite and boron (see spigot).

Fight The duel between angler and hooked fish.

Fixed-spool reel Casting reel on which the spool is mounted at a right-angle to the rod, and from which the line pays off over the front lip. Line is recovered by a hook or semicircular arm mounted in a revolving flyer, the spool, which is equipped with its own drag system, remaining stationary.

Flats Term to describe flatfish, as opposed to roundfish, ie plaice or flounders. Also very shallow, sandy or muddy areas of sea, particularly in tropical and sub-tropical areas such as the Caribbean and Florida Keys, but also in the United Kingdom, especially the Essex coastline.

Forged hook Hook on which the area of the bend has been hammered flat to better resist distortion when a fish is hooked.

Foul-hook To hook a fish, accidentally or deliberately, usually in the body or around the head, without it having taken a bait or lure.

Forrest, Nigel East Coast angler and expert tournament surfcaster. Co-inventor with Ian Gillespie of the Breakaway lead.

Free-spool System on a multiplying reel whereby the spool my be freed from the recovery gears system, for casting or lowering tackle to fish. Most are lever- or button-operated.

Fuji Japanese company which supplies hard-centred rod rings and reel fittings made from graphite and stainless steel, highly regarded in Britain.

G

Gaff Steel hook with a sharp point used to haul a large fish into a boat or on to shore.

Gammon, Clive Angling journalist and sports writer and until late 1976 a columnist in *Angling* magazine; now in America as a staff writer on *Sports Illustrated* magazine. A keen conservationalist.

Gillespie, Ian Respected angling writer, *Angling* magazine columnist of long standing, and tackle innovator (see Forrest).

Gimbal Slotted device built into the butt cap of boat rods which locate in the bar of a belly-pad and prevent the rod turning when fighting a fish.

Graphite Alternative term for carbon-fibre.

Greyhounding Term which describes the action of a fast-moving fish leaping forward at a low angle from a water. Usually applied to sailfish and marlin, but sometimes to garfish and even stingrays.

Ground Term used to describe the seabed configuration relative to the types of fish sought, ie, rough ground, smooth ground.

H

Hands The ability that comes with experience which tells an angler when to be gentle with a fighting fish and when to be firm. Cf. 'good hands' – as in horsemanship.

Hardy Hardy Brothers of Alnwick, Northumberland, world renowned tackle makers.

Hold, holding Term used to describe whether the leaded tackle will remain in position on the seabed . . .'Are you holding?'

I

Intermediate rings The rings on rods apart from the butt ring and tip ring. They are of larger diameter towards the butt end of the rod than at the tip, to minimise weight in the flexible tip.

J

Jig A heavy metal lure (sometimes adorned with feathers, hair or other fibres) which is fished in an up-down motion near the seabed. To jig: to fish a lure in an up and down motion.

Jumbo mackerel Very large mackerel which run westwards, very near the seabed in British and north-west European waters – usually in late summer and autumn.

K

Kelp Rubbery, ribbon-like fronds of weed that grow in relatively deep water with a rocky bottom. Cod fishermen, who have to fish into it, often lose both tackle and fish as a result.

Kevlar Another man-made fibre used in rod construction, mainly as a strengthening agent with graphite (carbon-fibre).

L

Lead The moulded piece of lead used to sink, project, anchor or otherwise help present a bait or lure to a fish.

Leger To fish a bait anchored to the seabed by a lead; also sometimes used to describe such a lead.

Lever-drag A braking system on high-class multiplier reels on which a lever on the frame operates a smooth and progressive disc-type drag system, rather like the disc brakes on a car.

Line capacity The amount of line a reel will properly hold.

Line-class A term used by the International Game Fish Association to classify various tackle systems. Lines in various classes must be tested to break at no more than the various figures listed, when the line is wet. For example, line for 20 lb (9 kg) class is usually made to break at about 17 lb (7.7 kg).

Linnane, Kevin Sea Angling Officer of Ireland's Inland Fisheries Trust. This respected sea angler is also an active conservationist.

Lip-hook Definition of having hooked a fish by the lip; also to describe method of using a live and dead fish, so hooked, as a bait.

Lesser-spotted dogfish A bottom-dwelling scavenger of no sporting value, but a valuable fish-and-chip shop food-fish.

Longline A long line of baited hooks used to catch big fish such as cod and halibut commercially.

M

Mark Location at sea where there is good fishing; found either by radar navigation systems or by lining up on landmarks.

Memory Quality of a line which enables it to stretch, then return to its former position, as curls remain in monofilament nylon.

Mincing-machine Slang name for a fixed-spool reel, used mainly by those who do not like using it.

Mitchell Famous French reel-making company; also make other tackle.

Moncrieff, Leslie Known as the 'Gentle Giant', the pioneer in Britain of long-distance surfcasting techniques.

Monel-metal A malleable material, used to make wire fishing lines, which does not corrode.

Mustad Norwegian company world-famous for its hooks.

Mylar A bright plastic material, resembling shiny metal; often made into a braided tube and used to make flies.

N

Nail-knot A whipping-type knot made with one line around another, into which the turns of the nail-knot bed, usually with nylon monofilament round a flyline. The monofilament may be passed into the flyline's core before the knot is formed, to make a straight junction, which passes smoothly through rod rings.

Neap A tide where the rise and fall between high and low is at a minimum.

Neish, Don Casting expert and tackle dealer of Edmonton, North London.

O

Over-run Line coming from the spool too fast (usually of a multiplier or fixed-spool reel), then getting caught up by winding itself round the spool the wrong way. Also backlash.

P

Partridge of Redditch World-famous British hookmaking company based in the English Midlands. Hand-made hooks are the company's speciality.

Paternoster Method of fishing with one or more hooks above a lead weight, the hooks on short links projecting from the main line at right angles.

Pirk A heavy metal or plastic/metal lure fished up and down, usually from a boat; used for predatory fish, such as cod, pollack and coalfish.

Play Similar word to fight – to battle with a hooked fish.

Policansky Name of a lever-drag reel made in South Africa.

Pump The action of lifting a fish by raising the rod, then winding in slack line rapidly as the rod is lowered again.

R

Ratchet Same meaning as check.

Recovery (of rod) The act of a flexed rod returning to its straight condition, as in casting, which helps to project the weighted tackle.

Recovery rate Of reels: The amount of line rewound on the spool or drum for one turn of the handle.

Reel seat The metal or plastic arrangement which secures the reel to the rod handle, either with a screw-locking ring which closes over the reel's foot (also called a saddle) or with a pivoting clip which locks into a series of grooves. Also, the point on the rod butt, often reinforced, on which reels with their own clamps may be positioned.

Reverse taper Feature of a rod on which the part below the reel tapers in the opposite direction to that of the rod. It was produced by Leslie Moncrieff to help people cast long distances without over-runs or backlashes.

Rig Name for terminal tackle.

Rings Fittings on the rod through which line runs and is supported.

Roller Revolving bollard in the pick-up arm of a fixed-spool reel to reduce friction; also parts of roller-rings used on boat rods.

Run The action of a hooked fish swimming away from the angler; also the movement of migratory fish to and from a region at a particular season of the year.

S

Set Bend that remains permanently in a rod after stress; also the action of sinking the hook in a fish's mouth.

Shooting-taper or shooting-head A short length of

flyline, usually between 30 and 40 ft (9.1 and 12.1 m), smoothly linked to nylon monofilament, braided monofilament or dressed thin flyline. Such lines are for long-range casting.

Sink and draw Lift and fall action of fishing a lure or bait.

Sound A fish diving towards the seabed.

Spade-end A hook with a spade-shaped flattened end to its shank and which holds a whipping-knot firmly.

Spigot joint A joint system used on tubular rods in which a strong male extension on the lower joint's end fits tightly into the open end of the upper (female) section. Spigots may be solid or hollow, but are usually reinforced, as may be the open end of the upper joint into which the spigot fits, by extra wraps of the rod material.

Spinning Method of fishing which involves casting a metal, plastic or other type of lure, and winding it in, so that it spins or wobbles through the water, simulating a small fish on which predatory fish species feed.

Spring tide A tide where the rise and fall between high and low is at a maximum; the opposite to neap tide.

Star-drag Capstan-shaped wheel, like a ship's helm, by which the drag on a reel can be adjusted.

Steep-to Description of a beach that slopes steeply from the water level.

Stop A knot or some other form of method by which a lead or a sliding float is fixed on the line at the correct fishing depth.

Storm-beach Atlantic-facing beaches, usually in west Wales or on the south-west coasts of the Irish Republic, on which several lines of surf are usually breaking but which are not necessarily produced by local wind conditions but by the ocean swell from storms way out in the ocean. Such beaches are shallow, composed of hard sand with dunes behind, and are haunted by bass, flounders, tope and dogfish.

Superglue Collective term used to describe cyanoacrylate adhesive, used in fishing to glue flylines instantly together and do quick, strong repairs to tackle.

Swash The shallow water left to recede after a wave has run up a shallow surf beach and expended its energy.

Swivel-chair Fixed to a boat's stern from which an angler plays a big fish.

T

Tailer Rope used to secure large fish, like sharks, by putting a noose over the tail.

Take Action of a fish grabbing a bait or lure.

Terylene British ICI line, of braided construction – Dacron is the American term.

Test The amount, expressed in pounds or kilograms, to which a line will resist linear elongation.

Test curve Optimum bend in a rod for safety, by which safe casting weight and safe line test to be used can be evaluated.

Thumb Action of braking a multiplier reel spool, when casting and fighting a fish.

Titanium A metallic chemical element, often used with stainless steel, to make strong, rigid butts for casting rods, and for reel components.

Tournament casting Casting on a field for distance and accuracy. (Some tournament casters do not go fishing at all!)

Trolling Term, of American origin, used to describe fishing a lure, spinning or wobbling, behind a moving boat, under engine or oar power. Also termed trailing, more correctly, in the United Kingdom. Trolling was an English term used to describe sink-and-draw fishing with a dead fish, for pike, in freshwater.

U

Uptide rod Casting rod, usually about 9–10 ft (2.7–3 m) in length, used for fishing uptide from an anchored boat, mainly in shallow water.

V

Vycoat Liquid vinyl used to coat splices and joints in flylines.

W

Whelm The disturbance visible on the surface caused by a mullet moving fast deep down and changing direction.

Whippings The wrappings with which the rings are attached to a rod; whippings may also attach or secure hook-keepers to the rod just ahead of the handle area.

Work-harden Means by which the molecular construction of a metal – such as a line – is altered and made brittle by constant friction over another unresistant surface.

Index

Italic type denotes an illustration.

239